Valerie's Journeys

Valerie's Journeys

Valerie Monkhouse
Peter and Duncan Monkhouse

ISBN-13: 978-1-7770085-2-9
Kindle/PDF: 978-1-7770085-3-6

Dedication

To my family, without whom, none of this would have been possible.

Acknowledgment

This book was made possible with the assistance of my sons, Peter, Duncan, and grandson Andrew. Able assistance was provided by Nick Monkhouse, David Sanger, Barbara Tose, and Pacific Ghostwriting. Peter and Duncan would also like to thank Valerie's grandsons Devon and Joseph, other family members, friends, and work colleagues who have shared their stories about Valerie with us as we completed this book. Finally, we would like to thank Valerie and Ben for the trip reports, Christmas letters, pictures, and records they kept, allowing us to complete the book.

Contents

About the Authors

Valerie Monkhouse—The eldest child of English parents, Valerie had an interesting early life travelling the world. After graduating from university, she married, and settled down to have a family. The family moved to Ottawa when the children were young. Once her two sons were older, she returned to the workforce as a librarian and manager in the federal government. After retiring she continued to travel, knit, do genealogy, and enjoy time with her family before passing away in 2022.

Peter Monkhouse—The first son of Valerie and Ben Monkhouse, was born in Toronto and attended public and high school in Ottawa. He earned a BSc (Eng) from Queen's University and an MBA from the University of Toronto. Peter has actively led projects and project managers in the areas including education, consulting, engineering, information technology, health, and organisational change for multinational organisations. Peter is an active volunteer with PMI (Project Management Institute) including Past Chair of the PMI Board of Directors. Peter and his wife are parents of two children.

Duncan Monkhouse—The second son of Valerie and Ben Monkhouse, like his brother, Duncan was born in Toronto and attended public school, high school, and Carleton University in Ottawa, graduating with a BSc. Duncan has worked in IT (Information Technology), as a programmer, computer security consultant and computer forensic examiner in both private industry and the federal government. He has now retired. His volunteer work included the High-Tech Crime Investigation Association and the British Isles Family History of Greater Ottawa. Duncan and his wife are the parents of two boys and have three grandchildren.

Preface

This book was the brainwave of Andrew Monkhouse, Valerie's grandson. He realised that his grandmother's life was an interesting one with many journeys and wished to pass on those experiences to his children. With the assistance of Pacific Ghostwriting, Valerie took up the challenge and completed Chapters 1 to 9 before her death on March 26, 2022. After her death, her sons, Peter and Duncan took up the torch and completed Valerie's biography.

As we wrote the book, we realised that Valerie's life consisted of multiple intertwined journeys, each impacting the other and affecting those around her. Firstly, Valerie was a daughter and a sister who travelled the world in her younger years. Then she was Ben's wife for over sixty years. She was a mother to Peter and Duncan and a grandmother to their children. Finally, she was a successful professional librarian, rising to be the Director of Library Services for the National Museums of Canada.

We hope you enjoy following Valerie on her journeys.

Chapter 1
The Beginning – Valerie's Childhood

1930 to 1935

1931 – Valerie – Portsmouth, England

Valerie's Journeys

The settlement in the market town of Tring, Hertfordshire, England, dates back to prehistoric times. According to The Concise Oxford Dictionary of English Placenames, the name Tring is believed to derive from the Old English Tredunga or Trehangr. 'Tre', meaning 'tree' and with the suffix 'ing' implying a slope where trees grow.

The town, located at the intersection of Icknield Way—an ancient trackway that runs from Norfolk to Wiltshire, thought to be the oldest road in Europe—and the Roman Akeman Street, hosts a myriad of age-old buildings. The tower of the Church of St. Peter and St. Paul—now classified as a Grade I "building of exceptional interest" by the Historic Buildings and Monuments Commission for England—was built in the early 1300s. And it was that very 14th century Anglican church in which Valerie Sanger was christened.

Valerie was born at home in The Cottage, Highfield Road in Tring, Hertfordshire, on Tuesday, July 8, 1930. Her mother, Kitty, was attended by the local doctor and nurse-midwife Eva Sanger, the elder sister of Valerie's father, Fred. The healthy baby girl, who weighed 6 pounds and 4 ounces, was adored by her mother and father.

Four months later, Eva became one of Valerie's godparents, along with Arthur Goddard. Arthur was a close friend of Fred, who had also served as the best man at Fred and Kitty's wedding. Fred and Arthur had met while attending the University of London.

In those days, a girl would typically have had two godmothers and one godfather. Valerie's second godmother was meant to be Arthur's fiancée, who unfortunately could not attend the christening and passed away just weeks after Valerie's birth.

Valerie's father, Frederick "Fred" James Sanger, was indentured, at the age of 15, as an apprentice shipwright at His Majesty's Dockyard in Portsmouth, Hampshire, England, where there was a large naval base, for a term of 6 years. During this time, he was schooled and worked in the dockyards. Portsmouth is now famous as the home of the HMS Victory, which Admiral Nelson commanded during the Battle of Trafalgar.

In Fred's day, apprentices worked on the ships during the day and went to school at night. In *The Royal Dockyard Schools and their Education System, The Mariner's Mirror,* Frank E. King notes that, initially, the purpose of dockyard schools was

> "to improve the technical competency of shipwright apprentices and to identify those that showed the most academic aptitude for further education in order to qualify as naval constructors. Later, as the Royal Navy went from wooden ships with sails to steel, electricity and steam propulsion, the mission of the schools expanded to include the technical education of apprentices in all the trades."

Competition to remain as an apprentice was fierce as the bottom half of the class was dropped every year, regardless of the student's marks.

Fortunately, Fred proved that he was more than capable of meeting the school's standards. In 1925, he received two scholarships and a special leave to attend the Imperial College, University of London, where he spent his time studying and getting to know the big city. Three years later, he graduated with an engineering degree.

Valerie's mother, Kathleen Mary "Kitty" Thorn, on the other hand, experienced a slightly more complicated upbringing. Her father served in the Royal Navy for seventeen years, and during this time, he spent only seventeen months at home. Kitty's mother, Lilly, who had been ill for years, died when Kitty was 12 in 1918 during the Great Influenza pandemic. Even before her mother's death, Kitty spent most of her time with her mother's sister, Rosetta, who was also ill. Kitty cared for her aunt until she passed away in late 1926 or early 1927. After Rosetta's death, her husband remarried. This left no place for Kitty, so she returned to live with her father and his second wife.

Fred and Kitty first met when they were twelve. They were next-door neighbours when they lived in Portsmouth. Kitty would talk about playing the piano while she and Fred would sing duets during their courtship. Fred and Kitty got married on September 1, 1928, in Fareham, Hampshire, England in a church ceremony and surrounded by their close friends and family. Post-wedding, the newlyweds ventured off to London, where Fred was working at the time. In 1929, Fred was offered a position as an Education Officer for the Royal Air Force at the Halton Air Force base near Aylesbury. Kitty and Fred moved to Tring, where the first of their three children, Valerie, was born. David followed six years after Valerie, and Diana was born two years after that.

One of Valerie's very first memories was from when she was 3 years old—the family had just moved to Wendover, near Aylesbury. She remembered a dull earache and her crib being brought down into the front room of their new home so she could see the activity along the street as a form of entertainment.

She began to show a knack for problem-solving from a young age—with help from her father and godfather, of course. Kitty recalled that by the time Valerie turned two years old, Fred had taught Valerie how to set up a chessboard and by the age of three, she was putting together jigsaw puzzles. According to the stories, she had a small puzzle with a picture of an aeroplane on the box. After she had completed it with the help of the picture a few times, they would turn the picture over and have her attempt to put the puzzle together again without the reference—and they would time her. Valerie enjoyed doing jigsaw puzzles for the rest of her life.

By 1934, Fred and Kitty were restless as they wanted to travel. Fred took a leap of faith and accepted a position at the new Henry Lester Institute in Shanghai, China—affiliated with the University of London—as Head of the Engineering

Department. He left England on July 31, 1934, soon after securing his position and five months later, on December 22, 1934, Valerie and her mother left England to join Fred in Shanghai on the SS Rajputana[1].

Valerie does not remember much from that voyage, despite it being her first international one, as she was only four years old at the time. But she does remember that during the six weeks that it took them to make it to Shanghai, they made numerous stops along the way, including Gibraltar, Marseilles, Port Said, Aden, Bombay, Colombo, Penang, Singapore, and Hong Kong. At a young age, she had seen more cities and countries than most adults.

Known as "The Paris of the East, the New York of the West," Shanghai was thriving in the 1920s and 30s. The city's economy was on the rise and numerous forms of Chinese art were flourished.

Valerie and her parents lived in a house on Kiao Chow Road in the International Settlement. It was home to many expatriate travellers like themselves. She remembers that the house was quite big—or at least it seemed so to her four-year-old self. In the summers, she slept on a screened-in verandah because it was cooler than her bedroom. She thinks that after David was born, the verandah became her room, and then it was glassed in. She had no complaints, though. She would often count the stars in the sky at night to kill time until she fell asleep. It was during the summer evenings that Valerie remembers hearing cicadas in the garden for the first time.

She attended the Girls' Public School in Shanghai, which was a short walk from her home. One of her memories includes seeing a long list of words on the blackboard arranged according to their endings.

While exciting, Valerie's new journey in Shanghai also

---

[1]A Peninsular and Oriental Steam Navigation Company (P&O) ship. See Appendix A - Valerie's Ships for more information.

came with some unpleasant hardships, especially for a child in a new school. For unknown reasons, she developed two boils on her buttocks. As a result, she had to sit on a chair in the circle while all her classmates sat on the floor. Unfortunately, this was the time before antibiotics, and she remembers having to lie on her parents' bed as Kitty cleaned and dressed her wounds every day until they healed.

However, it did not end there for poor Valerie. She also had to get vaccinated for smallpox at school, even though she had already received the vaccine before leaving England—local regulations required it. The first vaccination had left a prominent scar on her arm, so this time her parents insisted that it be done on her leg—and it did not go well. Valerie had a strong reaction to the vaccine and had to stay in bed for several days. Those days were difficult for all of them. Consequently, her parents decided against her having any more vaccinations or immunizations at school.

Valerie's days were not just limited to school. She spent ample amounts of time with her father. Sometimes he would walk her to school, and she had to run to keep up with him. The route they often took was filled with flowers and butterflies.

Valerie also enjoyed visiting her father's office. She remembers the space as being bright and open and seemed to have a sort of passageway to the main office. Her father's desk was just around the corner—she vividly recalls the aeroplane picture that was hung up on the wall opposite it.

She recalls the celebrations for the Silver Jubilee of King George V and Queen Mary at Jessfield Park, marking 25 years of the king's reign. Valerie also recalls a day trip they took to visit West Lake in Hangzhou, China. It is still known as "paradise on Earth". The lake there is divided into five sections by three causeways. With beautiful and crystal-clear lakes, high mountains, attractive towers, islands and banks, West Lake became one of her favourite destinations of all time.

Chapter 1 The Beginning – Valerie's Childhood

1933 – Valerie – Wendover, England

1934 – Valerie – Shanghai, China

Chapter 2
Temporary Relocation

1936 to 1937

1936 – Valerie – Shanghai, China

Valerie's Journeys

In the summer of 1935, Valerie and her mother travelled on Empress line boats to Hong Kong and back. It was a holiday to visit Kitty's friend, Jane Lunson. Kitty and Jane had met on their journey to Shanghai the previous year and, over those long six weeks, became fast friends. Jane had been asking them to visit for some time now, and after getting settled into their new life, they finally decided to make the trip.

Jane Lunson's husband managed a dairy farm, which was located on the Peak. There was sprawling greenery as far as the eye could see dotted with animals. Cows were grazing on the grass, occasionally speaking to one another or lying down for a quick nap. A few times Valerie got the chance to pet them; they were soft and gentle. She decided that she liked cows.

Valerie would accompany Mr. Lunson on his rounds. He would carry her in his arms because she did not like walking too far, and her little legs would give out quite quickly. He also introduced Valerie to the newest craze—Eskimo pies, a small bar of ice cream coated with chocolate. They were available at the local farm store, which was located at the bottom of the hill. Together, the two would stroll there after their explorations of the farm, ready for a nice treat. Valerie would run inside the shop's doors and be greeted by the cashier before getting lost in the aisles. She would get distracted by the variety of goodies she could choose from. But, more often than not, they would go for the Eskimo pies. They were a novel and delightful treat at that time. Each time she devoured them, she would be grateful to Mr. Lunson, savouring every bite.

After one week of enjoying the fresh air and the company of the farm animals—and Eskimo pies—Kitty and Valerie wished Jane farewell, thanking their host for a lovely getaway. They returned home to the city, quickly adjusting to their daily routine, though sad that their vacation had come to an end. Fred, however, was eager to have his two favourite girls back home with him. He always missed them, even while at the office. However, it was not long before that routine was disrupted once again.

In the early spring of 1936, Kitty was awakened by a terrible stomach pain in the middle of the night. They attempted to ease the pain at home with medication and hydration, assuming it was a stomach bug she had picked up from something she had eaten. When the pain did not subside, they decided to take her to the local hospital. After some back and forth in the emergency room, she was diagnosed with acute appendicitis.

She was speedily admitted and rushed into surgery as soon as a surgeon became available, for there was fear that the organ would burst at any moment. Fortunately, her appendix was removed in time. This was a surgery that was considered difficult in the 1930s. She needed to remain under observation as she was a few weeks pregnant. While her mother was recovering and beginning to feel better, Valerie's health became worrisome. She was writhing with stomach pain and also a fever and nausea. She was unable to keep her dinner down. So, like her mother, Valerie was rushed to the same hospital where they told her father she had bacillary dysentery, an intestinal infection caused by bacteria found in the human gut. She had to be treated immediately, so now both Fred's wife and his daughter were in the hospital.

After receiving a round of medicine, Valerie was quite indignant as they had placed her into a crib in the children's ward. Eventually, she became tired of fighting and fell asleep with her father by her side.

In the summer of 1936, Valerie and her father went to Tsingtao (now more commonly known as Qingdao) for a holiday. It was a beautiful, historic city and the journey from Shanghai along the coast was breathtaking. Valerie had not seen much outside of the city of Shanghai, so she was thrilled at the sight of the vast ocean. They went on to Laoshan in the mountains, where it was cooler than by the sea in Tsingtao.

Unfortunately, this year seemed to be producing a

pattern in her life. Two weeks before they were to return to Shanghai from Tsingtao, Fred came down with amoebic dysentery – a parasitic infection that caused him to experience similar symptoms to Valerie and her mother: stomach pain, fever, nausea, and chills. He was immediately taken to a hospital for treatment, but he was worried about leaving his child behind. Luckily, he had a good support system to turn to in time of need.

Valerie could not stay at the hospital with her father all by herself. With her mother not around to look after her, she was left in the care of her father's trusted friend, who lived in town. Still only a child, she could not quite grasp that her father was seriously ill, so she was not very concerned. She had seen her mother come and go from the hospital, so she knew her father would eventually return. She missed him but she enjoyed the company of her new friends. Once her father recovered, the two of them made their way back to Shanghai and met a very worried Kitty. She had been enormously stressed not being there for her family when she heard of Fred's illness. However, the sight of him, finally home and healthy, brought her relief.

The year 1936 continued to be an eventful one for the Sanger family. Vacations, sickness and now, another baby. On September 10th of that year, they welcomed David, Valerie's brother, who was born in the Cottage Hospital in Shanghai.

David's birth, when Valerie was only six years old, did not significantly change her daily life. She was quite interested in this new object that had become a part of her life. He was so small and dainty, did not speak, could not walk – could not do anything really, except cry. However, he did not provide her with any stimulus or entertainment. Valerie's parents had hired an amah, a local nanny, to care for their newborn, so they were still able to give Valerie attention.

That year Valerie spent a lot of time with her books. So much, in fact, that her parents wondered why she was so obsessed. It was great that she was fuelling her mind, but they were worried she would forfeit other experiences. She would spend hours in her bedroom quietly organising and reorganising books, removing them from the shelves one at a time, wiping them down with a cloth and then putting them back in alphabetical order. She would count all the books, making sure that none had gone missing. She was spending so much time reading that her parents decided to enrol her for horse riding lessons as a distraction. Fred had poor eyesight since childhood which was why he and Kitty were worried about Valerie straining her eyes spending too much time reading.

Valerie did not do very well at the riding school. She was terrified of the large and loud horses. She worried that as soon as one lowered its head, she would fall forward; if it raised its head too high or decided to jump, she worried she would tumble backward and hurt herself. She wandered around the stables with great caution so that no horse would sneak up on her or kick her by accident. It came to the point that she refused to ride any horse but the quietest one in the stable.

After horse riding did not work out, Valerie took up some other activities. She recalls the enjoyment of playing with her father's typewriter, which he would let her "toy around with" when he was not using it. He loved that she was interested in his tools. She was fascinated by its functionality and the ability to type one's own words onto paper.

It was around the same time that she also began to play mah-jongg with her father, who modified the game from four to a game for two. A game of skill, strategy, and a bit of luck, she would pull together the pieces, mulling over the Chinese symbols and characters, trying to absorb the instructions and techniques. When she was not practising the game, she would use the tiles to make buildings and forts. She never stuck to one purpose; she always tried to figure out what else she could do with the items before her.

When she did not have her nose stuck in a book or was not learning new games, Valerie would spend many hours playing hopscotch on the sidewalk right outside her home with her friend Joyce, who lived nearby. She would bump into the neighbours' children, children down the street, or sometimes even friends from school and invite them to play with her. They would spend hours chatting away and hopping along the chalk-drawn layout until they were exhausted and could barely walk back home. She would also show them a lovely glass stone she had with a pretty floral pattern in it. She was so proud of it and treasured that trinket for a long time.

One of the most vivid memories of her childhood was waking up one morning to find what seemed to her to be a large dead worm in her bed. She jumped out, squealing as she tried to get away from the unfamiliar bug that had made its way into her personal space. Apparently, she had been given worm powders. She supposed later that the worm was no longer than an inch or two, but to her at the time, it seemed about six inches long!

The family's streak of illnesses continued. Shortly after David's birth, Fred contracted mumps. Once again, he was tormented with fever, nausea, and body aches. In order to make sure his children did not contract it, given their young age and greater susceptibility, Valerie and David were banned from their parents' bedroom while their mother nursed Fred back to health. Luckily, neither of them contracted the disease, and Fred recovered with relative ease.

Valerie began to become aware of nature at this age. She would notice all the different kinds of trees, leaves, and flowers that she saw when they explored around Shanghai or when on vacation. She remembered the noise of the cicadas most vividly—the loud buzzing and clicking, which sometimes were so loud she could not pinpoint their location. Her father told her that there were thousands of cicadas in one of the trees in the garden, so he arranged for them to be removed. Men came with sticks with sticky ends and gathered up buckets full of the insects removing the load noise.

Valerie's parents had a gramophone in their home on which they would play music each evening. Her parents told her it was their favourite tradition and that when she and David were asleep, they would quietly play their music and spend hours just chatting away. Her mother was particularly fond of Paul Robeson's voice (an American bass-baritone known for Old Man River), and she sang Brahms' lullaby to her children.

Valerie also recalled her visits to the cinema. Her parents took her to see the movie Rose Marie (1936), and when the sad part began, she became so upset that her father had to take her out of the cinema. They walked around the upstairs lobby until the end of the film because her mother wanted to watch the movie till the end. She remembered the carpeted floors of the lobby and the plush sofas and easy chairs and, most importantly, how her father did not leave her side for even a moment and comforted her for as long as she needed.

1935 – Kitty and Valerie – Hong Kong, China

Chapter 3
To the Roots and Back

1937 to 1938

1937 – Valerie wearing a Kimono – Karatsu, Japan

In July of 1937, everybody, including Amah (David's nanny), went to Japan for a two-month holiday. The family was fortunate to avoid the societal strife going on in Shanghai during that summer. To get to Karatsu, they took a Japanese line boat to Nagasaki and then went by train to Karatsu, a resort town on the west side of Kyushu Island, where Valerie celebrated her 7th birthday and was lent a bicycle. The hotel staff gifted her a complete Japanese outfit—a kimono, obi, socks, and shoes—a perfect souvenir of her trip to Japan. In 2019, Valerie gave the kimono to her great-granddaughter, Maria.

She learned to ride a bicycle. She had no prior training in handling two wheels, so she could not balance herself and would fall off quite often. The other activity she enjoyed, apart from cycling, was swimming, which she did with a rubber ring floating device and riding the ocean swells before they crested into waves that crashed onto the shore. Valerie's parents had friends from Shanghai staying nearby, who were greatly impressed with their swimming prowess as they swam a long way to a cave. Valerie improved her swimming skills by getting some tips from them.

As the strife between the Chinese National Revolutionary Army and the Japanese Imperial Army worsened in Shanghai, the family decided to extend their stay in Japan. Things were not good in Shanghai as the Japanese were fighting the Chinese in the area surrounding the International Settlement.

Fred had to return to Shanghai early as it was the start of the school term. While Fred was there, it was decided that the teaching staff should take leave to visit England in three years instead of the standard five years.

The rest of the family, including Amah, stayed behind in Karatsu until it was determined that the family would return to England. So, Valerie, David, Kitty, and Amah boarded SS

Comorin[2] in Japan in October of 1937. Valerie surmised that SS Comorin stopped in Hong Kong where her father joined them for the rest of the trip to England.

On SS Comorin, there was a deep swimming pool above the deck next to the railing. There, Valerie enjoyed swimming with her rubber ring. One day, while Valerie was in the pool, the boat rolled severely, and she was afraid that she would be taken over the edge, considering the depth of the pool. It was not hazardous, however. Valerie also remembered being dressed like a gypsy for an egg and spoon race on the trip.

To avoid the rough waters in the Bay of Biscay, her parents decided to disembark from SS Comorin in Marseille, France. They continued their journey to England on a train to Boulogne on the north coast of France. There, they took the ferry to Folkestone, located on the south coast of England.

The crossing of the English Channel was very rough and took twice as long as usual. The family then went to London by train and stayed for a couple of days in a hotel in Wimbledon. It was an expensive hotel where they had to behave accordingly. She remembered a woman walking in with a couple of Pekingese, but Valerie was not particularly fond of them.

As the family arrived in England shortly before Christmas, Valerie's parents decided to split up and spend the holidays separately. Valerie then accompanied her father to visit his parents' home, a semi-detached house located at 34 Gladys Avenue in the north end of Portsmouth. Her mother, with David and Amah, went to Coventry to visit her parents.

Valerie got to stay in a room in her grandparents' house in Portsmouth, which had a large double bed and a deep feather mattress. The room was furnished with a bowl and

---

[2] P &O liner on the Asia to England route. See Appendix A – Valerie's Ships for more information.

ewer for washing, as there was not a toilet upstairs. Like many houses in England at that time, the bathroom was just outside the back door. A bath had been installed behind curtains in her father's old bedroom on the second floor. There was a parlour downstairs, which was rarely used, and a large dining room with a fireplace. Christmas dinner was held in the dining room with a roaring fire in the fireplace. At the end of the hall was the kitchen with a huge table where meals were served. It also had comfortable chairs where Valerie's grandparents spent most of their time. The back courtyard had a gate that opened to a back lane. While staying with them, her grandmother took her to visit all her friends in the back lane.

After Christmas, the family reunited in New Malden, where Valerie's parents had arranged to stay in a head gardener's cottage. She recalled a large living room with a huge fireplace. In the spring, Valerie discovered flowers. She collected armfuls of daffodils from the forest and recalled the floral bed around the cottage had plenty of forget-me-nots. She went to school in the vicinity, where she collected tadpoles and saw them become frogs.

Valerie also went shopping for a winter coat with her mother in Kingston-upon-Thames. There, she found a mustard-coloured jacket with a hat to match; it made her feel like a big girl. During her time in New Malden, she went to the Royal Albert Hall in London to see her father receive his master's degree. Valerie was thrilled to see that and was impressed with the building's structure. It was also at this time that Valerie's younger sister, Diana, was born in Kings College Hospital in London on April 5, 1938.

Moving back to England had been pleasant as Fred and Kitty's parents and siblings lived there. However, Fred had to return to Shanghai in May of 1938 because his home leave was over, and he needed to continue teaching at the Henry Lester Institute. Before Fred left, the family moved into a two-story house in Tolworth. Valerie's parents had decided it would be best for the rest of the family to stay in England since Diana was only a month old. This decision was made relying on Amah to help with the care of David and Diana. The plan was for the rest of the family to travel to Shanghai in December of 1938.

In Tolworth, right behind the house there was a railway line with a bridge under which Valerie could walk and picked wild blackberries.

By August, Kitty was concerned about the situation in England and the possibility of war. She wanted to be with her husband and decided to leave England early to be with him in Shanghai. After the Battle of Shanghai in 1937, the situation in the area around the International Settlement in Shanghai had stabilised.

As Valerie reflected on this time in England, she realised that four experiences significantly impacted the rest of her life. The first was her interest in nature, which grew with the collection of flowers, watching the tadpoles transform into frogs, and picking blackberries. The second was her interest in history, which started when she visited her grandmother, Ethel, in Portsmouth in 1938 on her own. For this trip, she travelled by train under the care of the train guard. Her grandmother took her on a tour of the HMS Victory (Nelsen's ship from the Battle of Trafalgar). Next was her understanding of the need for continuous education as she watched her father graduate from the University of London at Albert Hall. The fourth was the experience of learning another language – French at school.

To leave England, Kitty had to take what was available, which was a cabin on D deck – one of the lowest decks on SS Rawalpindi[3].

Sadly, Amah had to sleep on an even lower deck where there were even worse conditions. Upon seeing Amah's cabin, Kitty quickly brought her up to the cabin on D deck with the

---

[3]A P&O liner built in 1926. See Appendix A – Valerie's Ships for more information.

rest of the family to sleep on the floor until she could arrange for better accommodations.

On the journey from England back to Shanghai, the ship docked at Marseille. Here, Valerie heard about Chamberlain's famous quote on September 30, 1938, "Peace in our time", after his return from his meeting with Hitler in Munich. There was great relief on the ship with Chamberlain's announcement. It impacted everyone!

Valerie had a couple of memories of the journey. First, all the children, including herself, ate in a unique dining room before the adults. Whenever Valerie ordered soft-boiled eggs, they arrived with the egg white uncooked, so she would not eat them. She was finally convinced to ask for hard-boiled eggs to solve the problem. The ship stopped at many ports, and Valerie remembered the little local boats that came out to meet the ship, and the people tried to sell their goods to the passengers. The good news was that some passengers left the ship at these ports. This allowed the family to move to higher decks and better accommodations.

Upon arrival in Shanghai, Valerie and her family lived in a house at the end of the row of rowhouses on Great Western Road. Each home in the row was three stories high with a separate entrance. On the other side of the road that entered the complex of rowhouses was a wall, over which the family could look. On the other side of the wall was muddy ground and low buildings in a Chinese area, then a railway line which was the Japanese lines. In the night, the frogs could be heard croaking. The house was comprised of three stories – a living room, a dining room and a kitchen downstairs, a master bedroom with an ensuite bathroom in front and a second bedroom in the back. There was a second bathroom part way upstairs to the 3rd floor where there were two more bedrooms, one of which Amah used. Valerie used to sleep on the second floor while David and Diana were younger, but later, David took that room, and Valerie got one of the upstairs bedrooms.

Chapter 3 To the Roots and Back

The house was located relatively close to the Columbia Country Club, which was also on Great Western Road. The family spent most mornings swimming at the Club during the hot summer months. The treat afterward was to have a portion of a new food item—French fries and ketchup. In addition, she took swimming and diving classes and eventually, she was able to swim the width of the pool underwater. On Sunday mornings, the family often walked in the other direction crossing over the Japanese railway lines and entering the countryside. The treat was then to come home, where Valerie would sip her father's shandy. After that, Valerie often went to the swings at Jessfield Park, taking a road that smelled of burning rubber.

Upon her return to Shanghai, Valerie started at the Cathedral Girls School. Prior to the trip to England, she was a student at the Shanghai Public Girls' School from 1934 to 1937. While at the Cathedral Girls School, she played field hockey, usually on the wing, which required lots of running. She thought she spent many recesses doing cartwheels, which were her specialty, but other students did handstands. Being a larger school, it was much more organised than the one she had attended in England. She took classes in Algebra, Geometry, Latin, English, Geography, History, Arithmetic, French, Music, and Art. It was here that she had gym three times a week, used the balance beam, and came to know how to march and hang from the wall bars.

The highlight of this time was Gilbert and Sullivan's opera *Iolanthe*, which was initially scheduled for three days on the large patio of the school. However, the exhibition was so successful that another day was added. Valerie was a fairy with ruffles of white chiffon on her skirt. She wore a dark pink dress and loved every minute of it.

The school's colour was purple, and Valerie wore marine blue tunics with white blouses and purple ties in the winter. In addition, she wore a mauve princess-style dress with buttons on the front, no collar but white lapels in hot weather.

The school had lovely terrain where she discovered her talents in outdoor sports, a perfect fit as she was hyperactive. However, her actual love was for singing.

1938 – Valerie and David – Richmond Park, New Malden, England

Chapter 4
Exploring and Discovering

1939 to 1941

1941 – Valerie's 11th birthday party – Shanghai, China

Moving from one place to another during her growing-up years, Valerie had adventures wherever she went. Some of her greatest memories were during her childhood when she travelled, saw countless new places, and experienced new things.

Valerie had many memories, both good and bad, from when she lived in Shanghai. The house on Great Western Road, like the ones she had lived in before, also had a swing with two seats and a platform in between. However, the platform had disappeared for some reason, and only one seat remained on the swing. Since there was only one seat, Valerie and David had to take turns. Valerie was glad that Diana was too young to ride on the swing; otherwise, she would have had to wait longer for her turn. As David was very young, Valerie would push him on the swing. One particular day, as she was pushing David, she must have let it go too high because he fell off, and the swing hit her on the head. She was not seriously hurt, but that incident did remain with her for life, and she never pushed a swing too high again.

Another day, as she was entering her house late one afternoon, she saw some very dark, hard soil by the front door. Curious as to why it looked that way, she began digging and thought she had discovered coal. She immediately ran to her father to show him her discovery. After having a quick look at what young Valerie so eagerly claimed to be coal, her father informed her that it was actually something else. Needless to say, she did not go around digging in the garden after that.

Valerie also remembered the first and only time she received an Order Mark, a piece of paper given to students for some misdemeanour that had to be taken home and signed by the student's parents. The school had instructed students to bring cardigans to put on after gym class and that if anyone forgot, they would be given an Order Mark. Valerie was not one to break the rules or disobey them and she was always meticulous in remembering her cardigan except for once. That was the fateful day she received her first Order Mark. Her parents stood in front of the fireplace, debating whether to sign the slip of paper or not after Valerie had handed it to them. They did eventually sign it, however.

When Valerie lived on the Great Western Road, she had three good friends: Bunny, Daphne Butt, and Coryn Clark. Bunny was the first friend she made after moving there. They would meet every day and spend all evening playing together. One of their favourite things to do was to turn round and round and then fall to the ground while they watched the world around them spin. Then, when the world stopped spinning, they stayed on the ground and tried to make out the shapes of the clouds – Valerie always saw maps of different countries! Valerie and Bunny soon befriended Coryn and Daphne, and the group of four spent their time having parties and playing different games. Their favourite games were Sardines, similar to hide and seek, and Musical Chairs. They could spend all day playing those games!

Valerie distinctly recalled another game she was fond of called 'And the wheel came off'. The game revolved around the story of a carriage ride. One player was the designated reader, while the other players were each assigned a particular word from the story. When that word was mentioned, they had to stand up and turn around. If they failed to do so, they would have to forfeit something. When the reader said, "And the wheel came off," all the players had to stand up and turn around. Valerie did not recall what the players had to do to retrieve their forfeited items, but she remembered that it was a lot of fun.

The British Embassy would celebrate Queen Victoria's birthday every year, and Valerie would have to parade on the grounds of the Embassy in her brownie uniform. She especially disliked the activity because, even though it was very hot in Shanghai in May, she was required to wear a woollen hat in the sweltering heat. It was no surprise that she almost fainted one day. She was taken to the porch of the Embassy, where the staff looked after her.

Valerie did not dislike all traditions, though. For example, the Henry Lester Institute held a Christmas party every year where all the children of the faculty received presents. One Christmas, she received a lovely black box of watercolour paints in tubes. She was delighted because the paint set, when opened, had a place in the lid to mix the paints and a paintbrush holder at the front.

While art was not particularly appealing to her aesthetic senses, music was a different story. She enjoyed music, especially folk tunes, and loved singing. She would sing all kinds of songs, even if she did not know the words.

One of the most exciting things about Valerie's time living in Shanghai was travelling in rickshaws pulled by a man running. Valerie did not take a bus to school; she took a rickshaw. Countless rickshaws operated throughout the city. Whenever you had to go somewhere, you hailed a rickshaw like you would a taxi. Valerie's parents had hired a private rickshaw man, often called a rickshaw coolie, who catered to the family's travel needs when required. This also allowed the rickshaw coolie to earn more than the average rickshaw coolie because he would get paid for his services when he was called, and when they did not need him, he could carry on as a general rickshaw coolie. He made sure Valerie got to school on time, and when school let out, he would already be there, waiting to take her home.

Valerie seized any chance to have fun, and the rickshaws were no exception. Valerie and the other girls from school would often encourage their rickshaw coolies to race on the way home. Along the way, they would see countless things, such as men urinating on the sidewalks and others playing mah-jongg. Since she lived in a less-developed part of Shanghai, these were not uncommon sights for her.

A lot of stray dogs, called "chows", ran free in the streets, and the concern among the public was that these dogs were rabid, so, Valerie and her siblings were forbidden from touching them. Her parents eventually got so concerned about their children being afraid of the street dogs that they went and bought a pointer puppy to help ease the fright. However, the puppy did the exact opposite because whenever it came into the living room, Valerie and her siblings would jump onto the chesterfield and would not come down until the puppy left the room. The puppy soon became very ill, though, so they did not keep it very long.

At that time, Fred used to keep score for one of the cricket teams in Shanghai. Valerie enjoyed accompanying him and became quite a known figure at the games. Many of the spectators were kind to her, and she particularly enjoyed teatime at the games when her father came to visit her. When her father kept score at the home pitch, she was not allowed in the scoring box. However, when he scored at an away pitch, she was allowed in the scoring box with him and assisted by running errands. He also taught her how to score, and soon enough, she knew the names of all the players and was able to follow the game. It was here that Valerie learned to play cribbage, and, in the following years, her father taught her Russian Bank (Double Solitaire), Bezique and two kinds of solitaire, as well as a few card tricks.

While living on Great Western Road, Valerie's home was broken into one day, and her parents' silverware (cutlery) was stolen, among other valuable items. After the robbery, Valerie accompanied her father to the police station, where his fingerprints were taken. The police investigation determined that it had been an inside job and so her parents fired one of the servants.

Around that time, a large oil fire broke out at quite a distance from where Valerie's family lived, but it was clearly visible from her bedroom window. Seeing the huge fire at that age had a significant impact on Valerie as she remained concerned about fires all her life. After the fire, everyone was required to get typhoid shots. Because Valerie had reacted quite badly to her last shot, her parents decided against it. They had heard of pills, which could be taken in place of the shot, two hours before breakfast. For the next three days, Valerie was woken up by her parents at an unusually early hour to take the pill so that she could have breakfast.

One day, both Valerie and David experienced diarrhoea. This was of particular concern for her parents as Shanghai was experiencing a cholera outbreak at the time. The "cure" that the locals had come up with was taking castor oil followed by hot tea. Valerie remembers that her parents put her and her brother in their bedroom and administered the dosage. Once the castor oil and tea started taking effect, both children ran to the bathroom. Valerie was glad that they had two bathrooms!

In the late 1930s, Valerie's parents had a Wendy house built for her and her siblings. A Wendy house was a playhouse that was large enough for Valerie and a couple of her friends to walk into. Her father had designed it. Each wall was separate, and Valerie made curtains for the windows on the sidewall—with the help of her mother, of course. She remembers the curtains were made with a patterned cloth that had horses and riders on it. She also made a curtain for the front door. The Wendy house was painted yellow, while the roof was made of red wooden tiles. However, she did not remember what kind of furniture they put in it or even if they did.

Soon after that, in March of 1940, Valerie and her family moved to Jessfield Road. They lived in a large house in a compound of four houses that belonged to the American-owned and operated Saint John's University. Because of the political situation in China, many of the American faculty had returned to the United States. The University wanted some reliable tenants to move into the compound, so Valerie's family moved there.

The house the family lived in was the first one on the left as you entered the compound; it was a lovely big house. It consisted of a living room, dining room, den, kitchen with a refrigerator, and screened verandah on the main floor. The second floor consisted of three bedrooms and two bathrooms, one of which was between the two bigger bedrooms. The second bathroom, which was near David's room, had a unique bathtub that was round with high sides and not very long. It was so high that David had to be picked up and lowered into the tub. There was also a screened-in verandah above the one on the main floor. The house also had a third floor that had two small rooms and a large one. The large room was turned into David's and Diana's playroom, even though it was called the "nursery", and the Wendy house was kept there. Valerie's parents bought raffle tickets for a doll's house for each of their children, and Diana's ticket had won! So, the doll's house was another addition to their playroom.

One of the two smaller rooms on the third floor, one was Amah's, and the other one was kept for the seamstress who used to come once in a while to make the children's clothes. One of the bigger bedrooms on the second floor was Valerie's parents and the other one was shared by her and Diana. The smaller room was David's, and he had his own bathroom. Valerie and Diana shared their parents' bathroom as it had a proper bathtub.

From the upstairs front windows of the house, Valerie could see another compound of much larger houses on the other side of the unpaved alley. This compound was owned by wealthy Chinese residents.

The den on the main floor served as Fred's office. He had a large, framed picture of Lord Kitchener on one of the walls. It had been given to him as he had been awarded a Kitchener scholarship. He did most of his marking in his office, and Valerie remembers going there to watch him mark papers, develop a bell curve, and tell her about his expectations for each student. Of course, that was not very exciting for a child, and she would often get very bored and start yawning, much to her father's annoyance.

At the time they moved to Jessfield Road, Fred was working long hours, but he still spent at least half an hour with each of his children in the evening before they went to bed. It was "quality time", as it is now called. Their father would usually start by reading Diana a bedtime story, and then he would read adventure books to David, such as Climbing Mount Everest, which piqued Valerie's interest, so she would listen as well. Once her father was done with the younger children, he would play Chinese Checkers with her.

Fred used to entertain her and her siblings by making a tune with his hands clasped together. Another unintentional source of entertainment for the children was when their father gargled every morning. His theory was that this would kill any germs and help prevent illness. The sound was hilarious and would make Valerie and her siblings giggle, but what made it entertaining was that he would sing a tune, such as God Save the King, as he gargled.

Initially, Valerie was sad about the move because she had to leave her three dear friends behind. However, she soon settled into her new home and found two playmates in the compound: Yurie, the youngest daughter of artist Emma Bormann, and Sandy, the youngest son of Dr. Dunlap, an ear, nose, and throat specialist. Emma Bormann was trained in Vienna and had exhibited her work in Chicago. She was a friend of Mrs. Dunlap, who also was an artist.

Valerie and Sandy would go to Yurie's house and would sometimes roller-skate on her terrazzo verandah. Other times, they would go to Yurie's mother's studio and paint. Emma Bormann would prepare outline drawings for the children. The children would then use wax to outline the picture and then paint with different colours between the wax edges. Valerie remembers that she thoroughly enjoyed it. Behind the houses, there was a common garden with a grape arbour that they once got into trouble for climbing. Valerie had not been allowed to ride a bicycle on the streets when they were living on the Great Western Road, but now that they were residing in a gated community, her parents finally allowed her to ride her bicycle, which she had been given in Japan. She rode it around the compound on many days.

Their neighbour at the other end of the compound, Mr. Evans and his family, owned one of the largest bookstores in Shanghai. Many years later, Valerie contacted his daughter, Joyce, in Toronto. At that time, Mr. Evans was making a living as a travelling book salesman.

One time, Valerie was running along the driveway when she jumped over a stick. However, as the stick started wriggling, she realised that it was, in fact, a snake. Boy, was she shocked! Another time, it had rained a lot, and she was walking in the mud at the other end of the compound with Sandy and David. David fell over and got covered in mud. They hurried over to Amah to get him cleaned up before their mother found out. David and Valerie would often engage in tickling fights, which is when Valerie learned to control the tickling effect.

The summer after moving to the compound, Valerie celebrated her 11th birthday, and her parents threw a party on a large lawn at the other end of the compound with about ten of her friends. Valerie wore a new sunsuit with red taped edges and because it was hot, Valerie sweated, and the coloured edges of her sunsuit bled. They played games and ate outside under a large tree.

Valerie joined the Girl Guides Program and became a Brownie when she was about eight. The program was very well managed, and she graduated to a Sixer. The Brownies were split into groups of six, and the Sixer was the Brownie in charge of the other five in the group. At the age of eleven, in September of 1941, she completed the Brownie program and "flew up" to the Guides.

In the last year of living in Shanghai, the cholera outbreak worsened, so everyone had to get cholera shots. The Japanese insisted that all workers get the shots, and since Fred had to cross Japanese lines daily for work, he had to get them.

While she was living in the compound, a significant event occurred: a large fire broke out in a village just outside the compound. It originated in a ping-pong ball factory located on the other side of the high wall surrounding the compound and to the right of the compound's entrance. Valerie's house was on the left-hand side of the compound's entrance, so the fire was very nearby. The fire quickly spread throughout the village, destroying around 25 acres of property. The firemen used Valerie's house as their headquarters to put out the fire. Later that evening, her parents opened their garage for the people who had been rendered homeless by the fire. Valerie was already afraid of fires after witnessing the fire from her room back in her house on Great Western Road, but this one, being so close, absolutely terrified her. So, her father gave Valerie her very first drink—a brandy.

In September, it was back to school. This time, however, it was different as David joined Valerie in the rickshaw. He was five so he went to kindergarten in the same school as Valerie until he was old enough to go to The Cathedral Boys School. The curriculum was the same as in England. Valerie's real struggle came on Friday afternoons when the art teacher positioned a stuffed bird on a stand in the centre of the room. The class had to measure it with their pencils and draw it. Valerie just could not draw all the curves on the bird.

Although Valerie was very happy living in the compound, her parents became more and more concerned about the increasingly alarming situation in Shanghai. Her father wanted to join the British army in India, but the British government had asked him to stay and educate the Chinese. However, because of the circumstances at the time, he decided to go to India, and he submitted his resignation effective December 10, 1941.

As the situation in the city worsened due to the growing tensions between the Chinese and the Japanese, Fred managed to arrange for berths for Kitty and the children on a

Dutch motor ship called the Tjisadane[4] that would leave on November 30, 1941. Because Fred had to wrap up his work at the Institute and manage their financial affairs, he could not accompany them. The trip had been decided very quickly, so Kitty only had a week to pack up. On the morning of November 30, as Valerie's family headed to the harbour, they saw several Japanese tanks parked on Jessfield Road. Fred and his friend, Bill Ankerson, known as 'Uncle Bill', saw them off with 13 pieces of luggage. It was customary in Shanghai that if children had no other relatives in the city, to call good friends of their parents 'aunt' and 'uncle'. Included in the 13 pieces of luggage were two woodcut pictures done by Yurie's mother and given to Valerie and her mother as parting gifts. The one of the British Consulate in Shanghai was given to Kitty; the other of the racetrack, was given to Valerie. The two woodcuts are still in the family.

The Tjisadane was the last non-evacuee ship to leave Shanghai before the Japanese took over completely on December 8, 1941. Fred was due to leave on the 10th, but when the Japanese attacked Pearl Harbor on December 7, they also took over the International Settlement and French concession in Shanghai, and her father was trapped. Unbeknownst to Valerie's family at the time, he would remain in Shanghai for the next four years.

---

[4]See Appendix A – Valerie's Ships for more information.

1940 – Valerie, David, Kitty, and Diana – Shanghai, China

Chapter 5
On the Run

1941 to 1942

SS Tjisadane

Valerie's Journeys

After the SS Tjisadane left Shanghai on November 30, 1941, it stopped in Hong Kong before setting sail for Manila. Times were tough as most of the passengers had left at least one, if not more, family member behind, but the captain, WFH Burger, managed to uplift everyone's moods. He was particularly popular among the children. However, a day and a half after leaving Hong Kong, the Japanese attacked Pearl Harbour on December 7th, and the captain was instructed not to dock at Manila by the higher-ups and to go immediately to Surabaya, a port in the northeast of Java, Indonesia. The captain was never seen again by the passengers as he was occupied with getting the ship to port safely. They were originally meant to go to Batavia (changed to Jakarta in 1949) and this sudden change in plans was most fortunate. Another evacuee ship had arrived in Manila, and the captain had let the passengers go ashore. When word came that the ship was to sail in two hours, the captain was unable to inform the passengers, who ended up trapped there. They were later captured by the Japanese and put in camps. They were treated harshly as they had attempted to flee the approaching Japanese army. On December 8th, the Japanese took over the International Settlement and French Concession in Shanghai. The residents offered no resistance to the Japanese takeover and, thus, were not treated as harshly.

It was terribly hot in Surabaya, and upon reaching there, Valerie and her family had to spend the entire day in a customs shed, which was, unsurprisingly, not air-conditioned. All the adults were body searched, and Valerie remembers her mother bravely going into a cubicle to be searched, leaving David and Diana in Valerie's care. In the hotel that Kitty found, the children were introduced to Dutch husbands, long, thick pillows that were placed between people so they could sleep as comfortably as possible in the hot weather.

Valerie and her family were originally meant to stay in Java for a three-week holiday in the mountains with her father. They would then depart for Auckland, New Zealand, on a Dutch ship, while her father would join the British Army in India.

Chapter 5 On the Run

However, the family had not heard if Fred had left Shanghai or was trapped there. Kitty honoured her husband's last words to her—if there was ever a problem, she should go to the British Consulate. This she did. The British consul instructed her mother to leave Java as soon as possible, and so, the next day, they boarded a train to Tjilitjap (also spelled Tjilatjap or Cilacap), a port city in Central Java. The British consul had also assisted Kitty in obtaining a refund for the family's reservations on a ship to New Zealand. Valerie recalled that it took all day to reach Tjilitjap and that her family only had one banana each for the duration of the travel.

Upon reaching Tjilitjap, Valerie was very excited to see the scenery of the wooded mountains—something that could not be witnessed in Shanghai since it was situated on the Yangtze River Delta and was very flat. Since the only hotel in Tjilitjap had no vacancies, Valerie and her family were placed in army barracks a quarter of a mile away from the railway tracks. They had to sleep on straw mattresses, and there were no toilet facilities available.

The next morning, they went to the hotel, had breakfast, and waited in the hotel garden. At noon, they boarded the SS Gorgon[5]. The following days were spent travelling to Fremantle, the port of Perth in Western Australia. The voyage was not pleasant as the sea was rough, and the ship had to zigzag continuously as a safety measure, resulting in a tense atmosphere on the ship. The crew and the adults were concerned that Japanese submarines might be in the area. Some of the adult male passengers volunteered to go on watch to help out the crew. Alarms did go off, but these were due to whales, not submarines. Valerie remembered that during the six days she was on the SS Gorgon, they would have different boat drills every single day without warning. By the second day, the passengers got used to it, but everyone was completely

---

[5]A Blue Funnel Line ship. See Appendix A – Valerie's Ships for more information.

taken by surprise the first time it happened. During the drill, it became evident that Valerie, at age 11, was not quite dependable. Valerie shared a cabin with David, while her mother and Diana shared the one next door. Valerie's mother had instructed her to take care of David in case of an emergency, but the first time the drill happened, Valerie dashed out the door, leaving David behind.

Upon their arrival in Perth on December 20, 1941, Kitty contacted her friend, Renee Ankerson, who was living in Perth at the time with her daughter, Tricia. Her husband, Bill Ankerson, had accompanied Fred to see the family off in Shanghai, but neither Kitty nor Renee Ankerson knew what had happened to their husbands. Valerie would later find out that her father was first confined to their home in Shanghai. He was then given some freedom and assisted the British Relief Association in placing British families in civilian internment camps. Renee Ankerson also heard later that her husband had made it to Singapore.

Renee Ankerson and Tricia lived in a small two-bedroom apartment, but they readily took in Valerie's family. Tricia and her mother slept in one bedroom, while Valerie's mother and Diana slept in the other. Valerie slept on the chesterfield in the living room, whereas David's sleeping arrangement consisted of two chairs put together as a makeshift bed, also in the living room. Their first Christmas after leaving Shanghai was spent with the Ankersons. Valerie did not remember much about that Christmas except that it was not a very joyful one, as the men of the family were not present, and their whereabouts were unknown. She did remember watching Charlie Chaplin movies, which Auntie Renee had, and other things of the sort that amused children back then.

Originally, Valerie's family was headed to New Plymouth, New Zealand. Kitty decided to go there because she felt her husband would come looking for them there. So, after staying with the Ankersons for two weeks, Valerie's family boarded a train bound for Sydney on January 5, 1942. The sleeping cars were not air-conditioned, and it was extremely hot as they crossed the Nullarbor Plain in central Australia. There were only three air-cooled carriages where they would stay for part of the day before returning to the sleeping car. At times, when David would get too restless, Valerie would take him for a walk to an air-cooled carriage, to the sleeping car and back. They stopped at several stations, which were seemingly in the middle of nowhere. It always felt like Aboriginals would appear out of the blue to beg the passengers for things. Someone even told Valerie that Aboriginal women loved dresses so much that they would wear one on top of the other! Valerie never found out how ***true*** that was, though.

Along the way, Valerie saw a large pipe beside the railway line. She was told that the pipe supplied water to Kalgoorlie, a city in Western Australia in the desert. Because the widths of the railway tracks in Australia were not standardised at the time, they had to switch trains every time they entered a new state. Valerie also went through the worst dust storm that the region had experienced there in 50 years between Augusta and Adelaide. Luckily, the station in Adelaide had showers, and the family was able to clean up before their journey to Melbourne. They left Melbourne in the evening, and Valerie could not help but be amazed by the beautiful scenery in front of her—the wooded mountains and the greenery. Valerie was very disappointed when it grew dark, and she could not admire it anymore. They arrived in Albury in the late evening and had to change trains again. Valerie was used to it by now, but this time, the family had to walk about ten coaches before they reached their reservation for the night! Diana had insisted on carrying their mother's attaché case that contained medicines during the walk to their coach, and she had bruises on her legs for days. At Albury, Valerie remembered her mother stepping off the train to go to the station for a cup of tea. Valerie was terrified because the train was due to leave soon. In fact, the train did start to move, and her mother had not returned! As Valerie was wondering what to do, she knew that a family friend, Auntie Joyce, was going to meet them in Sydney. What Valerie did not realise was that her mother had gotten on at the end of the train just before it started to move and walked through the cars to where her children were. Valerie was very relieved to see her mother!

One of the best parts about living in Shanghai was that Kitty had made friends from all around the world. When they arrived in Sydney, her friend, Joyce Whittington, was waiting for them. While in Sydney, Kitty frequented the shipping offices until she got her family a passage on the SS Rimutaka[6]. The most memorable incident from Valerie's time in Sydney was when she spotted a tarantula on the wall beside her bed. It was quickly killed by Auntie Joyce since tarantulas are venomous. It was the biggest spider Valerie had ever seen!

A week later, they left for Wellington, New Zealand. On the way out of the Sydney harbour, Valerie saw the Queen Elizabeth, an 83,000-ton cruise ship, in her war paint. It took four days to cross the Tasman Sea to Wellington, and the voyage was rough. During that time, a man jumped or fell overboard, and the crew spent some extra time trying to rescue him but failed. When they arrived in Wellington, they boarded a train to New Plymouth on New Zealand's west coast. The arduous journey was compensated for by the beautiful scenery and fascinating Māori names.

---

[6]P&O ship acquired by the New Zealand Shipping Co See Appendix A – Valerie's Ships for more information.

Chapter 5 On the Run

1943 – New Plymouth Harbour – New Zealand

Chapter 6
Calm After the Storm

1942 to 1944

1942 – Kathleen, Valerie, David, Diana, and Friends – 179 Carrington Road, New Plymouth, New Zealand

On January 19, 1942, Valerie and her family arrived in New Plymouth with 28 New Zealand pounds and their 13 pieces of luggage. They were met by Ruth and Jim Blakelock, who took them to their home on Kitchener Terrace. Kitty contacted the local schools, but since it was summer, the schools were closed. Valerie's situation was special; in Shanghai, she was educated under the UK system whereas New Zealand was similar to the Canadian system. In particular, Valerie had taken French, Latin, Geometry and Algebra in Shanghai, but these topics were not covered in elementary school in New Zealand. The Head Mistress recommended that Valerie start at the New Plymouth Girls' High School in February. Although this may have made sense from an academic point of view, it meant Valerie was taking classes with girls two or three years older than herself.

Valerie and her family stayed with the Blakelocks for six weeks and, although the couple was very nice, the weeks they spent with the Blakelocks were unhappy ones. The atmosphere in their house was always very tense. The only redeeming factor about Valerie's stay at the Blakelocks' was a girl her age in the neighbourhood, Betty Shuttleworth, with whom she used to play. Since it was summer and the Blakelocks lived near the beach, Valerie visited the beach a couple of times where she rode lovely rollers of waves. The sand, however, was black as coal due to volcanic ash and, thus, hot.

Kitty arranged for them to receive social security from the New Zealand government. She was granted four pounds per week for herself and her family with the caveat that she would repay the amount at the end of the war. Kitty found a small, furnished bungalow for her family on Carrington Road, which was between Holsworthy Road and Selwyn Street, for 2 pounds 15 shillings per week. Her mother had to do a bit of persuading to get the older lady who owned the house to rent it out to her, which was why Valerie and her siblings had to be extra careful not to break or damage anything. A passionfruit vine grew by the back door of that house. It was new to them, but they all enjoyed the fruit they picked from it.

Valerie and her family had been in their new house for less than six weeks when her mother fell ill with a suspected gallbladder problem and had to be admitted to the hospital. The Blakelocks, who were kind despite everything, offered to take in the children while their mother recovered. So, for the next two weeks, Valerie resided with the Blakelocks again. During the few weeks Valerie's family had lived on Carrington Road, the Blakelocks had moved into a house opposite the boys' high school, on the edge of a gully. Their new home had two bedrooms on the lower level where Valerie, David, and Diana slept, while the couple lived on the level at road height with their family. During the entirety of her stay at the Blakelocks, Valerie was unable to visit her mother at the hospital because of a 'flu epidemic' scare, so she wrote her letters.

The Blakelock family and the Sanger children all ate their meals together, and Valerie helped dry the dishes afterwards. But, of course, the environment in the Blakelock household was much the same. Auntie Ruth and Uncle Jim would engage in verbal combat over the meal table and Auntie Ruth often walked away to her bedroom in tears. Once, Valerie broke the glass liner inside a silver salt cellar and was most distressed; however, it was not made an issue. While their mother was in the hospital, Valerie was tasked with caring for David and Diana. She would look after their baths and then carry them down to their bedroom via the outside stairs. She was very grateful when her mother finally recovered and returned home. Valerie did not remember, but her mother later told her that, after she returned, Valerie would not let her mother do anything out of fear that she would end up in the hospital again.

Valerie and her family lived on Carrington Road for about six months before they moved into an unfurnished two-storey, three-bedroom statehouse at 16 Somerset Street, where they would stay for the remainder of their time in New

Zealand. Built in the 1930s during the Depression, the house was used to provide work and housing to those who could not afford homes. This house was much cheaper, costing 1 pound 15 shillings per week, so that helped the four pounds a week last much longer. Kitty's friend from Carrington Road, Mrs. Symes, and her other friends helped gather odds and ends of furniture. With that and some beds that Kitty bought, their new house was set up. The house was built on about one-third of an acre. All three bedrooms were upstairs, but perhaps the best was the smallest bedroom which provided a beautiful view of Mount Egmont (now Mount Taranaki). A bathroom with a tub and washbasin was also located upstairs, whereas a toilet was on the way downstairs. The ground floor consisted of a living room, hall, dining room and kitchen. The kitchen had a hot water tank with shelves above it that served as an airing cupboard. They did not have a refrigerator, but they did have a larder on the kitchen's exterior wall that was essentially a cupboard with slatted shelves that had air flowing through it, which helped keep the contents cool. Outside the backdoor was a place to store coal on the left and a place to do laundry on the right. The coal was used only to heat the water for laundry.

Unlike the previous house, this one had a garden where Kitty grew vegetables. The garden also had a shed where they kept tools and the children's bicycles. Valerie would mow the lawn and help around the house while her mother tended to her vegetable garden. It was here that Valerie learned about compost heaps and how to grow apple cucumbers over them. There were bungalows on either side of the house, a street, and then one block that led to Brooklands Park (today it also has a zoo). The park had a huge chestnut tree with sprawling branches that the children loved climbing. Pukekura Park located across a field from Brooklands Park featured a lake where Valerie rented a rowboat and taught David and Diana how to row.

There was a corner store at the end of Cornwall Street

that Diana particularly liked. She would always bring Valerie along to buy candy. On Saturdays, David and Valerie would walk downtown to Devon Street to pick up groceries for their mother and would then take the bus home. There were woods behind the row of houses across Somerset Street. Valerie and her friend Joan, from across the street, spent countless hours making tree houses and playing in the woods. Valerie remembered that whenever they would have extra sugar in the pantry, her mother would buy wooden crates, the size of a cardboard carton, of the fruit in season and they would make jam. Her mother also bought Granny Smith apples for cooking, even though Valerie enjoyed eating them raw. Their daily source of milk was a man who supplied milk to the whole neighbourhood from his cart.

In the summer, Valerie and her friend Joan would go to the fields beyond the woods to pick gooseberries which her mother used to make jam. The bushes grew wild in the fields and were not high like the ones she had seen in England, where they seemed to form hedges. The fields also had gorse bushes which looked lovely at that time of the year. The gooseberry jam Kitty made was good but one time, Valerie got badly scratched while picking gooseberries. All her scratches turned septic, so she was given sulpha. Valerie recalled lying in bed, confident that the walls around her were swaying. However, she later found that they were not swaying, she was just sensitive to sulpha.

In the rooms upstairs, they had scatter rugs by the beds that moved when you stood on them. The children would use the beds as "ports" and the rugs as "ships". Since Diana and Valerie slept in the same room, they would be in one "port", whereas David would be in the other. They would then push the rugs to visit each other. The children were allowed to take the living room apart to aid in their imaginative play, but on the condition that they would put it all back together within the time set by their mother. At other times, they would have make-believe houses in the living room and visit each other.

Not long after they had moved to Somerset Street, the husband of a couple who lived down the road took Valerie and David to the beach along with his own children. Diana and the mothers would follow later with a picnic lunch. Since her mother would come later, Valerie was in charge of David. However, she did not realise just how strong the New Zealand sun was, having lived there for only a few weeks, and they both got burned badly. David had it the worst, with huge blisters on his shoulders, while Valerie's back was sore. Next time, they would remember to take proper precautions.

As the months passed, they settled down into their new lives and as February of 1943 approached, Valerie prepared to resume her education at the New Plymouth Girls' High School where, at age 11, she was the youngest by six months in a school of 500 girls. David and Diana, on the other hand, went to Vogeltown School, which was about a mile walk away over a hilly route.

The New Plymouth Girls' High School was a boarding school as well as a day school for girls. The students were required to wear a uniform: a navy-blue tunic, a white blouse, and a tie striped diagonally in silver and blue that represented the school's colours. Its five buildings consisted of classrooms, a gym, and a residence called Scotlands, while one of the smaller buildings was used for music. A path through the woods and by the river led to a swimming pool where Valerie had her swimming lessons. Assembly was held in the gym every morning, and Valerie went to the gym three times a week, which also included swimming lessons. Although Valerie swam like a fish back in Shanghai and could swim the width of the pool underwater, for some reason unbeknownst to her, she could not bring herself to put her face underwater here. Perhaps it was because of the arduous journeys across the sea and the emotions attached to them. Regardless, swimming lessons were pure torture for her.

During this time, Kitty arranged for them to get fifty pounds per month from England. This was a significant increase from the 4 pounds per week they were getting before. This made for some good improvements in their lives, like Valerie getting many presents and having hot lunches at school. However, less than a week later, the British Government stopped money from leaving England due to the war reducing their income to 4 pounds per week. It would be another year before the controls were lifted and Kitty would once again receive 50 pounds per month for the remainder of their stay in New Zealand.

While living on Carrington Road, Valerie's mother bought her a bicycle for 14 pounds. Valerie felt lucky because only six bicycles were delivered in all of New Plymouth, and she had been the proud recipient of one of them. From the day her new school term commenced, Valerie would ride her bike to school, a three-mile trip, every day along with Wendy and Airlie – two older girls who lived on Somerset Street near Brooklands Park. Their journey to school was a long slope down, then a very steep hill beside the boys' high school, riding through the suburbs. It was a long walk uphill all the way home.

Valerie's school started at 9, but she would leave around 8:15 to arrive on time. Although she managed to be on time in the morning, when she returned home depended on the activities, she participated in at school that day. For example, on Mondays she had to stay back for sports. She was also in the Glee Club, which often held practices after school. On days when she had to stay back, she would ride home alone since Wendy and Airlie would be long gone. Some days the wind would come off the ocean and other days off the mountain. On really windy days when the wind came off the mountain, Valerie would take the route through Pukekura and Brooklands Parks. Valerie really dreaded windy days because that meant she had to walk a good part of the way home as riding bicycles was not allowed in the park.

Valerie's time at New Plymouth Girls' High School was quite eventful. She had one good friend, Philippa, who lived on the other side of town, making it difficult for them to hang out after school. At those times, Valerie was grateful for her friend Joan, who lived right across the road. At school, she ***had*** to participate in Sports Day every now and then. She always entered the slow bicycle race as it seemed to require the least effort. Her participation in the slow bicycle race ran its course when Valerie realised that she could actually run quite quickly.

In her first year at the school, Valerie took cooking classes every Tuesday, her class would prepare the main meal at noon for the boarders at the school. Valerie was a day student who would go home at night. If the cooking class cooked the main dish one week, they would make dessert the next week. Valerie's mother thought it would be a good idea for her to have a main meal at noon. So, for the entirety of the first year, Valerie ***had*** to "enjoy" what the cooking class put out, most of which was not very appetising, to say the least, especially the burnt puddings. In the later years, Valerie would bring her lunch from home.

There were different streams in Valerie's school, where the students were categorised based on their skills. Valerie was part of the academic stream, where she studied Latin. She was expected to go to university eventually. There were other streams, such as the general stream that studied Geography instead of Latin, and those girls were expected to go to Teachers' College. There was also a secretarial stream and homemaking stream.

The one school activity that Valerie wholeheartedly enjoyed was the Glee Club. In her first school year, she participated in the operetta, "Merrie England," which she thoroughly enjoyed. In terms of academics, Valerie took English, Mathematics, Latin, French, General Science, Sewing, History and Gym. For the three years that she attended the school, she had the same Mathematics teacher who made a lasting impression on her, but not in a good way. Her name was Miss McMullen and due to her vicious tongue and rumoured propensity for hitting girls, she was known as Muck. Every week, she would hand out Geometry theorems for the students to learn by heart, and if anyone was unlucky enough to score less than five out of ten, they would first face her verbal wrath and then get detention. Detention meant staying for forty minutes after school and learning some Shakespearean lines by heart – an impossible task for Valerie. In order to avoid that fate, Valerie tried her best to learn the theorems. Her mother was especially helpful in Valerie avoiding detention by listening patiently to her recite the theorems, only to forget something mid-way and then start over again.

The first year went by with Valerie successfully avoiding detention. However, as the second year came around, Valerie had to write a poem about courage in English class. That was too abstract a concept for her, and she ended up getting detention. Her punishment was to write about courage yet again, this time a paragraph instead of a poem, which was just as bad according to her. That year, she also had to take part in a debate, which was another torture for her as she was not fond of public speaking. To make matters worse, although she did not remember the topic, she did remember that she was on the side she did not agree with, so the whole thing was a recipe for disaster.

During their time in New Zealand, Valerie's family went through many health-related crises. First, her family contracted measles, and David consequently developed pneumonia. Valerie recalled how worried her mother was when she took him to the hospital. Then, David and Diana got chickenpox and Valerie had to quarantine at home for three weeks even though she had contracted it twice! After that, Diana got whooping cough. The poor girl was very ill. Kitty stayed up many nights in a row caring for Diana. She would sleep during the day and Valerie would act as a babysitter for the daytime.

A kind lady named Mrs. Nielson lived down the road and Kitty would often visit her in the evenings, leaving Valerie in charge of her siblings. Her mother went over to Mrs. Nielson's on D-Day as well and Valerie spent a memorable evening listening to speeches by King George VI, Churchill, and Eisenhower on the radio. She wondered how Eisenhower had made the time to speak on such a day, not realising until she was a little older that it had been pre-recorded.

During their stay in New Zealand, Valerie made a scrapbook for her father. It contained newspaper clippings of important events pasted in with a flour paste. She did not think her father would hear about the war; this was her way of informing him of what had happened during the war. However, she never had the chance to give it to him as she lost it before they were reunited.

Valerie and her family stayed in New Zealand from 1942 to 1945, and during those three years, communication with her father was erratic. Until June of 1943, Fred stayed in their house on Jessfield Road along with Dr. Earle and Dr. Reid. During this time, he would send them letters once in a while through the underground route. One of his students would take the letter and arrange for it to arrive in Kunming, from which it would be airmailed to his family.

The Japanese had given the English a choice; they could be put in camps, or they could help organise them. Since Fred chose the latter, he was one of the last few people to go into a camp. Once the Japanese moved him to Lunghwa, one way he could send letters to his family was through the Red Cross, which provided a form with room for only 25 words. It was then sent to Geneva and delivered behind the war zone. In February of 1942, Valerie mailed her father a 25-word letter through the Red Cross[7]. In May of 1942, while at the Blakelocks, Kitty heard that her husband was still in Shanghai but that he was safe. A year later, in February of 1943, Valerie received a reply, also 25 words, from her father in which he asked her to help her mother and be nice to her siblings. Another way the internees in the camp could send out messages to their families was by putting them in a box and the Japanese would broadcast them.

---

[7] See Appendix C for a copy of the Red Cross Letter.

Chapter 6 Calm After the Storm

There was a man on the South Island of New Zealand who sat up all night transcribing these messages and would then send them to the families.

During their time in New Zealand, Valerie's family took three lovely holidays. Their first holiday was staying at the house of a sister of Mrs. Thomas. Mrs. Thomas, the lady who came to clean their house, was a family friend. Her sister lived in Eltham, a quaint little town at the foot of Mount Egmont (Mount Taranaki). The beautiful town had many old-fashioned buildings that caught Valerie's eye. However, the one drawback of staying there was they only had an outhouse, which Valerie did not particularly like. In Eltham, Valerie had her first experience in house painting when she helped the man of the house paint its exterior. He also took her to the rennet factory. Rennet is used in the making of junket, a type of custard popular in New Zealand. After the factory visit, Valerie lost her appetite for junket.

Their second holiday was in 1943 at Dawson Falls in Egmont National Park, halfway up Mount Egmont at a height of 5000 feet. Valerie's family drove to a lodge at Dawson Falls, where they stayed for a week. The family climbed about a thousand feet up the mountain, above the treeline, and came across a very narrow path with no railing and steep drops on both sides. This was when they decided to turn around and head back to the lodge. The high elevation triggered Diana's whooping cough again. This occurred despite Diana having fully recovered from her whooping cough, a fact Valerie's mother often had to emphasise to others.

In her third year in school, in 1943, Valerie took private ballroom dancing classes on the weekends and went to the weekly dances at the boys' high school. The Girls' High School and the Boys' High School were separated by a stream. For school dances, Valerie recalled going to the boy's school to dance with the boy boarders. Similarly, boys would go to the girls' school to dance with the girl boarders. Kitty would arrange for a taxi to drop her off and then pick her up at a specific time.

In the summer of 1944, Valerie threw a party to celebrate her 14th birthday with around seven or eight boys and girls, some from her class and some from her dancing lessons. Out of all the activities they engaged in that day, Valerie clearly remembered a travel game that her mother had come up with. She created multiple cards with names of different countries on them and placed them throughout the house, such as under the dining room table. The objective of the game was to find the right cards that would take the players to the next destination. All the children had a grand time!

After Valerie's birthday, her mother threw David and Diana a collective birthday party as well. For David and Diana's birthday party, unlike Valerie's, their mother did not have much planned. She expected the guests to entertain each other in front of the living room's high windows. When it came to Diana's turn, she got the giggles which were so infectious that pretty soon everyone was laughing uncontrollably.

Living in New Zealand, Valerie's culinary tour de force was date loaf. Even though there were times when her mother was down with the flu and she would have to look after everyone and feed the family, she could not remember making anything else. During such times, she would often have a hard time cleaning the kitchen counter and Mrs. Thomas would come to rescue her from her distress.

Valerie's last holiday in New Zealand was Christmas of 1944 when her family went to a seaside village called Opunake. They stayed in a small hotel by the beach. On Christmas Day, they swam at the beach and had roast turkey for dinner. For dessert, they only had fruit, much to Valerie's dismay. She was there when the New Year rolled around, and this was the first time since she moved to New Zealand that she saw the many New Year's celebrations. She remembered a long Conga line running through the hotel on New Year's Eve. She also participated in a snake dance around the hotel.

Chapter 6 Calm After the Storm

In January of 1945, Kitty received a letter from the New Zealand government suggesting that they return to England since that was where her husband would be repatriated after the war. This letter marked the end of Valerie's stay in New Zealand.

1944 – Kitty, Diana, Valerie, and David – New Plymouth, New Zealand

Chapter 7
Time in England

1945

June 1944 – Valerie – New Plymouth, New Zealand

Valerie's Journeys

Besides informing Kitty that her husband would be repatriated to England, the New Zealand government also alerted her that space on shipping would be tight after the war as the troops returning home would be given priority. Initially, Kitty thought of staying in New Zealand, her husband could join her and their children here. However, once she inquired about possible opportunities for her husband, the results were grim, and so she decided to take the government up on its offer.

Valerie was absolutely thrilled by this decision because even though she had completed three years of high school, she was threatened with having to repeat the third year. The school thought repeating the year would help Valerie do better on the national examination and also place her with girls her own age, as she was much younger than her classmates throughout high school. So, even though her mother told her that she would have to go to boarding school when they reached England because of the shortage of housing, she was still happy that she did not have to repeat the school year.

So, in February of 1945, instead of going to Rotorua for a holiday, as originally planned, Valerie's family took the train to Wellington and boarded the SS Rimutaka once again to begin their journey to England. The SS Rimutaka had just been refurbished for the Duke and Duchess of Gloucester's travel from England when the Duke of Gloucester was named the Governor-General of Australia. The band played 'Now is the Hour', as was the tradition in New Zealand when a ship departed. It took three weeks to cross the Pacific to Panama and an additional three weeks to reach England. For this trip, the family had two adjacent cabins. Valerie and David shared one cabin and her mother and Diana shared the other. In Kitty's cabin, there was a long corridor to the porthole. On the other side of the passageway were cabins for the senior members of the crew.

Approximately half of the passengers consisted of a naval draft returning home, while the remainder were civilians. A high-ranking official from the British High Commissioner's office in Wellington, his wife and their two sons around the same age as Valerie and her siblings, were also on board, leading to plenty of enjoyable interactions. Among the passengers were four teenagers who commonly engaged in games of deck quoits or darts in the mornings. In the afternoons, they would gather with Valerie and other children to play Monopoly, a highly popular game at the time. During mealtimes, Valerie delighted in being regarded as an adult. Her mother established a dining arrangement with a woman she met on the ship named Kath, and a boy named Olaf, who was around Valerie's age. Before leaving New Plymouth, Valerie's mother had made a couple of dresses for her, so she would change into a different dress every day. During the trip back to England, Valerie also picked up knitting. She knit a sweater for one of her aunts when she had no one to play with; knitting became a lifelong hobby for her.

After leaving Wellington, the ship sailed a route through the southern Pacific to avoid any Japanese submarines. This made the first week a rough sail, filled with large waves accompanied by bouts of seasickness. However, the next two weeks, when the ship turned east, were pleasant with calm seas; it was a much-needed reprieve from the first week's conditions. Thereafter, the ship sailed north-east and arrived in South America near Chile and then turned north to sail to Panama City. There were no stops between Wellington and Panama City. During their three-week voyage to Panama, Valerie would spend most of her afternoons playing Monopoly with the four teenagers on board. Her mother persuaded her to sign up for other activities and so she did. She took part in darts, table tennis, and deck quoits. For darts and deck quoits, Valerie was paired with a sailor known simply as "Red". He was a tall, kind man and the two of them made a great team. They even made it to the semi-finals in darts and deck quoits! Their last game of deck quoits was played while crossing the Atlantic. It was cool and windy and with Valerie undoubtedly being the weaker link in the team, the opponents took advantage of that.

Red did his best, but it was all in vain. Nonetheless, Valerie was glad to have made it that far in the competition.

After three weeks on board, the passengers were allowed to go ashore in Panama. It felt amazing being on land again! The next day, the ship transited the Panama Canal, and the passengers were allowed on the bridge to watch. They stopped in Colon overnight and then left for Kingston, Jamaica. They also had an overnight stop in Havana but were not allowed ashore as they were to join a convoy of three other ships and four frigates as escorts. The convoy was to travel a speed of 14 knots (26 km/hr), bound for New York.

Valerie's brother, David, remembers playing with the ship's gun. While in the Pacific, David had been allowed to go into the gun turret and move the gun. While docked in Havana, David was bored and decided to go and play with the gun. This created great excitement as the gun started moving and pointing at a building on shore.

Once in New York City, the passengers were not allowed ashore. It was especially frustrating because they could see the Statue of Liberty, but they had to remain aboard, moored in the harbour. To add to their woes, the passengers on a sister ship were allowed ashore. However, staying on board would prove to be a blessing as that ship went on the southern route and was attacked, whereas Valerie's ship went on the northern route. By now it was April, and the northern route was cold and windy. However, Valerie had her sea legs by then, so the journey was not too bad. They still, however, always had to carry life jackets. For Valerie, it would be many years before she returned to New York City.

The Rimutaka left New York in a different convoy with 40 ships and 8 destroyers headed for Cherbourg, France. Valerie remembered there being a few oil tankers in convoy and one of her pastimes was to watch the waves washing over the oil tankers' decks. As the convoy approached Ireland, the Rimutaka left the convoy and approached England from the south of Ireland, going north through the Irish sea to Liverpool. One evening, they dropped depth charges (a weapon dropped into the water to destroy any submarines nearby) in the Irish Channel but did not see any action. Finally, on April 12, 1945, the family arrived in Liverpool. This also happened to be the day the U.S. President Franklin D. Roosevelt died and the last day of the V2 rockets. Valerie recalled going up the river Mersey and seeing all the rows of dirty brick houses on the south shore. The realisation soon dawned on her that she had successfully travelled around the world!

Upon their arrival in Liverpool, the family had to stay on the ship for a day or two. Kitty made contact with Auntie Eva and Uncle Eric. Auntie Eva was Fred's eldest sister who lived in Sunderland in northern England. Once they could disembark from the ship, Valerie and her family headed to Auntie Eva and Uncle Eric's house in Sunderland. However, this was an arduous task as they had to take a train south to Birmingham, change trains to go north to Newcastle, and then get on another small train that would take them to Sunderland. Safe to say, it was a long day! Auntie Eva and Uncle Eric lived in a very small house and Valerie could not remember how they all managed to sleep there, just that they did. During their stay with them, Auntie Eva and Uncle Eric took the children and their mother to see the Sunderland Minster and the river below it. Valerie also remembered Uncle Eric playing the piano and singing "Trees" for them. While roaming around the city, Uncle Eric pointed out the initials "EWS" wherever they went. They were his initials, Eric William Sparkes, and the initials for Emergency Water Supply, which was where he worked. In addition to working for the water company, Uncle Eric was the assistant choirmaster and organist at their church. He also took them to Newcastle one day, where he received physical therapy. Auntie Eva, on the other hand, taught nurses and was on the National Board of Medical Examiners.

After two or three days, they bid farewell to Auntie Eva and Uncle Eric and Valerie and her family went to Coventry to visit her mother's father, Grandpa Thorn, and her stepmother, Gran. Grandpa Thorn worked in an aircraft plant and had a house on the side of a hill. Gran told Valerie that all the houses at the top of the hill had been bombed, but they had been lucky that their house had avoided the impact. In her grandparents' house in Coventry, Valerie recalled a horrible geyser (hot water heater) in the bathroom, so the trip to the bathroom would never be a pleasant one! She also recalled standing in queue for two hours to get some oranges, maybe four.

After leaving her grandparents' house, Valerie's family went to Ealing, just outside of London, to stay with Auntie Goddard. Auntie Goddard's son, Uncle Arthur, was Fred's best man and was not related to her family. Uncle Arthur never married and was living with his mother at the time. Uncle Frank, who was a dentist and Arthur's brother, also lived nearby. This was convenient for the family's dental visits.

They were in Ealing on May 8, 1945, when Victory in Europe (VE) Day occurred. On this day, cities in Great Britain, Canada, and the United States put out flags and banners and celebrated the defeat of the Nazis in Europe. At Auntie Goddard's house, Valerie shared a bed with her mother, while David and Diana shared another. While lying in bed, she remembered hearing everyone celebrating in the streets, distressed because, in her view the war was not truly over. For Valerie, the war would only end when her family was reunited. As for that, she would have to wait another seven months.

Chapter 7 Time in England

1946 – Eversley – Lymington, England

Chapter 8
Boarding School

1946

1946 – Valerie and Diana – Lymington, England

Valerie's Journeys

Before their arrival, they had been forewarned that England faced a housing shortage, and they could not live at Auntie Goddard's house forever. Auntie Goddard was kind, but she was over 80 years old and did not have much space in her house for the family of four. Kitty could not find any other suitable housing options for them, so she started inquiring about boarding schools. Consequently, in the middle of June of 1945, David and Valerie were enrolled in boarding schools. Valerie was to attend Eversley, just outside Lymington in Hampshire, whereas David went to St. Hugh's in Farringdon, Gloucestershire. Diana was too young, only seven years old, and so her mother decided against sending her off to boarding school just yet. Instead, both of them temporarily stayed at Kitty's friend's house. Later in 1946, Diana would join Valerie at Eversley. This did not completely surprise Valerie as her mother had mentioned the possibility of sending the children to boarding school.

During World War II, Eversley was repurposed to accommodate troops, causing substantial damage to the structure. There were numerous crosses in the vicinity, initially misconstrued by the students as graves. However, the crosses were later discovered to be warning signs for the troops. Valerie joined the school in the summer of 1945, following the European segment of the war, marking the school's return to its previous state. The school had approximately 100 girl students. Valerie's journey to reach the school involved a train ride from Waterloo Station in London, with a change at Brockenhurst, taking her to Lymington. Here, along with several other students, she alighted at Lymington Pier and trekked uphill to the renowned 'Eversley'. One particular time, as she went through Southampton, Valerie saw both the SS Queen Mary and SS Queen Elizabeth berthed there.

Valerie was a little concerned about going to boarding school, but her worries were soon forgotten when Eversley came into view. It was a lovely manor house built on beautiful grounds beside the Solent. There was an expansive lawn that went down to the river and was named the "Queen Mary" because it was as long as the ship! Beyond the lawn was a raised walkway to a dock that was out of bounds to all, except teachers and prefects. The school had multiple tennis courts and an area to play rounders (English version of baseball) and field lacrosse.

Classrooms were situated on one side of a long building, equipped with a science lab and gym, complete with a stage. There were also some smaller rooms on the other side of the building where students could have music lessons or practise their music skills.

The manor was a three-storey building with central heating. However, it was hardly ever warm because of the rationing of coal during those days. The first floor of Eversley consisted of a wood panelled music room, panelled library, a chapel, the Headmistress' drawing room and office, dining rooms, kitchens, and a large lobby with a winding staircase that led to the second floor. The second floor was home to the Headmistress' living quarters, two dormitories for six students each, the nurse's office that was called the "Surgery", the prefect's lounge, and two single bedrooms, one of which belonged to the Head Prefect and the other to the next in charge. The single bedrooms were constructed in such a way that the Head Prefect had to walk through the next in charge's room in order to reach hers. This floor also had a large room full of washbasins, and separate rooms each with a bathtub, or a toilet. Valerie recalled a hairdresser would come in once every six weeks to wash their hair.

Valerie did not recall much about the third floor, just that it had one dormitory for six girls. There were multiple buildings on the school grounds. The senior girls lived in the main house, whereas the junior girls lived in a different building. There was another building where the teachers resided. Furthermore, there was a smaller one intended for use as a hospital. However, as far as Valerie could recall, it was never used as such and was instead used for writing exams.

As for Valerie, she slept in a six-girl room on the second floor in the main building, right at the top of the stairs. Valerie had to walk through the prefects' lounge to get to her room. That meant knocking on the door every time, even to go to the bathroom! Thankfully, the prefects' lounge was eventually moved, and Valerie could come and go as she pleased.

The girls at Eversley had their meals in the dining room, and each week, a different table was assigned to them. All tables were given equal amounts of food, regardless of the table size and number of people. Keep in mind that this was the time of the severest rationing of food during the war, and all the girls would hope to be assigned a smaller table because the smaller the table, the more the food. The two best tables were the Headmistress' table, which seated only five and the French teacher's table, seating four. Both the headmistress and the French teacher only came in for lunch, so lucky students assigned to these tables would leave the dining room with full stomachs. However, the students at the French table were required to speak French in the presence of the French teacher. Perhaps the worst of the bunch was the largest table of 14. Whenever Valerie was unlucky enough to be assigned that table, she would often leave with a growling stomach because there was never enough food.

All students had access to three meals a day, and the menu was fixed throughout the term. For breakfast, three days a week oatmeal porridge was served, which was made with water and usually burnt. On three of the other days, they had pork and beans. Sundays were special because they had scrambled eggs made from powdered eggs. Breakfast was always served with toast and the girls had an option to choose between a jar of jam or marmalade at the beginning of each month. Since it had to last them the whole month, the girls did not dare share their jars with anyone. Lunch was the main meal of the day, and, as far as Valerie remembered, it was a balanced meal consisting of meat, potatoes, vegetables, and dessert. Valerie also remembered that they had a sweet ration which would be locked up in a cupboard—all well-labelled—and the girls had to line up to take some from it.

Every morning after breakfast, the students would attend a short service in the chapel, perform "wake-up" exercises on the patio at the back of the building, and then head to class. On days when it rained, the exercises would take place in the gym. If the Headmistress ever had any announcements, an assembly would be held in the gym before class. Valerie had classes in the morning followed by lunch, two hours of free time to play games and then more classes before supper. After supper, they had another short religious service, followed by their homework time, which they called "prep". Afterwards, they would sit on the floor in the Headmistress's drawing room where she would either read to them or give them a lecture. Finally, they would go to bed.

Valerie had gym twice or thrice a week and also classes on Saturday mornings, while her afternoon would be spent in music, ballet, or horse-riding lessons, depending on what the student was interested in. On Sundays, they had a regular church service in the morning. Valerie was in the choir and was the leader of the altos. She was also a sacristan and even though she had not been confirmed, she had to get the robes ready for the chaplain before the service commenced. After the service, if the weather was nice, the girls went for a walk, crocodile style (walking in pairs). Valerie especially liked taking a stroll on the school grounds during the fall when blackberries were ripe. Valerie and her friends knew all the places where they were! There would be another service in the evening. So, Valerie's days at the boarding school were packed!

Valerie went into the fifth form at Eversley and so she had to repeat her last year in New Zealand in preparation for what was known as the "O" levels. After the first six weeks, Valerie had half term, and her mother came to visit her. Valerie was terribly homesick, not used to being away from her mother for so long, and so seeing her mother was a much-needed reprieve. Valerie took the ferry to Yarmouth with her mother.

However, since it was a Sunday, all the lunch places were closed. However, the lovely weather compensated for it, and Valerie spent her day at the beach talking with her mother.

The students at Eversley were divided into groups called "Houses", which met once a week. Each house had a designated name and colour—Valerie's were Faraday and red. Each of the houses was regularly given projects to compete against the houses. The one activity that Valerie dedicated a lot of time to for her house was a ballet where every girl in the house had to participate, whether or not they had ever done it. They were fortunate enough to have a few dancers on board who had some ballet training. The ballet was based on the 10 Little Indians. From designing the set and costumes to choosing the music and doing the choreography, they managed everything. It took them quite a while to prepare, but it went well from Valerie's perspective. Another activity Valerie willingly took part in was a Christmas concert of selected arias and choruses from "The Messiah", specially arranged for girls' voices. Valerie sang the aria, "For He Shall Feed His Flock".

The first term came to an end, and for the summer break, Kitty had arranged for herself and her children to stay at a farm near Lymington belonging to Mr. and Mrs. Jackson. Mrs. Jackson was willing to take the three kids but not their mother and so, Kitty did not accompany them on the trip. At the farm, the Jacksons had another boy, Benedict, living with them for the holidays whose parents were in Nigeria. He was a little older than David, but they got along very well. Valerie recalled that the Jacksons' farm was not a typical one, it was more of a hobby farm. They did, however, have hay in the barn onto which the four children would jump. Valerie had a fun time at the farm but the most unforgettable memory from this trip was when the end of the war was announced in August. The Jacksons had lived in Malaya and so there was a great celebration. Valerie was also allowed to toast with the adults but with Benedictine.

At Eversley, Valerie had courses in Scripture, English,

French, Geometry, Algebra, History, Science, Geography, and Latin. Valerie did not get along well with the school's minister, who was also the Latin teacher. Miss McCall, the headmistress, arranged for Valerie to take Latin from Reverend Hooper at the church in Lymington twice a week. Valerie was able to ride her bike to the church. The transition to school subjects was not difficult for Valerie as many of the textbooks were the same as the ones she had in New Zealand. While at Eversley, Valerie was working to complete her school certificate. Valerie did not find the adjustment to being at boarding school very difficult, but it was hard for her to fit in. Her experience living in China and New Zealand was very different from the other girls who spent the war in England. Miss McCall had noticed this and when Valerie returned to school after the summer break, she was made a junior prefect. The position came with some advantages and disadvantages. First, Valerie was moved to a six-girl room on the third floor and was responsible for making sure that the rest of the girls did not talk after lights out. She was also allowed to use the prefects' lounge and could manage her own sweets! As a prefect, Valerie had a number of other duties such as shepherding the girls to various places, ringing the bell to signify the end of class, and taking the lead in her house's activities. Because all the prefects would have a private session with Miss McCall every evening, this meant Valerie went to bed later than the other girls. It was quite an adventure for her, with the lights being out by the time she went to her room. There were often obstacles in her way, created by the girls in her room, such as an apple pie bed (a short-sheeted bed) and string strung between the beds, on the way to hers.

One exciting thing Valerie remembered from her time as a prefect was being awakened by the school nurse and a doctor in the middle of the night in November of 1945. They came to examine her and set up screens around her bed. Valerie had not been feeling well the whole day and so they surmised there was something wrong with her appendix. Valerie was taken down to the surgery, where she waited for an ambulance. When it arrived, the attendants were most solicitous and insisted that she lie down on their gurney. Valerie obliged, and off they went to the nearby hospital. At around 4 o'clock in the morning, Valerie's appendix was removed by Dr. Pitt. Miss McCall could not get in touch with Valerie's mother, who was spending the night at the home of Lionel, one of her father's cousins, and Valerie did not know their last name. So, Miss McCall had to take responsibility for Valerie. The next morning when Valerie's mother returned to Auntie Goddard's, she called the school to get the news. Kitty travelled to Lymington and was by her side by noon. Valerie stayed in the hospital for two weeks, and for ten of those fourteen days, she was instructed to rest and was not allowed out of bed.

When the school asked Valerie what she wanted, she simply requested an egg. Coincidentally, her mother had visited friends in Devon and brought back half a dozen fresh eggs. She gave two to each of her children. Valerie cooked one over an open fire in the prefects' lounge, while the other one was cooked in the hospital kitchen for her.

During the school holidays in January of 1946, Kitty had managed to rent a house and so, when her father arrived in England in December of 1945, she was able to stay with her family for the whole month.

In August of 1945 Fred was released from the Lunghwa Internment camp. He decided to stay in Shanghai, in hopes that the Lester Institute would reopen, living in an apartment on the top floor of the Institute. However, as November rolled around, it became apparent to Fred that the Institute would not reopen. So, he packed his bags and headed to England. In December of 1945, Fred arrived in England, before the start of the school holidays. This allowed Valerie's parents time together alone before they were joined by their children. Valerie and Diana met their father at Waterloo Station in London. When Fred saw his family, he knelt to greet them. But in four years, they had all grown, and he did not have to kneel. The biggest change was in Valerie as she had become a young woman. The family was finally reunited after four years!

During their month together, Fred took Valerie to the Royal Albert Hall for a Tchaikovsky concert, where she heard Myra Hess play for the first time. Valerie was awestruck by her poise. However, that feeling was quickly overshadowed by her chilblains. When the room warmed up, Valerie's feet itched dreadfully, and she could hardly keep them still. Her father, trying to enjoy the concert, was very annoyed.

Valerie attempted the O-level exams in the school 'hospital' at the rate of two a day in July of 1946. She did not pass that first time. By then, Diana had also joined Eversley. By the summer holidays, Fred was working on his doctorate thesis but had no job. When Miss McCall from school was searching for a science teacher, she offered the job to Fred, who accepted it promptly. When summer break ended and Valerie, Diana, and David went back to school, her parents rented rooms with kitchen privileges in a little house just up the road, owned by Reverend John Ferguson, who was also a well-known writer of detective stories. Every Sunday, either Diana or Valerie would go and have lunch with their parents. Her mother used to save up all her meat ration coupons for the week so they could have roast beef on Sundays.

By the summer of 1946, Valerie had become a Senior Prefect and was assigned a room of her own on the second floor, next to the Head Perfect's, which was accessed through Valerie's room. The funniest thing about it all was that the Head Prefect's name was also Valerie!

In her last term, Valerie once again prepared to attempt the O-levels. She was even in one of her father's classes for the general science exam preparation. She sat for the exams in December of 1946, but at the time, she did not know she would not be in England by the time the results were announced in February of 1947. In December of 1946, Valerie graduated from Eversley, having attended seven different schools in three countries!

During this time, Fred was looking for jobs to better suit his qualifications. He had been away from England for over twelve years, and it was hard for him to get an interview, let alone a job. Finally, he had an interview with a professor from the University of New Brunswick (UNB), Canada and was offered a position there. Once everything was finalised regarding his new job in December of 1946, plans were made to travel to Canada. Valerie's family took the train to Liverpool and stayed in the Lord Alfred Hotel overnight. The only thing Valerie remembered about the hotel was the long corridor one had to go along in order to reach the bathroom.

The next day, they boarded the SS Cavina[8], a banana boat that only took a few passengers, Valerie's family being among the lucky few. They had a stateroom that also had a small living room, so there was plenty of space to walk around. There were four bunks in the stateroom where Valerie, her mother, and her siblings slept while her father stayed in another cabin with three men. However, they arranged for her father to sleep on their cabin's living room floor.

The voyage was rough, with the boat springing two leaks and losing one of the propellers; thus, it took fourteen days instead of 10 to reach their destination. Because of the unstable conditions on board, only two of her five family members were able to enjoy the Christmas dinner. The SS Cavina arrived at Pier 21 in Halifax, Nova Scotia, on January 1, 1947, on a glorious sunny morning. Valerie was stunned by all the snow and the deep blue of the water, a sight unlike that in England. It was on January 1, 1947, that Canadian law changed, and Valerie did not automatically become a Canadian citizen, which she would have if she had arrived a day earlier. Consequently, she was required to apply for Canadian citizenship at a later date.

In Halifax, Valerie's family was given a warm welcome by the Immigration Officer, who had been informed about their

[8]See Appendix A – Valerie's Ships for more information.

arrival by his daughter, a UNB student. He drove them back to his house, where his wife served them a delicious supper. From there, he took them to the railway, where they boarded a train to Saint John, New Brunswick. The train's heating system did not work properly, and when Valerie's family woke up early due to the excessive heat, they looked out the window and marvelled at all the snow in the fields. It was a beautiful sight! They spent a day in Saint John, mostly at the New Brunswick Museum, before they boarded the train for Fredericton, New Brunswick, where they were met by the President of UNB, Milton F. Gregg, and his wife.

S.S. Cavina

Chapter 9
O Canada

1947 to 1951

1951 – Valerie – Fredericton, New Brunswick, Canada

Although Valerie's family enjoyed their time in Canada because of the change of pace and weather, the first six months were not happy ones for Valerie. This was primarily due to the fact that her family had very little money when they reached Canada. Most of her parents' savings had been spent to support the family in New Zealand and then the year and a half in England, when her father did not have full-time employment.

In Canada, Valerie's family lived temporarily in Alexander College, where first-year classes were held. It also housed a residence for single students and families of veterans. The college buildings were built in 1940 as residences for the families of soldiers and converted into Alexander College (a part of UNB), in January of 1946. Valerie and her family lived in one of these furnished buildings until their home was ready to move into. This provided them ample time to buy furniture and other essentials for their new home.

After a week or two of living in that building, Valerie and her family moved into half of the Women's Auxiliary Army Corp (WAAC) officers' hut, which consisted of three bedrooms, a kitchen, dining room, living room, and a single bathroom. The other half of the hut consisted of single rooms for bachelor faculty. One really surprising thing about their new living arrangement was the lack of household appliances. There was no washing machine in the home, so everything had to be hand-washed in the bathroom. The clothes would then be hung outside on a clothesline that extended from David's bedroom window. Washing clothes in the winter in the freezing temperatures of Canada was a challenge, as the clothes would literally freeze on the clothesline!

A washing machine was not the only near-essential thing missing from their new home. The hut also lacked a refrigerator and, instead, had an icebox. They had always had a refrigerator wherever they lived, so Kitty found it hard to believe that Canada was so far behind. Valerie remembers, during the winter, David was sent out to collect icicles to be used in the ice box. However, despite its lack of appliances, the WAAC Officers hut was built better than the other huts and the family would remain there until August of 1948.

Another adjustment Valerie had to make was the cars drove on the right side of the road. In all the countries she had lived in, the cars drove on the left side of the road. Although Valerie did not drive at this point, she had to be careful in crossing the road. To ensure she could cross the road safely, she developed the habit of looking right, then left, then right again, which she continued for the rest of her life.

Besides adjusting to a new country, Valerie's family also had a hard time adjusting to living with each other. This was the first time in five years that they were all living together under one roof. A lot had changed in those five years.

In terms of school, Valerie was enrolled in grade 11 in a high school in Fredericton. This meant that she was studying the same material for the third time after having previously passed it once in New Zealand and then obtaining her O-level in England. Moreover, she was teased by other girls because of her accent, so her school life was less than ideal.

In March of 1947, Kitty got sick and was prescribed bed rest at home. Valerie, being the eldest child, was pulled from school to take care of the family. That was actually music to Valerie's ears, as it allowed her to leave high school. Of course, she would have preferred the circumstances to be different, but she made the most of the situation.

Valerie was not worried about getting into college. She had passed every subject for her O-level in England, except for Latin, which secured her admission into the UNB. Because of that, Valerie did not return to school for the rest of the term, even after her mother recovered. However, her parents would only agree to that if she talked to the school superintendent about her plan, which she did. The only question the superintendent asked her was if she was 16. She replied she was, and so she was allowed to leave school.

Although not having to attend school was fun at first, Valerie realised that all that glitters is not gold. The lack of activity and interaction with others eventually got to Valerie, and by late spring, her mother suspected she was depressed. So, Kitty arranged for her to visit a friend's parents who lived near Montreal in Châteauguay for a month. The family had a daughter a few years older than Valerie, so her mother thought she would provide her with some much-needed company. Valerie did enjoy the time spent with the family. The daughter, along with her fiancée, took Valerie around Montreal on the weekends.

In the summer of 1947, Fred travelled to Urbana, Illinois, to study with the esteemed civil engineer, Ralph Peck, for updates in the field of soil mechanics and to learn about recent advancements made during the war.

While Valerie was able to enter the UNB, her father did have to talk to the UNB registrar about her O-level Latin failure. However, they determined that the Latin taught in England was much more advanced than that taught in New Brunswick, and since Latin was only required in the first year, Valerie was accepted into UNB. She received a 75% score in her first-year Latin course!

So, in September of 1947, Valerie started her four-year Bachelor of Arts program at UNB. Those four years at university would go on to become some of the best years of her life. The University of New Brunswick was the first English language university established in Canada. It was founded in 1785 as the Provincial Academy of Arts and Sciences. Although it received provincial government support, the university did not receive a charter until 1800, when it became known as the College of New Brunswick. About three decades later, in 1828, it received a royal charter and, in 1859, officially became the University of New Brunswick.

At the time Valerie joined, there were about 1,000 students at UNB, and Valerie was one of only 100 female students there. A proud moment indeed. After WWII ended, the Canadian government offered to pay the university tuition for returning soldiers. This increased the number of students at UNB over the years. The incoming students were also older and more focused; many of them were even married.

At UNB, there was a girls-only room for the female students to rest or have discussions. On her first day, Valerie learned that at the beginning of the year, the new female students had to stand on top of a table one by one and entertain the seniors. Most of the freshmen took what Valerie considered the easy way out by singing a song. When it was her turn, the other students asked her where she had lived before moving to Canada. To their surprise, she had lived in many places and had many stories to tell about her adventures. By the time she was done, the head of the group claimed that Valerie had entertained them enough with her travels and so she did not have to sing for them, which greatly relieved her.

Because of the degree for which she was enrolled, Valerie was able to study a wide variety of courses. In her first year, she took Chemistry, Latin, French, English Literature, History, and Mathematics at Alexander College. Alexander College was separate from the main UNB campus. It closed in 1950. The buildings were converted back to their original use for the Fredericton Exhibition Company. Although all the classes in her first year were held at Alexander College, Valerie's Chemistry lab was on the main campus, so she had to take a bus to get there.

From the second year onwards, Valerie attended all her classes on the main campus. In the second year, she took English Literature, French, European History (1500–1815), Biology, and Political Science. In third year, she took Canadian and American Literature, French Literature, American History, Introduction to Sociology, and Social and Abnormal Psychology. In her fourth year, she took French Literature, Classics in Translation, European History (1815–1939), Sociology, and Political Science. A fun fact about her Classics in

Translation course: it was taught by the Latin professor who interviewed and hired Fred for UNB.

Among all her courses during her four years of university, Valerie enjoyed her final year Sociology course the most, partly because of the professor, who was very knowledgeable and made the course interesting. Valerie remembered writing a paper about the Japanese in Canada for this course.

Valerie had a very active social life at UNB. The events held at the university also helped her thrive. UNB had three formal dances every year, which were held in the gym: the Fall Formal, The Con, and the Graduation in the spring. Valerie attended all of them every year, and since she was somewhat of a social butterfly, she never had trouble finding a date to accompany her.

Besides the formal dances at UNB, two formal dances were also held at the Lady Beaverbrook Residence every year. Valerie eagerly waited for them as they were much better than the ones at UNB. Tables, each with four chairs, were placed against the walls in the dining room. A band played from the balcony while downstairs, there were lowlights and sofas set up around the pool. It had a delightful ambiance and was definitely better organised than the dances in the gym.

In terms of her personal life, Valerie had a boyfriend named Jim in the first year. They had a good time together. Jim's mother happened to work at a mill in St. Stephen. He would bring Valerie some material with which she made some dresses for herself. However, the sparks that had once flown when they first met soon died down and the two broke up at the start of the second year.

A few months later, Valerie met Ralph, who was one year her senior, and the two soon began dating. However, that relationship also came to an end when Ralph graduated at the end of her third year and left Canada on scholarship to attend a university in Scotland. This was the longest Valerie had been with anyone, so she was understandably a little heartbroken at Ralph's departure.

Valerie also made friends with other women attending UNB, including Betty Cork, who became a life-long friend.

In the summer of 1948, Fred went to Sackville, New Brunswick to teach a summer program at Mount Allison University while the family stayed back in Fredericton. During that time, Valerie enrolled in a secretarial course, which included typing and dictation. Valerie was glad she took up this course as it allowed her to fill in for the secretary of the Dean of Arts when he went on vacation. Dr. Alfred G. Bailey was the Dean of Arts and Honorary Librarian, and his office was situated in the library, where Valerie simultaneously began working as well.

At the library, one of Valerie's co-workers was a fellow student named Bob Hanson. He had a good personality and the rest of the staff seemed to like the idea of them as a couple and were hoping they might get married. However, Valerie had no romantic interest in him and saw him only as a friend. She later found out that Bob was gay, and they remained good friends.

In the fall of 1948, Fred was offered a job at the Worcester Polytechnic Institute (WPI). Since it was a much better opportunity than his current job, Fred decided they would relocate to Worcester, Massachusetts. While the others were excited about her father's new job, Valerie was not excited. By this time, she had grown tired of moving around. Moreover, she was now 18 years old and was enjoying her time at UNB with her friends and she was reluctant to leave them behind.

After much discussion, which included some pleading and begging on Valerie's part, her parents decided to let her complete her education at UNB, and since UNB did not have a women's residence at the time, they left her in the care of Mrs. Clark. The move to Worcester allowed Valerie's parents and siblings to become American citizens.

Mrs. Clark was a widow whose husband had passed away in March of 1948. Before his death, the couple had taken in boarders to help with the finances. Mrs. Clark continued this after his death. The cost of accommodation at the Clark residence was $14/week, but since Valerie was working at the library, she was able to pay for it herself.

The three-story Clark residence was located on Charlotte Street and was about a 20-minute walk to UNB's main campus. The first floor had a parlour with a piano, behind which was a living room and then a dining room. Adjacent to the dining room was the kitchen. The kitchen had a wood stove for cooking. There was also a door that led to the backyard which had a shed and a lovely garden.

The second floor of the house consisted of five rooms. One of the two larger rooms was occupied by Mrs. Clark herself, while the other was rented out to a professor at UNB. The third room, which was above the front hall, belonged to Valerie. The room was rather small, just spacious enough to contain her single bed, a dresser, and a small desk. At night, Valerie would leave her door open to let the heat in.

There were two other small rooms at the back on the second floor. The only bathroom in this three-story house was located at the end of the hall. Imagine the rush outside the bathroom in the mornings! The third floor only had two rooms and a wood furnace. Valerie recalled that one of the tenants got a really good deal on the rent because he volunteered to look after the furnace.

The rent agreement at the Clark residence included three meals a day: breakfast, lunch, and dinner. All the tenants usually ate all meals together, even though some of them did not pay for them. Just like in the WAAC Officers' hut, there was no washing machine at Mrs. Clark's, so everyone had to wash their laundry by hand. In the winter, the clothes would be hung in the shed to dry. Valerie boarded there for the remaining three years of her university.

Chapter 9 O Canada

The Presbyterian church was very close to Mrs. Clark's house, and she was an active member there. Her example meant Valerie also felt obligated to go to church. However, she opted to attend the United Church as the minister there was more in tune with the university students. The church also had a good choir, so Valerie was more drawn to it than the Presbyterian Church.

Valerie worked at the library for three years, from her second year through to her final year. In the first year of her job, she worked 4 hours a week as a Student Assistant. In the summer of 1949, she worked full-time in the Order Department. During the second year (1948–1949), Valerie worked with Bob on creating a list of periodicals. In her third year, she worked eight hours a week as a Student Assistant: four hours in the Circulation and Reference Departments and four hours in the Cataloguing Department. In the summer of 1950, Valerie worked one and a half months in the UNB Library Catalogue Department.

During school breaks and in the summer, Valerie would go to Worcester to visit her parents. To get to Worcester, Valerie had to take the train from Fredericton to Fredericton Junction, where she changed to the main train from Saint John to McAdam, New Brunswick. From there, Valerie had to walk across the border into the US and catch the train to Boston. In Boston, she had to change stations going from North Station to South Station to catch the train to Worcester. To get back to UNB from Worcester, she did the trip in reverse.

Valerie recalled being on a date one summer Saturday evening. While she was out, another gentleman was trying to reach her on her parents' home phone. Her father had to wait until Valerie returned after 1 a.m. to let her know. Valerie remembered her father being very amused that two men were pursuing his daughter at the same time!

In her fourth year (1950–1951), Valerie worked in the Catalogue Department again for eight hours a week. She worked from 5 p.m. to 9 p.m. on Wednesdays, and from 9 a.m. to 1 p.m. on Saturdays. She worked with Eleanor Wees, who was a few years older and was the Head of Cataloguing at the UNB library. Valerie and Eleanor worked on catalogue subject headings. They became good friends and kept in touch for over 70 years. Valerie had a lot going on with school and work, but she enjoyed every bit of it.

Ma Bailey's was a coffee shop just off-campus and a short walk away. It was frequented by UNB students, but Valerie never really went there. However, one day in the fall of 1950, at the start of her fourth year, she randomly decided to go. That day, standing in line behind her was Andrew Duncan Monkhouse, better known as Ben. As the two waited in line to be served, they started chatting. They hit it off and started dating soon after.

Like Valerie, Ben was also a serious student and so the two quickly settled into a routine that accommodated their studies and part-time jobs. Ben would call Valerie on Wednesdays to make plans for the weekend, as they would usually know by then what the rest of the week entailed. Then on Saturdays, they would go to a movie or to a dance, while Sundays were reserved for a walk in the park and then a trip to the Beaverbrook Hotel coffee shop for tea.

The more they talked, the more Valerie found out about Ben. Ben was born in London, England, on July 2, 1929, to Isabel, also known as Dot or Em, and Harold, also known as Bill or Flump, Monkhouse. The family lived in Wallasey, Cheshire, until 1940.

Flump's brother, Sir Edward Monkhouse, was the Deputy Controller of the Timber Board of England and he sent Flump to Halifax, Canada, in April of 1940 to coordinate the shipping of lumber from Canada to England during the war. On July 2, 1940, Em, Ben, his brother Nick - who was five and half years younger than him, and their grandmother Isabel

Henderson, arrived in Quebec City. From there, they took a train to Halifax. They lived in Bedford, just outside of Halifax.

Towards the end of the war, Flump realised that Canada had better opportunities and moved the family to Chatham, New Brunswick (which became part of Miramichi in 1995). There, he established a wholesale lumber company (Monkhouse & Company) that sold Maritime lumber into Central Canada, New England, and Great Britain.

In September of 1947, the same time as Valerie began university, Ben started the five-year Forestry program at UNB. From the second year onwards, he stayed at the Lady Beaverbrook Residence, which was where the formal dances were held. In 1948, a little after the end of his first year, Ben suffered from a serious medical problem that required intervention. He underwent three operations on his back, one in Fredericton, one in Montreal and the third one in Chatham—all three were successful; however, he spent over a year in the hospital to recover, which delayed his graduation until June of 1953.

After Valerie's classes ended in May of 1951, she found herself in a rather tough predicament. She could either take a full-time job at the UNB library, or she could move home to Worcester and work. Since Valerie and Ben's relationship was still fresh at that time, she decided to head back to Worcester and live with her parents. Her mother had also been pressuring her to return home.

In 1950, for his 21st birthday, Ben got a BSA motorcycle from his mother, Em. He had promised Valerie a ride on it, but the day never came as he sold it in the spring of 1952 to buy a car. During her last few weeks in New Brunswick, Valerie and Ben spent as much time together as they could. In June of 1951, Valerie returned to Worcester and finally, after three years, was reunited with her family.

1951 – Valerie Sanger graduation picture – Fredericton, New Brunswick, Canada

Chapter 10
The Marriage

1951 to 1953

1953 – The bride, Valerie Sanger – Worcester, Massachusetts, USA

Valerie's Journeys

In June of 1951, Valerie returned to her parents' home, which was now located in Worcester, Massachusetts, after three long years. While Valerie's family seemed to move to a new location every other year, it seemed like they were here to stay in Worcester this time around. They had settled into a colonial two-story wooden house which had been constructed in 1934. Their house was located on Berkman Street, and theirs was a quiet, residential neighbourhood.

The house had three bedrooms, which were located on the second floor, while the kitchen, dining room and living room were on the first floor. It also had a garage and a basement beneath the living room. Upon her return, Valerie had to share a room with Diana like in the old days, since the other two rooms were occupied by her parents and brother.

Valerie was happy to be reunited with her family, and especially her sister. She believed she was a very supportive and loving big sister and was sure that Diana would also agree. Valerie remembered playing cards with Diana in the evenings and teaching her how to play Patience (Solitaire) with two decks.

While Valerie was happy to be back home with her family, that happiness did not last very long. Valerie was unhappy, for the most part, as things were not easy. Her father was still trying to build his career after his return from Shanghai, but things did not seem to be going his way. It got to a point where he started teaching extra classes at the Worcester Polytechnic Institute, took on consulting work, and served as an expert witness in court cases. Valerie recalled one highly political case, where he was called as an expert witness for the City of Worcester who successfully sued a road contractor over the quality of work on a road repaving project. This just added to the stress at home.

During all this, Valerie thought about Ben and where their relationship was headed. The last time she had seen Ben was in May of 1951, when he left for Beaver Cove on Vancouver

Island to work a summer job cutting trees in a forestry operation.

To help the family and keep herself busy, Valerie decided to find a job for herself. Initially, she began working in the Circulation Division of the Worcester Free Public Library (WFPL), thanks to her prior work experience at UNB. During this time, Valerie worked on the bookmobile, which travelled all around town, delivering books to the community. It was a very fun experience indeed!

Valerie and Ben continued to write letters to each other throughout 1951 upon Ben's return from Beaver Cove. They fell into a routine of writing every day and mailing every second day. The more letters they exchanged, the more Valerie realised how much she loved Ben.

With her summer job at WFPL coming to an end, and Ben still busy with his studies, Valerie started looking for a more permanent job and settled on the Memorial Hospital Library in Worcester, where she worked for two years from the fall of 1951 to the fall of 1953. Valerie's job was to wheel a book cart around the hospital, taking books to patients. She really enjoyed working at the library because it gave her a chance to interact with the patients and bring a smile to their faces amidst the health battles they were fighting, big or small. Valerie's sister, Diana, volunteered as a candy striper at the hospital, and she would often go to the library to hang out with Valerie.

Ben's mother Em came from a highly educated and wealthy family. Her father had been a very successful and wealthy businessman in England up until the market crash in 1929. When Ben's father, Flump, had asked Em's father for her hand in marriage, he refused the proposal, saying that he would not let Em marry him until he was earning 500 pounds a year. They were unwilling to give up, resulting in a seven-year-long engagement, until Flump met his future father-in-law's expectations.

Naturally, Em also had high expectations for the future wives of her two sons. And while Valerie also came from a highly educated family (her father ***was*** a professor!), she had not been exposed to "the way for a young woman to behave in the upper classes of England," as Em liked to call it. The first meeting with Ben's parents was held at the Lord Beaverbrook Hotel over a cup of tea. However, knowing Em's mindset, the meeting proved to be quite difficult for Valerie, who felt Em did not approve of her. Em commented later that the girl did not eat very much.

By the end of 1951, Ben decided to ask Valerie's father if he could marry her, when he visited Valerie during the Christmas break. Valerie and Ben decided that they should wait until after Ben graduated from UNB in 1953. Despite Valerie's fears about what Em had thought about her, the two-faced no objections from either family.

After their engagement, things were quiet for a few months, with Valerie and Ben keeping in touch through letters. A big surprise came in the spring of 1952 when Ben sold his motorcycle and bought a car instead—an Austin A40, which they promptly named "Austin." With a car at his disposal now, Ben could travel to Worcester to visit Valerie and even drive her to Chatham to his parents. That news was music to her ears! While she was a little sad that she never got a chance to ride Ben's motorcycle, she could not be happier because she would be able to see him more often now. And while the visits were not very frequent, Ben still managed to visit Valerie a few times a year.

Whenever Ben announced a visit to Worcester, not only Valerie, but her entire family, would be elated. Ben fit in quite well with her family. He also had an excellent sense of humour that made everyone laugh and so they all admired him. However, there was one thing that Valerie's parents were concerned about – the car, Austin. It seemed Ben was always working on it, and it was always breaking down. Ben really loved Austin, but Valerie's parents were right – it required a lot of repairing. Those were just some issues that came with a second-hand car.

On December 27, 1952, Ben's cousin Judy (the daughter of his Aunt Joyce "Bump" and Uncle Jack Berry) married Grant Warner at the Chateau Laurier in Ottawa. The wedding was an extravagant affair, as Jack was an important person in the Canadian Government. For Valerie, this was her first introduction to Ben's ***whole*** family. However, the wedding was fun, and Valerie got along well with Ben's cousins and other family members.

On one trip back to Worcester in the winter, Valerie remembered that it was very cold and the heater in the car was not working properly. To top it off, the radiator froze, and Ben had to find boiling water to unfreeze it. Fortunately, their car had stopped near a farmhouse and not in some secluded area. The farmhouse was a short walk away, shivering from the cold, the young couple made their way to the farmhouse and knocked on the door. They were met with the curious faces of two women, who quickly ushered them inside. The women were very kind and hospitable. They immediately served them some piping hot tea, and to Valerie, it was one of the best cups of tea she had ever had! Valerie stayed in the warm confines of the farmhouse and chatted with the women while Ben got the car going. They were able to make their way home safe and sound.

In early June of 1953, Valerie travelled to Fredericton for Ben's graduation and then to Chatham to stay with his family. On June 2, while in Chatham, Valerie remembered watching the coronation of Queen Elizabeth. Ben's younger brother, Nick, took an immediate liking to Valerie. He honoured her by showing her the cannon, which he and his friends had made. Valerie was one of the lucky few to see the cannon outside of the group. Valerie also recalled walking in on Nick and his friends one day lying on the living room floor, examining a model train engine; Nick was very passionate about things of that nature.

While Valerie was in Chatham, an extremely powerful tornado, an F4 on the Fujita Scale hit Worcester on June 9th at 4:25 pm and lasted a good 90 minutes. Ninety-four people were killed, over 1,300 were injured, and more than 4,000 buildings were damaged in its wake. When Valerie returned home later that month, she felt as if she was looking at a war-torn city. It was that bad.

As the affected residents of Worcester began to rebuild their lives, Valerie and her family prepared for her wedding, to be held in Worcester. There was a discussion as to where to hold the wedding. Since Valerie's parents were not regular churchgoers and were relatively new to Worcester there was not a logical church for the wedding. Luckily, Diana was involved with the First Baptist Church. Because of her involvement, Valerie's parents approached the minister, and he agreed to hold the wedding at the church.

Back then, there was a residency requirement in order to get married, so Ben had to arrive in Worcester a week or two before the wedding. He stayed with Valerie and her family during that time.

Valerie and Ben were set to be wed on October 10, 1953, and the rehearsal dinner was held at her parents' house on October 9th. The rehearsal dinner included: Valerie, Ben, his parents, Em and Flump, Valerie's parents, Nick, Diana, David, and Ben's friend and best man, Stig Harvor, seated at one table; Jack and Joyce Berry, Colin (Ben's first cousin) and his wife Betty, and Ben's cousin, Michael Henderson (from Zimbabwe) seated at a second table.

Chapter 10 The Marriage

1953 – Family picture at the wedding (from right to left Nick, Stig Harvor (best man), Flump, Em, Ben, Valerie, Fred, Kitty, Diana, David) – Worcester, Massachusetts, USA

And so, on Saturday, October 10, 1953, Valerie and Ben were married at the First Baptist Church in Worcester. The marriage was officiated by Gordon M. Torgersen and was registered on October 13, 1953. The wedding was small, with Diana as the bridesmaid and Nick and David as the ushers. After the wedding, everyone headed to Valerie's parents' house for a two-hour reception.

David was 17 at the time of the wedding and, from the moment Ben had been staying with them before the wedding, he had wanted to have some fun and "decorate" Ben's car. He had planned to put up a 'Just Married' sign, among other things, on Austin. Normally while visiting, Ben's car was parked on the driveway. However, on the day of the wedding, Valerie's father suggested Ben park his car in the garage instead to make space for the guests.

That morning, David went looking for Austin, all set to 'decorate' it but, much to his dismay, he could not find the car in its usual place. David asked his father if he knew where it was; his father shook his head. When he asked if he could take a look in the garage, his father convinced him not to, saying the garage was full of things that had been taken out of the house to create more room. Taking his father at his word, David abandoned his plan. Valerie and Ben were grateful that her father had protected the car from David.

Right after getting married, Valerie and Ben went on their honeymoon to Yarmouth, Maine. The honeymoon lasted for a week, and then they drove to Toronto, Ontario, through Niagara Falls. It was a short honeymoon as Ben had to get back to work in Toronto. After 2.5 years apart, the two finally got to spend some quality time together.

The plan was for Ben to join his father's company, Monkhouse & Company, and to open an office in Toronto when he graduated from UNB. Flump thought that with a presence in Toronto, it would be easier to sell New Brunswick lumber in Ontario. After Ben's graduation, he went to Toronto to get things started. Upon his arrival in June, he stayed with his cousin Colin and his family (wife Betty and daughters Ann and Sue) on Gwendolen Avenue in Willowdale, now part of Toronto. Colin was also in the lumber business, being a junior partner in Hanford Lumber, a Toronto lumber company. By October of 1953, Ben had things set up and had found a studio apartment in the building at the corner of Havelock and College streets in the west end of Toronto. The next step was for Valerie to move to Toronto.

Chapter 10 The Marriage

October 10, 1953 – Valerie and Ben – Worcester, Massachusetts, USA

Chapter 11
True Calling

1953 to 1957

1954 – Valerie, Six-month anniversary – 3 Havelock Street, Toronto, Ontario, Canada

The housing market was quite tight back in the early 1950s and, based on how much Valerie and Ben were willing to spend on accommodation, they did not have a lot of choices. Prior to their wedding, Ben worked hard to find a place for them to live after their marriage. Fortunately, he was able to find a cosy studio apartment in a building at 3 Havelock St., located at the corner of Havelock and College streets in the west end of Toronto. It was constructed sometime between 1903 and 1914 as an apartment building with larger apartments. However, with the onset of the shortage of housing, the owners were quick to split the original larger units into multiple smaller ones.

Valerie and Ben rented Apartment 3 in the building. It had one room and one bathroom, and they quickly settled into their new home. The room had a fireplace and a Murphy bed that would fold into the wall during the day and could be pulled down at night. This room served as their bedroom, living room, dining room and office.

Although the apartment was small, it did have some advantages. Firstly, it was located on the streetcar line, providing easy access for Valerie to go downtown, to Eaton's College Street Store, in particular. It had much better-quality products than the Eaton's Queen Street Store, which is why Valerie favoured the former. Besides that, the apartment building was in the Grove Park area of Toronto, which had numerous houses with garages and some of the owners actually rented them out. This was perfect for the young couple because not only did Ben need a garage for Austin, but he also wanted one to make furniture in.

Chapter 11 True Calling

3 Havelock Street, Toronto, Ontario, Canada

Valerie and Ben had been formulating a plan; they wanted to buy a house. However, since money was tight, they decided to prepare, and making furniture was one of the ways to do that, in addition to saving. Because of his profession, Ben had easy access to the materials required to build the things he wanted. They started building a dining room table in Colin's garage. Then Ben rented a garage near their apartment. With Valerie's help, he built four chairs for the dining table, a coffee table, an end table, a double bed with a headboard and side tables, a chest of drawers for him and a vanity for her. They made it all using particle board. Their preparations were in full swing; all they needed now was a house to move all this furniture into!

Valerie and Ben's weekends would be reserved for chores, and boy, were there chores to be done! They had befriended a young couple named Derek and Margot Lovejoy, who lived in the same apartment building. Margot was a very multi-talented young woman. She was an artist, a film illustrator, and an author. Like Valerie and Ben, the Lovejoys were also newlyweds. Since they did not have a car, Valerie and

Ben would give them rides to and from the grocery store on Saturdays. For Christmas of 1953, Valerie and Ben decided to stay in Toronto instead of visiting family and they invited the Lovejoys over for dinner on Christmas Eve. Valerie's first Christmas present to Ben was an electric drill to help build the furniture.

While their Saturdays would be spent grocery shopping and doing other chores, their Sundays were often spent at the home of Ben's cousin Colin. Valerie and Ben also invited Colin, his wife Betty and their daughters, Ann and Sue, for dinner at their apartment. The space was barely big enough to fit them all, but they managed somehow. Needless to say, Valerie did not have many visitors.

While the apartment did have its perks, it also had some disadvantages, most significantly the paper-thin walls that separated the units. Valerie could hear each and every word from her neighbours, a couple who would almost always be quarrelling. As a joke, Valerie and Ben nicknamed them the "Bickerings." Valerie could not recall their actual names.

However, the Bickerings' bickering did not bother Valerie and Ben too much because they were often away as Ben's job involved him driving all over Ontario, selling boxcar loads of lumber from New Brunswick to wood retailers. Since Valerie did not have much to occupy her time at the apartment and wanted to be with her husband, she accompanied Ben on his business trips, which were quite frequent, when Ben would go into lumber yards to make a sales pitch, Valerie would wait patiently in the car, reading a book.

Accompanying Ben proved to be a great adventure for Valerie as they got to travel all around Ontario and discover it together. The first week, they went down to Southwestern Ontario, visiting Windsor, London, and Hamilton. In the second week, they travelled to Eastern Ontario, visiting Peterborough, Ottawa, Kingston, and Cornwall. The week after that, they made a trip to Northern Ontario, going to Sudbury, Sault Ste.

Marie, and as far north as Hearst. The fourth week was spent in Toronto, where Ben would visit lumber yards and finish up his paperwork.

With the goal of saving up for their house always in the back of their minds, Valerie and Ben were very frugal with their spending and managed to pay for both their meals on Ben's daily food allowance during these trips.

During this time, the freeway system of the 400-series highways, a network of controlled-access highways throughout Southern Ontario, was being constructed. This meant that Valerie and Ben had to drive on two-lane highways, such as Highway 2, through all the small towns in Ontario. While the roads provided a scenic view, it was not enjoyable being stuck behind a slow-moving truck, as it was difficult to pass or avoid heavy traffic.

The new year brought with it new interests. By the time 1954 rolled around, Valerie quickly realised that she did not know how to drive. So, that was yet another project for Valerie and Ben to work on that year, with Ben's help, Valerie was able to learn all the basics. She remembered taking her driving test in downtown Toronto, which was not the easiest place to drive, especially for a novice driver, because of all the streetcar tracks in the city and the plentiful construction projects, including the new subway line. The test proved to be very difficult as Valerie was required to drive up the big hill on Spadina Avenue. Valerie was nervous about the driving road test. However, she was well prepared, passed the test and obtained her driver's licence.

Ben did not have much vacation time. Whenever he was able to get time off, they would make a trip to Chatham to visit his parents, including going to Kent Lodge for the annual visit in August, and then they would be off to Worcester to visit Valerie's family.

Perhaps the most memorable trip Valerie and Ben had started on Monday, October 18, 1954. That week, they were on their way to Southwestern Ontario, which meant that they had to take Bloor Street (Highway 5) and head west out of Toronto. When they reached the Humber River, they found that the bridge was closed. Confused, they drove north to Dundas, where the bridge was also closed. They tried their luck again at Eglinton, Lawrence, Finch, and finally Steeles, but all of the bridges were closed. Before giving up, they made one last stop at Highway 7 where, thankfully, the bridge was open, and they were able to continue on their journey.

But why were all those bridges closed, one might ask? Unbeknownst to Valerie and Ben, Hurricane Hazel, a Category 4 hurricane, had made a direct hit on Toronto on October 15, 1954. It dumped a good 214 mm of rain, along with high winds, on the west end of Toronto. The storm resulted in 81 deaths, left 4,000 families homeless and caused over $137,000,000 in damages. Today, this would equate to more than 1.5 billion dollars! While Valerie and Ben were aware that it had rained a lot, they had been busy with their weekend chores and did not know the extent of the damage it had caused until they headed out on Monday.

As the year 1954 neared its end, Valerie and Ben's plans were finally falling into place. It was decided that it would be better for Ben to work for a larger company to sell lumber instead of his father's company. So, in November of 1954, Ben got a job at Burger Lumber in Montreal as their Ontario Sales Representative. With the stability that working for a larger company brought along with all the connections Ben had developed around Ontario during the past year, Valerie and Ben decided that they now had enough money to buy their first house.

Upon their return from a visit to Valerie's family in Worcester for Christmas 1954, Valerie and Ben began house hunting. However, once they started looking for a house, they realised that they did ***not have that much money*** after all. However, they had one big advantage; since Ben's job involved him travelling around Toronto and they did not stay in their apartment all that much anyway, they decided it was not essential to buy a house in Toronto.

With that thought in mind, Valerie and Ben were able to find the perfect house within their budget. The house was located at 1236 Echo Drive, halfway between Toronto and Hamilton, in an area called "Lorne Park" near Port Credit in modern-day Mississauga. Lorne Park was a small burg created to support the local logging industry. The house was located in a residential neighbourhood near Lake Ontario and Highway 2, with an elementary school just a block away.

Valerie and Ben bought the house in March of 1955 for $16,000. However, since they did not have that kind of money, Flump lent them the money they needed to make up the difference between the first mortgage of $10,000 and the price of the house. The couple was very grateful to Flump and wanted to pay him back as soon as possible, which they did within three years.

When Valerie and Ben moved into their very own house in April of 1955, they only had $50 in the bank. They immediately began renovations and painting. The next step was to furnish it with the furniture they had built together. Soon after they moved, Ben's parents announced that they would be coming to visit them in July, and so, $32.65 out of the $50 had to be spent on buying two single beds to accommodate Ben's parents when they arrived.

Valerie and Ben's house was a two-bedroom bungalow built on a large lot. Upon entry through the front door, there was a small entryway. To the left, there was a living room, which had a fireplace, with the kitchen right behind it. There was a window over the kitchen sink that looked out over the backyard. There was also a side door in the kitchen that went into the breezeway (a covered area between the house and garage that was about 4 metres wide).

1955 – 1236 Echo Drive, Lorne Park, Ontario, Canada

The dining room was straight in front of the kitchen on the other side. To the right of the front entrance, there was a short hallway that led to the bathroom on the right, the second bedroom on the left, and the master bedroom at the end. The house also had a full basement.

Valerie and Ben saw a lot of potential in the house. It had a lovely large backyard that they turned into a vegetable garden that bore them plenty of vegetables. Valerie remembers that Ben bought an Irish Sweepstake ticket (a kind of lottery) one day, and they spent the evening in the backyard discussing what they would buy for the house if they won. Sadly, they did not.

Besides the backyard, another great feature of the house was the neighbours. On the west side lived an older retired couple, Mary and Jack Wilson. Valerie adored Mary. She was like her second mother, always ready to lend a helping hand and answering any queries she had about being a housewife. William and Annabelle Heppenstall lived on the east side with their son, John, and two daughters, Janet and Ann, who were between 3 and 6 years old. Ann and Janet remember that their mother Annabelle had a special connection with Valerie. Both of them had immigrated to

Canada as young women and had faced similar challenges adapting to the Canadian way of life. Across the street from the Heppenstalls were the Woods. There were actually quite a few young families that Valerie met in the neighbourhood.

Even after Valerie and Ben bought the house, their routine remained much the same, with Valerie accompanying Ben on his work trips around the province. The economy was strong, and business was going well. In fact, 1955 was one of Ben's best years, as he sold a record amount of lumber. This was a good thing because there was still plenty to be done around the house, such as adding shutters and buying storm windows, which needed money.

The house was low on the ground and there was a slight slope in the backyard towards the house. After a heavy storm, water leaked into the basement. Noticing the window-well was full of water, Ben did what anyone else would have done—he opened the window and got soaked! So, there were also some protective and preventive measures that needed to be taken around the house.

In 1955, David was accepted into UNB and decided to visit his sister and brother-in-law on his way from Worcester to Fredericton in August. Valerie and Ben had a good time with David driving him around town. Valerie's memories from that time included a trip to Niagara Falls and the sight of David sitting in their backyard eating fresh cantaloupe.

Valerie and Ben continued to visit Ben's cousin, Colin, and his family. Although the trip was longer, now that they had a house, it was much easier to entertain Colin and his family at Lorne Park.

By the spring of 1955, Ben's brother Nick had moved to Toronto with his wife, Pat, who was pregnant with their first child. Their daughter Pamela was born in July of 1955. Nick and Pat first lived in an apartment in Rosedale but then moved to a basement apartment in Vinci Crescent, in the north end of Toronto. Every two weeks, the two families would take turns visiting each other. When Nick, Pat and Pam would go to Lorne Park, Ben would have a list of projects for Nick to work on around the house. With the men busy, Valerie had time to chat with Pat and play with Pam. Similarly, when Valerie and Ben would visit them in Toronto, Nick would have a list of projects for Ben to help with. Again, Valerie and Pat would be left to catch up.

Valerie and Ben had wanted to start a family and spending time with Pam had further intensified those feelings. Unfortunately, Valerie had a few miscarriages in the previous year. However, by the end of 1955, Valerie was pregnant and had made it past the first trimester. She was not willing to take any risks, so she stayed home while Ben travelled for work. However, Ben being away meant that Valerie did not have a car at her disposal so she would rely on the neighbours to drive her into Port Credit to go shopping or to Long Branch at the west end of Toronto to get the streetcar to go downtown. They spent Christmas that year in their new home in Lorne Park and visited Nick, Colin, and their families.

Valerie was very careful throughout her pregnancy. Her patience and care proved fruitful when her first child, Peter, was born on June 12, 1956, in Toronto General Hospital. Valerie and Ben could not have been happier at the birth of a healthy baby boy. Valerie recalled that Peter was born on the fourth day of an intense heatwave, with temperatures reaching over 32°C.

Back in those days, since expectant fathers were not allowed in the delivery room, Ben received the news of his firstborn's arrival from the hospital staff. Those were some of the most nerve-wracking hours of his life!

After the birth, Valerie had to stay in the hospital for five days before she could go home with the baby. As soon as Valerie was discharged from the hospital, her parents came to meet their first grandson. While Ben's mother, Em, was also desperate to see her grandson, she was unwell and could not travel the long distance to their house.

With Peter to take care of, Valerie's travelling days were over. Although Ben tried to adjust his schedule so he could be home more with Valerie and Peter, it was difficult, and ended up on the road more than he wanted. On the days when Ben was home, he would volunteer to get up at night to take care of Peter. However, Valerie recalled many times when she was awakened by Peter's cries in the middle of the night, Ben was fast asleep. She would sometimes poke him to wake him up, after which he would get up and tend to Peter. Other times, she would let him sleep and go to Peter herself.

For Christmas 1956, Valerie and Ben decided to travel to Chatham to spend Christmas with Ben's parents, who were eager to meet their grandson. Em was not well and could not travel to Toronto. This was the first time they were travelling with their now six-month-old son—quite the adventure with all the baby supplies.

Soon after Christmas, Valerie discovered that she was pregnant again. As the day of the delivery drew nearer, having already gone through the process once, Valerie and Ben were more prepared this time around. First, Valerie arranged for a cleaning woman, Ida, to come and help with the housework while she looked after Peter. Next, she asked her mother to come to Toronto to take care of Peter while she was in the hospital.

Valerie vividly remembers that in late August or early September of 1957, she, nine months pregnant, had to run after Peter who was running towards Echo Drive. Shortly after, Hugh Duncan (Duncan) arrived on September 6, 1957.

As planned, Valerie's mother had arrived in Toronto to take care of Peter. He had just started to talk and gave her the nickname "Idasan", which stuck.

Meanwhile, Ben's mother was still quite ill. So, Valerie and Ben, along with their two infants, flew to Chatham to spend Christmas with his family. This was an even greater challenge, logistically speaking, than the Christmas before, but the couple managed somehow and spent a lovely time at Ben's parents.

1956 – Kitty, Ben, Peter, Valerie, Fred – 1236 Echo Drive, Lorne Park, Ontario, Canada

Chapter 12
Boys' Childhood

1958–1961

1958 – Peter, Valerie, Duncan – 1236 Echo Drive, Lorne Park, Ontario, Canada

After spending a lovely Christmas with Ben's parents in Chatham, Valerie and Ben returned to Toronto. It had been a very busy two years, and now the young couple was looking forward to settling down into a routine with their two toddlers, Peter and Duncan.

Along with Valerie's sons, her siblings were also growing up. Her sister Diana followed in her footsteps and enrolled at UNB in 1957. That same year, her father started working with the U.S. Army Corps of Engineers in Waltham, Massachusetts, with a focus on building on permafrost.

As for Ben, business was still going well, and he would spend two or three weeks of each month travelling to sell lumber. By June of 1958, Valerie and Ben were able to repay Flump for the loan they had taken for the house.

After Ben started working at Burger Lumber, he sold Austin as he received a company car which also served as the family car. However, since Ben was often away with the only car, it was challenging for Valerie. Fortunately, the neighbours were very supportive and would lend a hand whenever she needed help or give her a ride to the grocery store or perhaps the hospital if one of the boys got sick. Naturally, no one likes asking others for help all the time.

Ben understood Valerie's struggles and after Flump's loan was paid off, he bought Valerie her very own car! It was a Morris Minor station wagon with wood trim that they called Polly. Polly gave Valerie the much-needed freedom and flexibility she desired. However, she did not usually venture too far. She would mostly go grocery shopping or take the boys out for a drive during the day. Valerie also recalls taking the boys to Port Credit Harbour in the summer to watch the sailboats.

When Ben was home, they did things together as a family. While Valerie and Ben realised it was important to spend time together as a family, they also recognized the need to do things together as a couple—without the boys. To have the opportunity to spend time together, they took up square dancing, which they both really enjoyed.

With the boys growing up, Ben finished working on the basement in the fall of 1958 to create a playroom for them, which was called the "No-No" room. It was a space that was never off limits to the boys and had no rules.

Family vacations continued to be visits to Valerie and Ben's parents throughout the years. To make things easier while travelling, Ben put together a platform that fit between the front seat and the back seat of his car. This created an area for the boys to play and sleep during the long drives. A brilliant solution that allowed for carefree travels involving long drives. This was well before the days of children's car seats or even seat belts.

In November of 1958, Nick and Pat moved to Holland Landing in south-central Ontario, about one hour north of Toronto. They welcomed their son Neale shortly after. The long distance meant that the two families did not get together as much. As both Ben and Nick had sales jobs, they managed to meet every other week and catch up over lunch.

In 1959, Fred joined the Cold Regions Research and Engineering Laboratory (CRREL) in Evanston, Illinois. With her parents now in Illinois, it was easier for Diana to visit Valerie during her school breaks. Of course, her nephews were an added bonus during these trips. For Valerie, these visits provided a much-needed reprieve from her busy schedule. Raising two boys under the age of three was challenging, so any help was welcome.

The initial years of motherhood were very hard for Valerie, but, once Duncan turned two, things got easier as they began to play together, leaving Valerie with some time for herself. Peter and Duncan shared a great relationship. Not having a very significant age gap, the two brothers got along very well. They were almost the same size too, which may have been amusing for them, it did not simplify things in the clothing department, as clothes could not be handed down.

Another amazing thing about the boys' bond was that they created their own language to communicate with each other. One of Valerie's memories from that time was working in the kitchen and watching, through the window, the boys play in the backyard while Ben was busy building a sandbox, a swing set and a climbing frame.

In the summer, Valerie remembered being in the backyard with the boys while working in the garden. They had some everbearing strawberries in the garden and it was always a race between Peter and the rabbits to see who would get to them first. Peter always managed to get his share.

With things going well financially, Valerie and Ben were looking to make another investment. Ben's cousin Colin owned a cottage on Lake Couchiching, which was about one hour north of Toronto. Colin enjoyed having friends and family over but, when Valerie and Ben visited him, the cottage did not appeal to them. However, the idea of having a place to go outside of Toronto in the summer did.

When they drove around Ontario selling lumber, Valerie and Ben got to see much of the province. They really admired the Kawartha area northeast of Toronto, near Peterborough. Stoney Lake, in particular, had caught their eye. They had mutually agreed that the Lake Couchiching lifestyle was not for them and decided to buy a cottage on Stoney Lake.

Starting in late 1958, Ben wrote to all the cottage owners on Stoney Lake, inquiring whether anyone was interested in selling their cottage. However, it was not until June of 1959 that he received a response.

David graduated from UNB in 1959 and was accepted into a master's program at the University of British Columbia (UBC) shortly after. While at UNB, David met Mary Jo Elson, and they fell in love. After David graduated, the two decided to get married. Their wedding was set for December 29, 1959, in Mary Jo's hometown of Hespeler (amalgamated with Cambridge, Ontario in 1973).

Chapter 12 Boys' Childhood

Since Hespeler was only an hour away from Lorne Park, Valerie's parents and Diana spent Christmas with them before driving to Hespeler for the wedding. Unfortunately, a major snowstorm swept across the Toronto area during that time. As Ben was driving David and Mary Jo to the airport, Valerie rode back to Lorne Park with her parents. She remembered being in the passenger seat, looking out the window and letting her father, who was driving, know where the edge of the road was. Fortunately, they all made it home safe and sound.

As 1960 approached, the economy in Ontario began to slow down, leading to a reduction in Ben's commissions. With two growing boys, and a wife to look after and a house to maintain, Ben decided it was best to start looking for a new, better-paying job.

In his job-hunting attempts, he wrote to the Government of Canada, where his Uncle Jack worked. Having not heard back from the Government, he received a job offer as the Ontario Sales Manager for Campbell MacLaurin Lumber, which he gladly accepted. However, his time at the company was short-lived because soon after being hired his salary was slashed by one-third. This meant that Valerie and Ben had to dip into their savings while Ben looked for another job.

In June of 1959, the owner of 260 Island 4A expressed an interest in selling their property at Stoney Lake – the lake Valerie and Ben had their hearts set on. Despite their unstable financial situation, Valerie and Ben decided it was best they not let go of this opportunity and used their savings to buy the cottage. Valerie and Ben were now the owners of a cozy little cottage in Stoney Lake.

Their cottage was approximately a 10-minute boat ride from McCracken's Landing to the west. Throughout the rest of the summer, Ben visited different lumber stores in the east end of Toronto, Oshawa, or Peterborough on Friday afternoons so the family could be closer to Stoney Lake for weekends at the cottage. Being on an island, Valerie always had to plan ahead and make sure that there was enough food and other supplies for the weekends. As for visitors, they had to book a ride at the marina in advance, so they had no surprise visitors, thus allowing them to spend some quality family time together.

In August of 1961, Ben prepared to bid farewell to Campbell MacLaurin Lumber as he had been offered the position of Trade and Commerce Officer in the Department of Trade and Commerce, Forest Products Division, Ottawa, Ontario. While this position came with less pay as compared to his previous jobs, it did promise a steady income and a pension.

Still in August of 1961, Valerie and Ben headed to Chatham with the boys to spend time with Ben's parents as well as Nick and his family. After their time in Chatham, they headed back to Toronto via Worcester. On August 26, 1961, Diana was set to marry Ken Maxwell, whom she had met at UNB. Although Valerie's parents had long since moved from Worcester, Diana and Ken decided to get married there in the same church as Valerie and Ben, as Diana felt comfortable in the First Baptist Church.

Valerie served as Diana's matron of honour, while Ken's brother was the best man. Unfortunately, as fate would have it, he did not make it to the wedding as his car broke down. So, Ben was asked to stand in as the best man. With Valerie and Ben busy with their duties, the boys were left in the care of Kitty, also known as 'Idasan', sitting in the front row of the church. After the wedding was over, Valerie, Ben and the boys headed back to Toronto so Ben could wrap up his work with Campbell MacLaurin Lumber before heading to Ottawa.

Ben started his new job on September 1, 1961, which was the Friday preceding the long Labour Day weekend. However, Ben had been informed he needed to show up in order to confirm his job. So, the couple decided to make the best of the situation. The family went for an extra-long weekend in Ottawa, where they stayed at the Green Valley Motel which had cabins.

Chapter 12 Boys' Childhood

On September 1, 1961, it was an extremely hot day, but Ben had to report to work. Upon his arrival, he learned that the office had no air conditioning. Moreover, there was a policy to send employees home if the temperature rose above 80°F (27°C). A few hours later, the temperature rose over 80°F (27°C), and everyone was sent home. Imagine Valerie's surprise when Ben showed up at the motel for lunch!

Before leaving for the motel, Ben had asked his co-workers about a good place to go for a swim. Mooney's Bay was suggested, which was quite close to the motel. After changing and having lunch, Valerie and Ben headed to Mooney's Bay with the boys, where they spent a very enjoyable afternoon.

With Ben now working in Ottawa, the decision was taken to sell the house in Lorne Park so the family could relocate to Ottawa. They mutually decided that Valerie would stay in Lorne Park with the boys until the house was sold, while Ben would stay with Auntie Bump and Uncle Jack. He visited his wife and children in Lorne Park on the weekends.

While Ben started his new job on September 1, Peter started kindergarten on September 5. He attended Owenwood Public School, which was a short walk from 1236 Echo Drive. And while kindergarten only lasted half a day, it gave Valerie time alone with Duncan.

Unfortunately, the family would have to wait four months to properly reunite because the downturn in the economy meant no one was interested in buying or renting their home. Finally, in December of 1961, they found someone to rent the house, which meant Valerie and the boys could finally move to Ottawa.

In the fall, Ben found a one-and-a-half-storey house for rent, located at 1380 Micmac Street. It was a block away from a bus to downtown Ottawa and a block and a half away from the local elementary school, making it the perfect location for the family.

With Ben not earning as much as he used to and the added expenses of moving to Ottawa, Valerie and Ben needed to make some budget cuts. Since Ben had a desk job and did not need to travel for most of the month, they decided that there was no need to maintain two cars anymore. He could simply take the bus on days when Valerie needed the car and, since they were in the city, shops were nearby. Consequently, Polly was sold. Furthermore, since Stoney Lake was quite far from Ottawa, they also decided to sell the cottage at the end of 1961.

However, to sell the Stoney Lake cottage, they had to take back a second mortgage on it. In 1964, the cottage burned down, and the second mortgage was paid out. This allowed them to buy new dining room furniture replacing the table the two had handmade together back in 1954.

After everything was settled and the whole house packed, Valerie and the boys embarked on their journey to Ottawa on December 2, 1961. A kind neighbour drove them to Union Station, where they boarded the overnight train to Ottawa. The train ride was rather uneventful. They went to sleep soon after boarding and woke up the next morning in Ottawa, ready to start a new chapter of their lives.

1959 – Cottage – Island 260 4A, Stoney Lake, Ontario, Canada

Chapter 13
Back to School

1962–1963

1962 – Duncan, Valerie, Peter, and Ben – 1373 Micmac Street, Ottawa, Ontario, Canada

In December of 1961, Valerie and her family started a new phase of their lives in Ottawa. As the days passed, the family settled into their new routine, with the boys attending school and Valerie managing the household.

With the money they received from the sale of the Stoney Lake cottage, which they sold at the end of 1962, Valerie and Ben decided to invest in a house. Fortunately, they were able to find one with relative ease right across the street from their rented house at 1380 Micmac Street. And so, in June of 1962, they purchased 1373 Micmac Street for $16,000. Although the house was not exactly ideal, but since it was in the same location as their previous dwelling, they hoped it would not disrupt their lives too much. The boys could continue going to the same school and keep their new friends. Since both Valerie and Ben had moved around quite a bit as children, which undoubtedly affected their education and social lives, they did not want their sons to experience the same thing.

The house at 1373 Micmac was one-and-a-half storey, as the roof was high, and the second storey was not the full width of the house and had sloping ceilings. It was a detached home with a front and back yard, which was ideal for the boys to play in, but there was no garage. Ben always mentioned adding a carport to the house, but he never got around to it.

Although the house was not their dream home, it was still well laid out. The main door of the house was located in the middle. Upon entering the house, there was a small entrance. Beyond the entrance, on the left was the living room, while the dining room was on the right, with no walls separating the two. Walking straight ahead from the entrance led you to a coat closet. The kitchen was located on the right side of the closet. The kitchen was a decent size and had enough room for a breakfast table. A short hall on the left of the closet led to a fourth room which doubled as a guest room and home office.

There was a door in the middle of the house at the back

too. Upon entering the back door, the kitchen was on the left while the stairs to the basement were straight ahead.

The U-shaped staircase that led upstairs was located on the right side of the hall. The second floor consisted of three rooms, the master and two other bedrooms. The master bedroom was on the left and actually went the full width of the house! The two other bedrooms were on the right; the bigger one at the front was Peter's, while the smaller one at the back was Duncan's. The house had one bathroom, which was located between the master bedroom and Peter's room at the top of the stairs.

When it came to the interior, Valerie and Ben had their work cut out for them. All the walls were painted dark colours with the ceiling and one wall in some of the rooms were painted different colours. For example, the back room on the main floor had white walls but a purple ceiling. The stairs transitioned from dark to light brown as you ascended the stairs, which was a shame because there was more light at the top of the stairs than there was at the bottom.

All the windows in the house were double-hung and most, if not all, had a broken pane of glass. So, the first order of business was to paint the entire house lighter and brighter colours and to fix all the windows, giving it the feeling of an actual home. While there were no real changes required other than that, Valerie and Ben continued to make small changes to the house every now and then. For instance, a kitchen cabinet was removed later to make space for an under-counter dishwasher, and the basement was also finished.

1373 Micmac Street, Ottawa, Ontario, Canada

Just like at Lorne Park, the family was fortunate enough to have great neighbours on Micmac Street, too. An older couple, the McCartens, lived in 1377 and, much like Mrs. Wilson from Lorne Park, Mrs. McCarten was also like a second mother to Valerie. Unfortunately, Valerie did not get to spend much time with her as she developed cancer and passed away soon after they moved to 1373.

Then there was a couple in 1369 who had two daughters five or six years older than the boys. Across the street from the McCartens lived the McLarens, who had a lively house with four children—three daughters and a son. Their son, Leslie, was Duncan's age and they quickly grew to be good friends.

After Mrs. McCarten's death, her husband sold the house to a couple, the Griffiths, who had a daughter the same age as Peter. So, the boys had plenty of friends growing up in the neighbourhood.

Because Ben's job with the Government of Canada

entailed promoting Canadian forest products around the world, he often attended trade conferences in other countries. He also led trade missions to foreign countries to help Canadian companies find potential customers.

Whenever Ben travelled, Valerie along with Peter and Duncan would drive him to the airport. Valerie and the boys would then watch him board the plane from the viewing area. And the family would pick him up from the airport on his return. Ben always made sure to bring back presents for his wife and sons whenever he travelled. Occasionally, he would bring a brooch for Valerie which she would add to her collection.

Ben's professional commitments often led him on trips to the US and Europe. On one of the trips to England, the family joined him as it was a posting of three months.

The most memorable trip was probably the one to Latin America in October of 1962. It was a three-week trip, starting on October 6 and ending on October 27. From Ottawa, the group embarked on a journey to Mexico City, Lima (Peru), Caracas (Venezuela), Trinidad, and Puerto Rico.

Although this was a three-week trip, Valerie was not overly worried as she was used to Ben being gone for extended periods of time for work. However, that changed on October 16 when the Cuban missile crisis started. A million thoughts rushed through Valerie's head, wondering what would happen if war broke out while Ben was on his trip. Further intensifying her worries was the fact that Ben was extremely close to Cuba—in Trinidad. The only thought that brought Valerie comfort during that time was knowing that Ben was travelling on official Canadian Government business, meaning he would be provided with the necessary help if the need arose. Fortunately, the crisis was resolved on October 27, and Ben returned to Ottawa the same day, safe and sound.

In 1958, Valerie's parents moved from Worcester to Belmont, which is just outside of Boston. After a year of living in Belmont, they moved to Evanston, Illinois. Fred was offered a job at the US Army Corps of Engineering in Hanover, so her parents ultimately moved to Hanover, New Hampshire, in late 1962.

Following Valerie's parents' move to Evanston, Illinois, Diana came up to Ottawa from Springfield, Massachusetts, where her husband Ken was working on his master's degree in psychology at the University of Springfield. She spent Christmas with Valerie's family, their first at 1373 Micmac Street. However, more memorable than the Christmas festivities, was that Ken's car, a Volkswagen Beetle was stolen from the driveway on Christmas Eve. Fortunately, it was found a few days later.

After spending a winter in Ottawa, with cold weather and snow from November through March, Valerie and Ben decided that Ottawa had a real winter. However, since they could not avoid it, they learned to embrace it.

Not long after moving to 1373 Micmac, Duncan started kindergarten in the fall of 1962. Initially, Valerie enjoyed the free time to herself while both boys were at school. However, she was never one to spend the whole day cleaning the house or chatting with the neighbourhood ladies. She started thinking of ways to utilize her free time and considered going back to school for Library Science. However, it was not easy for a mother of two young children to go back to school and, apart from choosing the right program, she first had to convince Ben.

Luckily, Valerie found that she could schedule her classes in a way that would allow her to either leave for classes after the boys left for school and be back for lunch or leave for her classes after they went back to school after lunch and be home by the time they got home.

Having convinced Ben and worked out a schedule that would accommodate everyone, Valerie began her Bachelor of Library Science at the University of Ottawa in the Fall of 1963. Other than coordinating her schedule with the boys', the most challenging thing for Valerie was having to take some of her classes in French, as the university is bilingual. There were also times when Valerie would have classes during lunch. On those days, Mrs. Griffiths would be kind enough to have the boys over for lunch.

Valerie was very excited about this new journey and quickly made friends with most of her classmates. If one of the boys was ever sick and she had to miss classes, she could always count on her friends to give her class notes.

At the beginning of her program, Valerie did not hire anyone to help with the cleaning or to look after the boys as she felt she was managing just fine. However, as the days progressed and her coursework increased, she realised a helping hand could do wonders for her. And so, Mrs. Trudell was hired to come on some weekdays to prepare lunches and clean.

Some of Valerie's classes were held in the evening, and on those days, Ben would be tasked with putting the boys to bed. However, Ben was also attending university during this time. Once he started working for the government, he realised he needed to learn more about how the government worked and how public policy was developed. So, in 1961, he registered at Carleton University to pursue a diploma in Public Administration.

Ben was not good at typing. Given his wife's typing proficiency, thanks to her days as a secretary at UNB; Valerie often typed and edited Ben's papers for him. These were busy years for the couple!

Winter, although very cold, made for fun activities for the family, especially the boys. Their school had two ice rinks; one was an outdoor hockey rink, while the other had a hockey rink with a skating oval around it. Ben had learned to skate when he came to Canada, but Valerie had not. So, the family would often go to the skating oval for Valerie, Duncan, and Peter to learn how to skate.

With the help of their bob skates, which have double blades on each boot, the boys picked skating up rather quickly, while Valerie would just cling onto Ben as if her life depended on it. In the end, she never did learn how to skate.

As the boys grew older, they started spending more and more time at the nearby ice rink. They would go over in the morning on the weekends, come home for lunch, and then go back in the afternoon.

Another one of the boys' favourite outdoor hobbies was tobogganing. Hog's Back Park was a 10-minute drive away from their school. It had a great hill for tobogganing and a small ski hill as well. Valerie remembered that on one particular tobogganing run with either Peter or Duncan, she went over a bump and crushed her tailbone. It was not very serious, but it did bother her for many years.

For Christmas 1963, the family decided to visit Valerie's parents in Hanover. Valerie and Ben had planned on gifting the boys skis for Christmas, yet another fun activity they could do together as a family. Ben expertly hid the skis in the car, and although the boys were very attentive to everything that went on around them, they did not find the skis. To this day, the boys recall that Christmas and wonder how their parents pulled it off.

Diana and Ken also came to Hanover and Ken, who was a good skier, taught the boys the ropes with some skiing lessons. However, David and Mary Jo were absent making the family reunion incomplete.

1962 and 1963 were very busy years for both Valerie and Ben but it was just the start.

Chapter 13 Back to School

1962 – Duncan, Peter, Valerie, and Ben – Ottawa, Ontario, Canada

Chapter 14
New Adventures

1964

1964 – In front of Windsor Castle with Cyril Rourke's (work colleague of Ben's) daughters – Windsor, England

Valerie's Journeys

The hustle and bustle of 1963 carried over into 1964, with both the boys going to school, Valerie attending university, and Ben working. Life was very busy, bordering on hectic sometimes, but Valerie somehow made it work. Life went on as usual for the family but, little did they know, they would soon embark on various new adventures.

In 1964, Ben was presented with a new work opportunity. The Trade Commissioner in London, England, was scheduled to take a three-month leave, and Ben was asked to fill in for him for the months of June, July, and August.

When Ben discussed the opportunity with Valerie, she was overjoyed and thought he should accept it immediately. It had been almost two decades since Valerie had last been to England. Ben's last visit was in 1948, when he got to see the Opening Ceremonies of the Olympics. Valerie thought this would be a wonderful opportunity for multiple reasons. The first was the opportunity to meet her relatives back in England after so long. The second was that the timing was perfect, as it would not affect the boys' education. Finally, she felt that Peter and Duncan, who were 8 and 6 years old, respectively, would be old enough to remember the trip.

So, once Ben accepted the temporary position, the family started preparing for their trip to England. However, a dark cloud was headed toward the family. In the spring of 1964, Flump received a diagnosis of stomach cancer. Nick had moved to Edmundston, New Brunswick, which was about 300 kilometres from Chatham, so he helped his parents and kept Ben up to date about their father's health.

Even though the family was concerned about Flump's health, the months passed in anticipation of the impending adventure. Ben left for England in late May to start his posting and to establish living arrangements for his family, while Valerie and the boys stayed back until the school term ended.

After school finished on the last Thursday in June, Valerie and the boys flew to London, where Ben had acquired a flat in Embankment Gardens in Chelsea. They boarded a plane in Ottawa and flew to Montreal, where they took a DC-8—a narrow-body aircraft popular with airlines at the time—to London.

Valerie recalled that their flight on the DC-8 was delayed for several hours, so they had to wait on the benches in the lobby. She remembered the boys lying on the bench, their heads resting on each of her legs as she read to them. Finally, they were able to board the plane and made their way to London, but not before stopping in Gander, Newfoundland, and Shannon, Ireland, to refuel the plane.

Valerie and the boys were met at the airport by Ben, who had been waiting there for three hours because of the delay. Ben drove them back to the flat, which was on the sixth floor. There was no elevator, so making the trip upstairs with all the luggage was quite a challenge!

Although Valerie was tired and jetlagged from the travel, and Ben was tired from the week's work, the boys were as energetic as ever. And so, Valerie and Ben decided to take them to the London Zoo the following day. Despite being a little low on energy, Valerie managed to have a good time.

Valerie would be in England for a little over two months, and she wanted to make the most of it. So, while Ben would be off at work during the week, she would take the boys sightseeing all over the city. They saw Buckingham Palace, Westminster Abbey, St Paul's Cathedral, the British Museum, Big Ben, and Trafalgar Square.

Since it often rains in England, the first thing Valerie did before they embarked on their city tour was to buy two yellow raincoats for the boys, which they had to carry with them everywhere in case nature struck. When Peter and Duncan had their own children, they suspected the raincoats were more for Valerie to keep an eye on them than to combat the rain, which Valerie denied vehemently, of course.

As luck would have it, the summer of 1964 was one of the driest summers ever recorded in London, and it only rained two days while they were there.

Wednesdays were shopping days when Valerie and the boys would go to Chelsea Bridge Road to buy groceries for the week. The boys would help carry the groceries all the way up to the flat. There was a cricket pitch on the grounds of the Royal Chelsea Hospital, which was about halfway to Chelsea Bridge Road. On their way home after doing the groceries, they would stop to rest there and watch cricket. Valerie explained the rules of the game to her sons, but it also served as a pleasant reminder of her time in Shanghai, when she helped her father score the cricket matches.

Determined to take advantage of the time she had in London, Valerie made sure that the family was always doing something. One week, she and the boys took a train to Plymouth to visit her father's younger sister, Aunt Dorrie, her husband, Uncle John, and their teenage son Brian. Unfortunately, that trip was not very fun. Perhaps it was due to Valerie travelling on her own with two boys, aged 6 and 8, to a home that was not well-suited for boys their age. Fortunately, Valerie's cousin Brian managed to keep Peter and Duncan entertained throughout the visit. He even had a pet hedgehog!

One day, Valerie heard that Queen Elizabeth II was visiting the Royal Chelsea Hospital, so she took the boys. They were able to catch a glimpse of the Queen inspecting the troops.

Valerie saved some trips for the weekends when Ben was home. The weekends consisted of more trips to the London Zoo, Whipsnade Zoo (when the boys got to ride at the front of the second floor of a double-decker bus), Greenwich, and Hampton Court. On other weekends, the family visited Ben's Uncle George, as well as his cousin Jean, her husband Edwin, and their children Tony and Carol.

Chapter 14 New Adventures

Upon hearing that Valerie was in London after so long, her father's older sister, Auntie Eva, and her husband, Eric, came down from Northern England to pay them a visit.

Apart from family visits and tours around the city, there were also several events held at the Canadian Embassy, which Valerie attended during her time in London. One of the events included a reception for the Canadian Prime Minister of the time, Lester B. Pearson, when he visited London.

The two months in London were like a vacation for Valerie and the boys. Valerie enjoyed every minute of her time spent in London, exploring the streets with her children, seeing what and how much had changed over the years, and visiting her family members. For Ben, unfortunately, it was all business as usual.

To remedy the situation, Valerie and Ben decided to take a trip to Paris on the way back home. And so, at the end of August, when Ben's assignment came to an end, the family flew to Paris. They spent two full days looking around the city. They went to the Zoo, the Eiffel Tower, the Louvre, and Versailles. On the third day, they took a flight back home to Ottawa via Montreal, just in time for the boys' new school term.

While Valerie and Ben were away, Flump underwent a series of operations; unfortunately, none of them proved to be effective. As soon as Ben returned from Paris, he was informed that his father's health had deteriorated to the point that he was near death. He rushed to Chatham, but sadly, Flump passed away soon after Ben arrived.

Em, Flump's wife, was also quite ill at the time, suffering from multiple diseases, including asthma. With her husband now gone, she could not manage their house in Chatham alone. Although Flump had left everything to his sons, he had done so on the condition that they take care of their mother. So, Ben and Nick were presented with a dilemma: what to do with their mother and Cannie (their parents' purebred collie).

After a discussion between the brothers and their wives, it was mutually agreed that Em should move to Ottawa since Nick was allergic to dogs and Em would not leave Cannie behind. Since their house was not very big, and all three bedrooms were occupied, Valerie and Ben decided to build an addition to the back of the house to accommodate Em.

Ben left for Ottawa first, with Cannie in tow. He took a train, and Cannie was in the baggage car. She had been very close to Flump, so she was visibly upset, and being in the baggage car just made things worse. She made sure everyone knew! Eventually, a porter had to call Ben to calm Cannie down. So, Ben stayed in the baggage car for the remainder of the trip. When Valerie came to pick up Ben, she was not sure who was worse for wear, Cannie or Ben.

Em arrived in Ottawa a little later in an unmarked ambulance. Since the planning for the addition had yet to commence, she was temporarily placed in a nursing home until Valerie and Ben were ready to look after her.

The planning for the addition began in the fall of 1964 and work finally began in the spring of 1965. It was a 20' x 20' addition connected to the house through the back door. The addition consisted of a large room with a window overlooking Micmac Street, a bathroom by the back door, and a small "bar" kitchen. Back then, Ottawa did not allow second kitchens in a house, so this was Valerie and Ben's way of beating the system. The "kitchen" was a small area off the main room that had a bar fridge, a sink, and a two-element stove but no door.

Valerie and Ben's lives got busier in 1965 with the added responsibility for Cannie and the addition's construction. Cannie was a very well-trained dog, and the family, especially the boys, got along with her just fine. Duncan, in particular, enjoyed the idea of having a pet dog and taking care of her. Cannie stayed with the family until 1966, when she had to be put down.

With so much going on in their lives, Valerie and Ben

planned a weekend getaway in the spring of 1965, which they had not done since Peter was born a little less than a decade ago!

Ben's job description included attending furniture shows and industry meetings. There was an upcoming event in Montreal that Ben had to attend, which also included a formal dinner. Since Montreal was only a two-hour drive away, Valerie and Ben decided to attend the dinner together.

Since the boys were young and with no family in Ottawa, Valerie and Ben hired a woman to look after the boys and the house while they were away for the weekend. The woman arrived at their house just shortly before they were to leave for the event. Valerie immediately had reservations. Something about the woman was off, but Valerie could not seem to put her finger on it. However, she really needed a well-deserved break, and so, hoping that everything would be alright, she left the boys in the woman's care. She figured that if a problem were to occur, the neighbours could lend a hand. Valerie's intuition turned out to be true; the woman barely lifted a finger all weekend. However, no damage was done, and the boys survived the weekend.

That year, Valerie and Ben started talking about attending church. Although neither of them was religious, Valerie still felt that it was important to introduce the boys to formal religion and leave it to them to choose how they wanted to take it forward. After going to a few churches in the area, they settled on the Unitarian Church at the corner of Elgin and Lewis Streets, because they had a nice minister.

Every now and then, Valerie and Ben would treat the boys to lunch at the nearby A&W after Sunday morning service.

In late 1965, the addition was finally completed, and Em moved in with Ben, Valerie, and the boys. While the addition was being built, Valerie and Ben made sure to fence in the backyard so Cannie could go outside. Cannie had a lot of freedom in Chatham but not so much in Ottawa, since she had to be on a leash for walks.

Also, in December of 1965, Valerie's brother, David, was completing his Ph.D. thesis in Archaeology from the University of Washington and got a job with the Canadian Museum of Man (renamed to Canadian Museum of History in 2013) that allowed him to be paid while he finished it. David moved to Ottawa with his wife, Mary Jo, and daughter Jennifer. They stayed with Valerie and Ben until they could find a house.

One of the most memorable days during David's family's time with them was Christmas 1965. Valerie's family had not gotten together in years since all siblings were now married with children, and no one had a house big enough to accommodate the whole Sanger family.

Now that the addition was complete, Ben was confident they could accommodate Valerie's whole family so, they were all invited to their house for Christmas. Of course, a lot of planning went into making sure that everything went off without a hitch.

Valerie's parents and Diana and her family arrived in Ottawa but chose to stay in a hotel, since David's family and Em were staying with Valerie and Ben. Christmas day arrived and everything went smoothly. Em had allowed Valerie and Ben to move things around in her room to arrange a very long series of tables that could accommodate everyone—9 adults, 4 children and one infant! Fred created name tags for everyone's place setting. By the time Ben had finished carving the Christmas turkey, everyone was coming back for seconds.

Two months after moving in with Valerie and Ben, David found a house and his family moved out. The house was a nice little residence about 4 km from Valerie and Ben's place. It was nice having David and his family nearby, and they often got together over the weekends.

Although 1964 and 1965 were tough, with the passing away of Flump and lengthy, disruptive work on the house to accommodate Em, the family ended the year 1965 on a good note, hoping for better days to come.

1965 – The main room of the addition – 1373 Micmac Street, Ottawa, Ontario, Canada

Chapter 15
Back to Work

1965 to 1969

May 1967 – Valerie and Kitty – Ottawa, Ontario, Canada

As the new year approached, life continued as usual for Valerie and her family. It was as busy as ever. With Em also living with them now, Valerie had one more task to her growing list of jobs. On top of being a mother, wife, and a student, she was now also a caretaker for her mother-in-law.

Valerie did not mind looking after Em, but it did take a toll on her sometimes, although Em usually made her own meals, Valerie had to look after other things, such as shopping for her, going to the library to get books for her (seven books a week) and also driving her to and from appointments.

Ben would take the paper back to Em every evening after dinner and would stay with her for an hour, leaving Valerie to do the dishes and then help the boys with homework. On Saturdays, Em would come over for dinner and play Scrabble with Valerie and Ben. It was never a good game for Ben or Valerie since Em was quite the player. However, they never declined an offer to play Scrabble as Em really enjoyed it.

Although things were hectic, Valerie took it all in her stride and made things work. By the middle of the year, things started to become more eventful. Perhaps one of the most memorable events of 1966 was Ben graduating from Carleton University with a Diploma in Public Administration in June of 1966.

The same month, Ben had a furniture show coming up in Montreal and wanted Valerie to come along. However, instead of opting for a babysitter, Valerie and Ben decided to ask Ann if she could come and take care of the boys. Ann is the eldest daughter of Ben's cousin Colin and his wife Betty. Since Valerie's family often visited Colin's family in Toronto, they knew each other quite well. Furthermore, Ann had come up to Ottawa on her own a few years before to visit Valerie and Ben. The boys were fond of her too, so they felt comfortable leaving them in Ann's care.

Ann was quite surprised when Valerie and Ben asked

her to look after the boys while they went to the Furniture Show. Not only did they trust her to take care of their children but also allowed her to drive their car so she could do errands. Other than that, Ann was only supposed to look after the boys' lunch and dinner—but things did not really go as planned. Right after Valerie and Ben left for Montreal, Peter got sick and could not attend school. Fortunately, Ann had just finished her first year of nursing school, so she had no trouble caring for Peter while he was sick.

While the boys did not accompany Valerie and Ben to Montreal in 1965, they took the boys to Montreal a few years later during winter break. They stayed at the Queen Elizabeth II Hotel and went to see their first live NHL hockey game in the Montreal Forum. The boys were amazed by the sheer size of it and had the time of their lives. Although Valerie was not a hockey fan, she had listened to hockey games on the radio while living in Lorne Park, so it was not difficult for her to understand and keep up with the game. She even recognized some of the players from the radio.

In 1966, David and Mary Jo welcomed a new addition to their little family, a baby boy they named Patrick. Patrick was very curious. As he grew up, he would investigate all nooks and crannies. Whenever David and his family visited, Valerie would ask the boys to "Patrick proof" the house. This meant placing everything out of Patrick's reach around the house and moving the furniture with sharp parts to rooms where the door could be closed.

Another memorable thing that happened in 1966 was that Ken got a job with the Longmeadow Board of Education in Massachusetts and so he and Diana moved to East Longmeadow. Their move started the annual two-week summer vacation for Valerie's family.

As mentioned before, Valerie had a lot on her plate, and Em was very grateful to both her and Ben for taking care of her. She was very considerate and to give Valerie and Ben a break, she would leave for Edmundston, New Brunswick, every August to spend a month with Nick and his family. So, August marked the start of the family's two-week summer vacation.

First, they would drive to Edmundston. Em would sit in the front seat, and Valerie would be in the middle of the boys in the back. They would spend a few days with Nick before spending a few days in Nova Scotia on their own. The next stop was Maine to visit David and his family, who had moved there in 1969, and then East Longmeadow to Diana's. The last few days were spent at Valerie's parents' house in Hanover. When it was time for Em to return home, Ben would drive to Drummondville, about halfway to Nick's; where they would meet in a park and Em would change cars.

Valerie recalled it was great catching up with her parents and siblings during these trips but there was not a lot of family time since they were travelling half the time. During one particular visit to Diana's in East Longmeadow, Valerie remembered it was hot and humid and the "cherry on top" was that the dishwasher was broken. Needless to say, with eight people in the house, washing all the dishes manually in that weather was a tough feat.

Although a lot of incidents and fun events took place in 1966, perhaps one of the sadder ones was that Hog's Back Park was closed that year to allow for a bridge over the Rideau River and the boys had to go to the small ski hill in Carlington Park. It was not as exciting, but it was better than nothing.

The year 1967 marked Canada's 100-year anniversary. Although celebrations were at their peak on Dominion Day on July 1, 1967, the event was followed by a year-long celebration, known as the Canadian Centennial.

To ensure their sons experienced some of the numerous celebrations across the country, Valerie and Ben initially took the boys to Parliament Hill on December 31, 1966, to watch the then-Prime Minister Lester B. Pearson light the centennial flame.

Chapter 15 Back to Work

Centennial Year is remembered for numerous events, such as the Centennial Logo, Centennial coins, the Confederation Train, and the Centennial caravan. Perhaps the main event was the Expo 67 World's Fair, held in Montreal from April to October of 1967.

Expo 67 was one of the biggest exhibitions of the 20th century and Valerie and Ben bought a five-day pass for the family. On the first day, they left home early in the morning, spent the whole day at Expo 67 and then returned home late in the evening. On one of the days, they left for Expo 67 later in the day and stayed to watch the fireworks when it closed for the day. The drive home that night was quite late, and Valerie remembered the boys falling asleep on the way back. Although Ben was also drowsy, Valerie ensured he did not fall asleep while driving.

As the boys grew older, they started getting involved in different after-school activities. This meant that Valerie had her hands full as she would often help her sons in these activities. For instance, Duncan took piano lessons for two or three years, and Valerie would help him practise. Both boys were also in Cub Scouts and would meet at Alta Vista Public School.

Duncan participated in organised hockey for a year while Peter competed in swimming events. In the summer, Valerie wanted the boys to do something productive, not just stay at home all day, so she arranged for them to have swimming lessons at the Recreation Association (RA), which was a short drive from their home. The RA, a facility catering to families of government employees, featured two outdoor pools, one of them very large, a curling rink, a gym, and other spaces which could host a variety of events. As the boys grew older, they also started going to overnight camps.

In 1967, upon completion of the new Unitarian Church in Ottawa's west end, Ben continued the tradition of treating the family to the occasional lunch at A&W after Sunday service.

One Sunday in the fall of 1967, after lunch, Valerie dropped Ben and the boys off at Lansdowne Park to attend an Ottawa Rough Riders football game.

A few years after the church moved to the west end, the minister, who was the reason Valerie and Ben had chosen the Unitarian Church, changed. The two were not happy with the direction of the new minister and, since the boys did not seem to be showing any interest in church, they eventually stopped going. After that, their Sunday mornings would be spent working on finishing the basement to turn it into a space where the boys could watch TV. Later, Valerie and Ben also added a wood-burning stove in the basement so they could enjoy the cold winter evenings.

In the spring of 1967, Valerie graduated from the University of Ottawa with a Bachelor of Library Science. It was a big accomplishment, and her parents travelled from Hanover to attend her graduation. Valerie's research paper "The Role of the Ombudsman in Canada" [9] is available online.

Having finally graduated after years of juggling her education, home, and family, she wanted to go back to work. However, she faced the challenge of convincing Ben that she should work. Ben was of the opinion that his wife working would give off the impression that he was not able to support his family. Furthermore, Em also did not think that Valerie should work, so Valerie had a challenging task ahead.

Since Valerie had already been studying and managing her family duties for the last few years, she was able to convince Ben that working part-time would mean she would leave after the boys left for school and be back by the time they returned. The growing independence of the boys, now older and more self-reliant, worked in Valerie's favour.

---

9 https://books.google.ca/books/about/The_Role_of_the_Ombudsman_in_Canada.html?id=-yiDHAAACAAJ&redir_esc=y

Chapter 15 Back to Work

Valerie planned to use the money she earned for things that the family would enjoy, like a day out, a trip, or some other activity. So, having convinced Ben, the next step was to go about looking for a part-time job. Soon enough, she landed a job as a cataloguer for the Ottawa Collegiate Board, the governing body for high schools in Ottawa, in the central office. Valerie often brought home stacks of library cards that needed sorting, and the boys were always eager to help.

Once Valerie started working and earning, Ben realised that not only was the extra money nice, but Valerie was also much happier. One of the first 'extras' was saving for a family vacation to drive across Canada.

Valerie now working meant that she would not be home during the summers, so she planned some activities for the boys to keep them busy. One of the very first summer activities the boys did after Valerie started working was going to visit their grandparents in Hanover. Since Peter was older, he travelled to Hanover on his own via bus. Ben gave some extra money to the bus driver in Ottawa to help Peter get on the Hanover-bound bus from Montreal. While Peter did manage to get on the right bus, it was no thanks to the bus driver!

The next year, it was Duncan's turn to visit his grandparents. Valerie recalled the family driving to Lake Champlain in New York State and meeting her parents to transfer Duncan. The boys really enjoyed their time with their grandparents, especially their grandmother, who spoiled them with all their favourite foods. The boys' visits to their grandparents also allowed Valerie and Ben to spend some alone time with the child who stayed home.

When it came to the boys' education, Valerie took the lead. She helped them with homework, attended the parent teacher meetings, and handled any issues that arose. Luckily, the boys were good at school and did well, so there were not a lot of issues.

The boys attended Alta Vista Public School, located only a block and a half from their home. Alta Vista was a huge school that went from kindergarten to grade 8 and had well over a thousand students.

When Duncan was in the first grade, he was made part of the accelerated program, meaning he covered most of the coursework from grades 1 to 4 in three years. As a result, Peter and Duncan were in the fifth grade at the same time. After that, Duncan joined an advanced class for grades 6 to 8.

Although this was a great learning opportunity, it also presented many challenges for Duncan as he was the youngest in the class. So, he required Valerie to provide some emotional support to help him through the advanced classes.

While Peter was not part of any advanced classes, he had his own challenges. He had trouble with spelling throughout school so, every summer before the new term started, Valerie would review words from the previous year to prepare Peter for the upcoming school year. It was not until Grade 12 that Peter was identified as dyslexic, which explained his challenges with spelling.

As Peter and Duncan got bigger, Ben wanted to get them outside more. One idea he had was to buy a canoe. In 1968, he bought a Chestnut Canoe that was specially designed so it could be sailed. The canoe also had a V-stern so a motor could be attached. Ben planned to travel the Rideau Canal from Ottawa to Kingston. On pleasant summer weekends, Valerie would drive Ben and the boys to a spot on the Rideau Canal where they could launch the canoe and set out with a picnic lunch. Ben would plan where they would be picked up and Valerie would drive to the pickup spot and wait for Ben and the boys. Valerie enjoyed this time by herself as she could read or study. She would then enjoy hearing about the adventures they had on the trip. The family never made it to Kingston, but they did get about halfway.

As the boys got bigger, it became clear that more space

was required. In the Winter of 1969, Valerie and Ben decided to finish the basement. They planned to spend Sunday mornings working on the renovations. Ben would plan the work and arrange for the supplies and then assign work out to the family members (and himself). The project took three winters to finish, but in the end, it was a pleasant space with a wood-burning stove that Valerie and Ben enjoyed during the cold Ottawa winters, a pool table that could be converted into a ping pong table, a dart board and a television where the family could watch TV.

When Peter started Grade 4, a new boy named Malcolm Crerar sat behind him in class. Malcolm and his family had just moved to Ottawa that summer and his parents had bought a house on Micmac Street. The two families were introduced to each other and Valerie and Malcolm's mother, Mary Lou, became good friends. Mary Lou was an artist, while her husband, Alistair, worked for the Government. As the boys got older, Malcolm would join Peter for part of the family's vacation and Peter would join the Crerars for some of their vacations. In 1969, Peter joined the Crerars on a trip to Newfoundland for two weeks.

The boys would get a break-week every March around Easter. After Valerie started working and began to save money, the family would use this week to get away from their routines. For one trip, they went down to Toronto to visit Colin and his family and for the boys to see the city. On this particular trip, they took Em along to also give her a change of environment and so she could visit her sister Joyce.

During this trip, Em stayed at the Inn on the Park, a nice hotel away from downtown Toronto at Eglinton and Leslie, while Valerie and her family stayed with Colin. Valerie remembered being shocked when she saw the hotel bill after Em checked out, as she had truly enjoyed her stay and liberally used room service!

In 1969, both of Colin's daughters were married. Ann

was married in June and Sue in December in the same church in Toronto. Valerie remembers that Ann's wedding took place on a very hot day with no air conditioning in the church, whereas for Sue, the day was very cold and the heating system in the church was broken. The family attended both weddings, and it was great fun as the boys were old enough to stay up late and remember the weddings.

In the fall of 1969, Peter got a job delivering the Ottawa Citizen after school. The next year, in the winter of 1970, Duncan also got his own paper route. Valerie recalled the boys returning from school and having a quick snack before heading out to deliver papers.

In 1969, the National Museum of Man moved its offices to Stittsville, a community just west of Ottawa. To be closer to work, David and his family moved to Stittsville, about an hour's drive from Valerie and Ben. With this move, the visits were less frequent, but it was still nice when they all got together. That year, David and Mary Jo also welcomed their second daughter, Stephanie.

As the end of 1969 drew closer, Valerie looked forward to what the next decade would bring.

Chapter 15 Back to Work

1969 – Valerie and Ben – Ottawa, Ontario, Canada

Chapter 16
Busy Days

1970 to 1971

1970 – Ben, Peter, Valerie, and Duncan – Duncan, British Columbia, Canada

In the summer of 1970, Peter and Duncan went to Camp Tawingo for two weeks. Although Valerie missed the boys, she enjoyed some much-needed time alone with Ben, which was not a lot in the end, as both of them had to work.

Valerie remembered that after the boys left for camp, she made sure that they both received a letter from her while at camp. So, the Monday after they left, she made sure to mail the letter. However, there was one problem with that: she did not know what to write. It had only been a few days, and there was not much news to share, so she had to work hard to come up with something interesting.

A week after the boys went off to camp, Valerie and Ben really felt their absence around the house, not having been away from them for this long before. So, they drove to Huntsville, where Camp Tawingo is located, to visit the boys.

The drive to Huntsville from Ottawa was a good four hours. Going to and from Huntsville would have made for a very tiresome day, so Valerie and Ben planned to begin the drive on Saturday so that they could visit the boys on Sunday afternoon and then be home and get enough rest for the next workday.

When the boys returned, they shared how much they enjoyed the camp, and they went there the next year (1971) as well.

In the spring of 1970, both boys graduated from the 8th grade and were preparing to enter high school in the fall. To celebrate the big milestone, Valerie and Ben decided to go on a special family vacation, since they figured the boys would get busier during the summer in the coming years. This time, they decided to drive across Canada.

The plan for the family vacation was to leave at the end of the school year and get to Calgary, Alberta, just in time for the Calgary Stampede, a 10-day exhibition and festival, held in July every year. They would slow down once in Calgary, enjoying the Stampede and the Rocky Mountains. The trip would end in Vancouver, where they would spend the third week.

With much excitement, the family began their trip on July 3, 1970. Meanwhile, Em went to Edmundston to stay with Nick and his family for the month. They drove for three days through Ontario, which included spending half a day in Sudbury, until they arrived in Winnipeg, Manitoba. Everyone was tired and needed a break from all the driving, so they spent two nights in Winnipeg to relax. After they were all well-rested, they once again resumed their journey, driving for two more days to Calgary.

The family got an early start during the drive and stopped in a motel on the way. The motel had a swimming pool and the boys cooled off in the pool. While the boys enjoyed themselves, the early start also proved beneficial for Valerie, as the heat caused her migraine headaches, and the stay at the motel allowed her to get some much-needed rest.

After checking out of the motel, the family went on their way, with Valerie and Ben sharing the driving. Their usual routine consisted of two hours of driving and then a two-hour break. The parent not behind the wheel would sit in the back seat and was tasked with entertaining the boys.

When the family was about to leave Calgary, they met with Valerie's parents. Fred was nominated by the Corps of Engineers to join the Department of Interior Technical Advisory Board for the construction of the Alaska Pipeline. This meant he had to move to Menlo Park, California. Since it was summertime, Valerie's parents decided to drive from Hanover to Menlo Park and go through Canada, since it would be cooler than the US routes. This decision allowed Valerie and the family to spend time with her parents in Calgary. The visit with Valerie's parents also included a day trip from Calgary to Banff.

The trip to Calgary was quite an eventful one. The family watched the Stampede parade, had a pancake breakfast, and attended the famous Chuckwagon races. The trip through the Rockies was also a wonderful experience. On their way to Vancouver, Peter insisted that they drive to Edmonton, so they could get a picture of the Alberta Capital building. Although Valerie and Ben were not happy with this detour, all their objections disappeared thanks to the spectacular drive along the Columbia Icefields Parkway. Halfway along the Parkway was the Athabasca Glacier, where you could take a tour of the glacier.

Ben had made a reservation in Golden, British Columbia, but with so many breathtaking views along the trip, there were frequent stops, which resulted in the family running behind schedule.

The last site the family visited was Emerald Lake late in the afternoon. Valerie loved the beautiful emerald colour of the water and since it had been a long day, there was nothing she wanted more than to stay there and admire the beautiful scenery. However, the hotel had been paid for, so the family drove on.

After a few days in Vancouver, British Columbia, which included visiting the Heppenstalls, their neighbours from Lorne Park, the family took the ferry to Vancouver Island. Prior to embarking on their trip, Ben had arranged to purchase a new car that they were meant to pick up at the Ottawa airport upon their return. So, while Valerie took the boys around Vancouver, Ben looked into selling the car. However, since the best offer he got was only $300, he decided to try his luck another time. When the family reached Victoria, Ben asked around and got an offer for $600 for the car. The car was sold in Victoria and the family flew from Victoria to Vancouver and then back to Ottawa.

In 1970, the Ottawa Collegiate Board, Ottawa Public Board of Education, Rockcliffe Park Board, and Vanier Board were amalgamated, and a centralised cataloguing system was started to be implemented across all the schools. At one point,

Chapter 16 Busy Days

Valerie considered becoming a school librarian. However, the idea of having to leave Ottawa in the summers to get the certification was not an idea that appealed to her, as she wanted to spend that time with her family. Therefore, Valerie started looking for other jobs.

As a first job after many years, the position at the Ottawa School Board gave Valerie the confidence to continue her career. It also allowed her to start building her professional network. One of the first women she met was Henne Schmitt. Henne was a couple of years older than Valerie and, like Valerie, had a very interesting life when she was young, as she and her husband were German. They kept in contact until Henne passed away.

Valerie applied to the Federal Government and secured a part-time job in the Department of Health and Welfare where she managed the Environmental Health Directorate library. The library was small and supported the research done by the Environmental Health Directorate. With her father and brother involved in research, Valerie felt right at home in this environment. The library was located in Tunney's Pasture, a complex of government buildings west of downtown Ottawa, meaning Valerie had to drive to work every day.

There were a few other library staff in addition to Valerie. The library had a small collection of books and scientific papers but most of her work revolved around obtaining material from other libraries to support the research being done by the section. When Valerie started work, she reported to the section head.

Valerie quite liked her new job; she enjoyed managing the library and working with the researchers. Finding the books, papers, and periodicals to support their research was a challenge but one she took up willingly. However, one thing she found particularly frustrating was that every scientist there had their own personal secretary, who did not appear to do much, while Valerie was always running around, fighting for additional staff to better serve the department.

Valerie had only been working at the library for six months when a major reorganisation took place. The government at the time decided to create a new Department of Environment by moving several agencies from existing departments. This decision impacted the Department of Health and Welfare as the government determined part of that agency would be moved.

For about a week or two, Valerie was uncertain where she would end up. Luckily, she stayed with the Department of Health and Welfare. The little library she was running was amalgamated with the existing Food and Drug Directorate and it was changed from the Environmental Health Directorate to the Health Protection Directorate. It also included several little sections of Health and Welfare.

While all this was going on, Valerie noticed that the boys returned home from high school, had a snack, and immediately left for their respective paper routes shortly after she rushed home from work. She thought to herself, "Why am I working part-time so I can be at home when no one else is at home?" She discussed this with Ben, and they agreed that she should start working full-time. This decision allowed Valerie to fit into the reorganisation plans for the Health and Welfare Libraries.

Em passed away peacefully in her sleep on December 20, 1970. She had been battling several illnesses for a few years, and her condition had significantly worsened in the autumn. Ann and her husband, Harvey, were in Ottawa at the time for a friend's wedding on December 19 and were staying with Valerie and Ben, which allowed them to provide help and support after Em's death. While Valerie helped Ben with the things that needed to be done, Peter and Duncan were sent to the Crerars for the day.

Nick and his family had been planning to spend Christmas in Ottawa but, considering the circumstances, they changed their plans to arrive in time for Em's funeral, which took place in the chapel at Beechwood Cemetery, where she was buried. The actual burial, however, did not happen until spring, when the frost left the ground.

The winter of 1970–1971 was one of the worst in Ottawa's history. There was snow on the ground for 139 consecutive days, and a total of 175 inches (14½ feet) (444.6cm) of snow was recorded that winter, 62 inches (157.5cm) in February of 1971, and 12 inches (30.5cm) of snow on February 13, 1971, alone.

Valerie remembered driving home one day in the winter while it was snowing. She was trying to get up a hill but was having trouble doing so. A television crew, who happened to be nearby filming the bad road conditions for the local news took pictures of Valerie while she was attempting to get up the hill. When Valerie finally got home, after struggling to get up the hill, she asked her family to turn on the local news to see her and the bad road conditions. While it was interesting to see herself on TV, she was quite furious that the crew did not bother offering her help of any sort.

February of 1971 was possibly the worst month that winter. Every evening after supper, the family would go outside to either shovel the driveway or the banks back from the side of the driveway to make more room for the next snowfall. Since the streets became very narrow due to all the accumulated snow, the City of Ottawa deployed large snow blowers to clear the snowbanks off the street. Valerie remembered Ben standing beside the snowbank at the end of the driveway after the city snowblower had been by. The snowbank was higher than Ben's outstretched arm—over 8 feet tall!

1971 – Valerie shovelling snow – 1373 Micmac Street, Ottawa, Ontario, Canada

There were also some fun times during that winter. Valerie remembered watching the boys shovelling the snow off the roof of the addition, creating a huge snowbank which they could jump into and build snow forts.

In 1970, Valerie and Ben's desire to own a cottage returned. Now that Valerie was working full-time, the couple wanted a place to occasionally go and get away from it all. However, considering their experience with the Island, they now wanted a place close to Ottawa and with indoor plumbing. The two began their search for cottages and were successful in February of 1971, when they found a suitable cottage on the Ottawa River west of Ottawa.

The cottage was only about a 45-minute drive from their home, making it an ideal place to drive to on the weekends. The location was also close enough to Ottawa for the road to the cottage to be plowed and mostly paved.

When Valerie and Ben first saw the cottage, they could tell it needed a lot of work. The cottage was rather small but had a large room with kitchen, dining room and living room areas. It also had two bedrooms, a full bathroom and a utility room with a water pump and water heater. In the main room, there was a fireplace and an oil stove. Although the current owners lived in the cottage year-round, it was clearly not designed for Canadian winters, as it had no basement and minimal insulation.

February 1971 – Valerie at the Cottage – Ottawa, Ontario, Canada

Despite its apparent flaws, Valerie and Ben still went ahead with the purchase as it met their criteria. They were not afraid of the work either, as the boys had proved themselves to be very helpful in such matters.

The cottage lot had some trees on it and a large mound covered in snow on the side of the cottage facing the river. At this point, the Ottawa River was very wide and almost looked like a lake. In the spring, however, the snow melted, and the snow-covered mound turned out to be dirt. Moreover, the family discovered a sandy beach, but once you got to the water, there was no sand, just a flat rock bottom.

Once the snow had completely melted, Valerie and Ben set out to create a project list for the cottage. The first thing on the list was building a retaining wall in front of the cottage and backfilling behind the wall with the mound of dirt. Besides that, there was a large tree that needed to be removed and numerous other repairs around the cottage and a general clean-up of the property because the previous owner owned a rifle and often shot at birds, leaving behind multiple empty shell cases. As for the repairs, they included replacing the broken glass in some of the windows, repairing the rotten wood and revamping the bathroom and kitchen. Among the longer-term projects were painting the entire cottage, adding more cupboards in the kitchen, installing a shower in the bathroom, and removing the oil stove.

February 1971 – Cottage – Ottawa, Ontario, Canada

With so many tasks at hand, the two-week summer vacation passed in the blink of an eye, as the entire family was busy working on fixing up the cottage. However, Valerie and Ben did not want the boys' entire summer vacation to be spent working on the cottage, so they decided to rent a motorboat and water skis for the boys to have some fun as well. Both boys enjoyed water skiing and even convinced Ben to try. Valerie, however, was not interested. Additionally, Valerie and Ben also took the boys to do some exploring of the Ottawa River.

The cottage was about halfway between a dam and a

set of rapids. These river obstacles were about 24 miles (38 kilometres) apart. In addition, there was a small island in the middle of the river in front of the cottage. So, there was plenty to explore.

After having a bit of fun, the family got back to work. As the weather improved, they started focusing more on the general clean-up of the cottage. On the weekends, they would go to the cottage and bring out a dozen cinder blocks to build the retaining wall. Building the retaining wall was of utmost priority for two reasons. First, to remove the mound of dirt that was blocking the view of the river from the cottage and second, to protect the property from the high water due to the spring runoff.

By the time summer rolled around, work started on the retaining wall. It was set to be the length of the property, about 100 feet (30m), and four blocks high. After the first weekend spent mixing cement by hand, which was quite arduous and time-consuming, Ben decided to buy a small electric cement mixer, which significantly sped up the process. Work continued throughout the summer (including during vacation) and by the end of August, there was a wall across three-quarters of the property. It was long enough to get rid of the mound in front of the cottage. To hide the cinder block wall, Ben planted cedar trees in front of it.

There was a large tree on the river that bothered Ben as he was afraid it would either fall on the cottage or the neighbour's boathouse. So, one weekend, with the help of the boys and neighbours, they felled the tree parallel to the river without causing any damage to either property.

At the end of August, Nick and his family came up to the cottage for their vacation. Nick was always eager to help, and when he saw the tree on the beach, he and his son Neale cut the tree up and removed it from the beach. Much to Valerie and Ben's amazement, they finished the job! Valerie and Ben were very grateful, and they had enough wood to burn in the fireplace for years.

In 1971, David got a job as a Professor at the University of Maine in its Department of Archaeology and the family moved to Orono, Maine, in September of 1971. That year, Fred was appointed Chairman of the Technical Advisory Board for the Alaska Pipeline and moved to Washington D.C. This made it much easier for Valerie to visit her parents.

With the boys returning to school in the fall and things getting busier at work for both Valerie and Ben, the cottage was closed for the winter, and planning started for the next year.

Chapter 16 Busy Days

1970 – Peter, Ben, Peggy Fenton (mother of Ben's friend, Gordon, from UNB), Duncan, and Valerie – Victoria, British Columbia, Canada

Chapter 17
Work and Relaxation

1972 to 1973

1973 – Valerie on Caramba, friend's sailboat – Ottawa, Ontario, Canada

Work on the cottage continued for a couple of years, but within a year's time, it had reached a point where Valerie and Ben could relax there on the weekends, to escape the workweek stress. It would always be refreshing, and Valerie looked forward to it the most.

Apart from the serenity and the feeling of freedom, those weekends involved more than fun and laughter. There were a lot of things that required their attention. When it was the first weekend of the season or when they went to the cottage after a long break, they had a lot of work piled up for them. In addition to the regular tasks in August, Ben trimmed the cedar hedges that surrounded the property on four sides: the road, neighbours, right-of-way, and river in front of the retaining wall. Then, the water pipe would burst every now and then, and Ben had to fix it. This occurred mostly in the spring when there was some water left in a low spot in the piping and it froze, cracking the copper pipe. It was quite challenging for Ben because the crack would usually happen either behind the toilet or the bathtub, in the most difficult place to get to. Eventually, Ben modified that section of the pipe to make it removable, which assisted in any necessary repairs.

Besides getting the water working, there were always small jobs to do to get the cottage ready for the summer. Just when they thought they could just relax, there was something else that had to be worked on. There was always something to do, but then again, Ben liked to potter at tasks to keep busy, so he found pleasure in doing small tasks.

Valerie enjoyed helping Ben and the boys, but she mostly did the house chores like cooking meals, washing dishes and other general ones. Mostly, the evenings of those days were the most enjoyable part for Valerie. The evenings provided a stress-free environment for the family to enjoy each other's company.

The family liked to play card games, such as Oh Hell! (also known as Contract Whist, a trick-taking card game), most of the time and Valerie loved joining in. She also loved putting together jigsaw puzzles with the family and sometimes just by herself while watching the river. She also spent some of those evenings on her knitting projects or playing solitaire. Time spent at the cottage was always a delight.

On several occasions, Ben took the boys for a trip in his canoe on the Ottawa River with a packed lunch. They would all come back and share stories about their enthralling experience. Later, Ben bought an Albacore sailboat, named *Ceta*, which allowed Ben and the boys to go for longer trips, but they never stayed overnight. This gave Valerie more time at the cottage by herself to relax and enjoy the view. She always yearned for more time like this.

Valerie's birthday was on July 8th, just six days after Ben's birthday. Since July 1st was Canada Day, a public holiday, it would give them a long weekend to prepare and celebrate their birthdays. And the best part was that their birthdays were always celebrated at the cottage. Most years, it would be just the family but there were certain times when some other relatives and friends would be invited too.

As Valerie was working, she had to figure out how to keep the boys occupied during the school breaks. During the Easter break in 1971, Ben had to go to an important conference in Montebello, which was close to Ottawa. He was rather thrilled about it. The conference had a 'wives' program, and it allowed children to be a part of it as well. Ben was thinking of taking Duncan and Peter with him on this trip, so he discussed it with the family. Duncan decided to join Ben as he was interested in it. Peter chose to stay at home with Valerie.

At the conference, Duncan explored a lot of new things and was introduced to a sport he would come to love ever since, curling. Curling is a popular Canadian sport. Participants are divided into two teams of four players each. The players take turns sliding 44-pound (20kg) stones along an ice sheet toward the targeted area divided into four concentric rings.

One player stands in the ring and calls the shots, one player throws the rock, and the other two players sweep in front of the rock, if required, to make it go further or curl less. The game is usually divided into eight ends, an end being over when all eight players have thrown two rocks. Points are awarded to a team for each rock that is closer than any of the opposition's rocks to the centre of the rings. It bears similarities to shuffleboard and lawn bowling.

Duncan had not known the game existed before and was captivated by it. He not only learnt how to play it in a few hours but was also quite good at it.

Since Peter stayed home, Valerie would take him to the office and would ask him to help with some basic jobs, such as photocopying and filing documents. He was quite responsive and alert as well, so Valerie liked taking him to the office. Weekdays would be work, home, eat, and then go to sleep. At the end of the week, Valerie and Peter went to see the World Figure Skating Championships Tour. They enjoyed seeing their favourite skaters, especially the speed of the skaters, which you do not really see on television.

May turned into June, a special time for Peter in 1972. He was about to turn 16 and was really excited as he could finally get his driver's licence. He had been waiting for this for several years, and now it was finally becoming a reality. He could not contain his excitement!

Peter's birthday was right around the corner, and he wanted to learn to drive before attaining his driving licence. So, Peter started taking driving lessons and Ben would take him to practise every day. Peter was a quick learner and picked up on things more quickly than expected and got pretty smooth at driving in just a few weeks.

Given these capabilities and his control of the car, Peter was allowed to drive for the family trips occasionally. Valerie still did not trust him and would sit in the back seat, her eyes tightly closed as she was scared and did not want to see an accident coming.

Peter had his own misconception about this. He thought Valerie had fallen asleep because he was such a good driver, and his rides always gave everyone pleasure. It was only years later that Valerie burst Peter's bubble and admitted why she would close her eyes whenever Peter was driving in those early years. However, once Peter got his licence, there was the advantage that he could run errands for the family, such as picking up cinder blocks to build the retaining wall at the cottage.

For the month of July, the boys enrolled in a computer programming course at summer school. Although it was a high school course, the classes were held on the Carleton University Campus. It was near their house, so they would ride their bikes from Micmac Street to the campus. That short ride to the campus would always be fun for the boys. Valerie was so pleased to have the boys take a computer course, as she and Ben had noticed a rapid increase in demand in this field.

That summer of 1972 was slightly different for everyone. Duncan visited David, Valerie's brother, in Maine to join him in an archaeological dig for two weeks. It was a highly anticipated journey for Duncan, and he could not stop bragging about it. After the dig was over, David drove Duncan to St John, New Brunswick, where Nick (Ben's brother) lived. Part of the reasoning was that Duncan desire to see Uncle Nick. So, David dropped him there, and Duncan had a blast, mainly hanging out with his cousin Neale, playing chess and golf. Ben and Nick's uncle, Jack, also came by to see Duncan and pass on his greetings to the family.

Time moved like a fast train that year. Summer had turned into winter and the Christmas bells were chiming. Christmas had always been an exciting part of their lives as they all spent it together. This year, the family decided to go to Washington and spend Christmas with Valerie's parents. Valerie's parents lived in an apartment. It was a good-sized apartment, but Kitty realised that it would feel cramped with her two teenage grandsons visiting. As soon as she knew the family was coming, she set to work to find activities for the boys to do to keep them busy. Fortunately, there are lots of interesting things to do in Washington, D.C., such as the Smithsonian museums, which kept the boys occupied and made for an enjoyable Christmas visit.

Another major development occurred in Valerie's life by the end of December of 1972. The Chief Librarian of the Department of Health and Welfare had Valerie move to the main Health Protection Branch Library as the head of Reader Services. Initially, she could not believe it as it was so unexpected, but once it sank in, she was so thrilled and could not be more eager to step into those new shoes. Her family was equally proud of her as well.

The year 1973 was full of uncertainties and turbulence. It was not as happy and busy as in 1972 and Valerie had to go through several hardships that were thrown her way.

It was the first month into the new year and the start was a little shaky. Valerie was enjoying her promotion. Things were going great until the day Martha Stone was promoted. As Martha took on her new role, she wanted to make changes. Valerie had to rise to the challenge and learn new skills.

The head of the Health Protection Library, Martha Stone, was promoted to the Chief Librarian for the Department of Health and Welfare at the start of 1973. Valerie decided to apply for the position of Head of Public Services in the Department of Health and Welfare Library and was successful. She would stay there for four years.

The Departmental Library was located on the second floor of another building in Tunney's pasture with a view overlooking the Ottawa River. The Departmental Library was going through a difficult period and lacked resources terribly. A lot of work had piled up, so getting her area back on track was quite challenging. In addition, Valerie had many human resource tasks, including writing job descriptions and organising her group.

Martha while presented challenges to Valerie, she was also a fair woman and played by the rules. Martha, like Valerie, was also fighting for the library and its staff. She was, in fact, very good to Valerie and would even help her out.

Martha was intellectual and always raised her voice for the right causes. She would fight for the people who worked with her and always took complete ownership of her responsibilities. Her discipline was quite exemplary. In short, she was a very interesting woman.

As Valerie and Martha had lunch together, they would often talk about their lives and the places where they grew up. Martha was born and grew up in New Jersey, USA. Even though they were born and raised in different parts of the world, the similarities they shared amazed them. Maybe it was because of their upbringing and the environments in which they were raised. They would even compare their upbringings and laugh endlessly after noticing the similarities.

Work-life, after the promotion, was quite hectic and tiresome. Most days, there would be a lot of work, and it would take her hours to finish the daily tasks. Sometimes, she would feel burned out, but it never stopped her from giving her heart and soul to the department. However, impressive progress was made in the department under her leadership. While working at the Department of Health and Welfare Library, there was an effort made to improve the sharing of books between the libraries in Ottawa. The Council of Federal Libraries, a new group, was formed.

Due to a large inter-library loan business within the Department of Health and Welfare, Martha, seeing the potential for a challenge, invited Valerie to join her. Valerie was hesitant at the start but, ultimately, she wanted to dive in and channel her abilities. Martha pushed and supported her to do it, too, so she ended up participating. When the group was formed, it took ten days to get books from the National Research Council Library to the Health and Welfare Library, which was just across the city. At the same time, the universities in Ontario and Quebec had set up delivery services, which included the National Library of Canada, which operated much faster. Valerie was now on the committee that worked on getting a similar delivery service within Ottawa. It was an exciting new venture and Valerie proved herself and shone brightly.

Also in 1973, Valerie's father suffered a severe heart attack. He was rushed to the emergency ward and the doctor said he was in serious condition. This stressed Valerie, as she was in Ottawa and her father was in Washington, D.C. He recovered soon enough and was discharged from the hospital. The doctor recommended that he avoid stress and rest for a few weeks. Since he was not supposed to have any stress or leave the house, he realised that it was time to retire, a decision Valerie supported.

The next year, her parents decided to move to Simsbury, Connecticut, which was about a 45-minute drive from Valerie's sister and about a 7-hour drive from Ottawa. Valerie was excited to visit them in their new house.

Chapter 17 Work and Relaxation

Cottage front view – Ottawa, Ontario, Canada

Chapter 18
A New Chapter

1974 to 1979

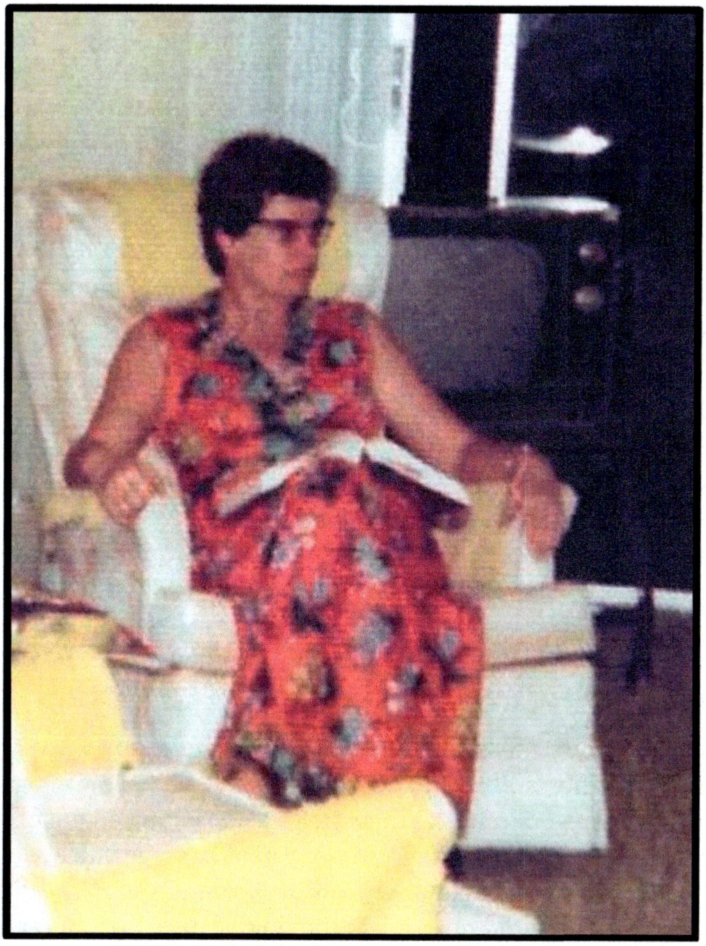

1977 – Valerie – Fort Myers, Florida, USA

In 1974, Valerie's parents finalised their move to Simsbury, Connecticut. Although they were still quite a long distance from Valerie, they were closer than before. So, the two sisters could visit their parents more often now.

Peter and Duncan were set to graduate high school in 1975 and as a treat for their final year, Valerie and Ben took the boys to Florida for the winter break in March. They went to Daytona Beach, which provided a stark but good change of weather. Valerie and Ben particularly enjoyed getting away from the cold and snow of Ottawa winters and basking in the moderate weather in Florida. The breeze was slightly warm, while the water was cool, making for a relaxing and enjoyable trip. From Daytona Beach, they made day trips to Disney World and the Kennedy Space Center. Valerie and Ben were so delighted by the weather during this particular trip that they started going south every winter, which would continue for the next 35 years!

After returning home from the trip, life went on as usual, and the boys finally graduated from high school in June of 1975. However, the road to graduation was not an easy one. One would expect the senior year of high school to be very stressful, with students aiming to attain the highest grades and get into the best colleges. However, it was perhaps even more stressful for Peter and Duncan as teachers in Ottawa went on strike for over seven weeks in the spring of 1975, beginning on February 27 and lasting until April 18, when teachers were finally given a salary increase.

During the strike, Valerie and Ben did not want the boys to sit idle, so they made sure the boys had something to do. Ben arranged for Peter to work for a consulting engineering firm in Ottawa while Valerie gave Duncan some jobs to do around the house. Fortunately, the strike ended sooner rather than later, and it did not impact the boys' future plans.

Although both Valerie and Ben went to university, they did not impose anything on the boys. They were very supportive and made sure the boys knew that all options were open after high school and that they could do as they pleased.

In the end, both boys decided to go to university, of their own volition. Peter went off to Queens in Kingston, Ontario, a two-hour drive, to study Engineering, so he would be relatively close to home. Duncan, on the other hand, enrolled in Carleton and chose Science as his major. While Peter lived in a residence in Kingston, Duncan lived at home.

Now, with Peter ready to leave, the cottage to take care of, and demanding jobs, Valerie and Ben decided it was time for a change. They decided to put the house up for sale and move into a condominium apartment (condo) in downtown Ottawa. When they had time, they would look for condos and after a bit of research, they found a new building being constructed at 151 Bay Street called Park Square. The details of the new project appealed to them, so they put down a deposit on a three-bedroom suite on the tenth floor with views north and west, up the Ottawa River. They were told the construction would finish in a few months' time, and it would be ready to move into by the summer, which meant that Micmac Street had to be sold—and fast.

Luckily, it did not take them long to find a buyer for the house. Coincidentally, the new owner had an elderly parent living with them, so the addition that had been built for Em, made it an ideal purchase for them.

Although Valerie and Ben were happy with how quickly things were falling into place, the whole process of relocating seemed a daunting task; furthermore, after Em passed away, the addition was turned into a family room. Now the family was downsizing; they realised they had to get rid of a significant number of things around the house.

With Ben's motto, "If in doubt, throw it out!" the process of packing and discarding the "useless" things began. This made for a very busy June—just as the boys were finishing high school, furniture was being sold. The last day of high school was when the family moved out of Micmac Street. However, they did not move to Park Square, as originally planned. Contrary to the builder's promises, the construction was facing delays, the extent of which they did not realise at the time. So, Valerie and Ben made alternate arrangements, renting a small two-bedroom apartment in downtown Ottawa at Bronson and Laurier. Unbeknownst to them at the time, they would end up living in this apartment for the next two years before finally moving into Park Square.

In the new apartment, one bedroom belonged to Valerie and Ben, while bunk beds were set up in the other one for the boys. During the summer of 1975, Peter had a summer job that started early in the morning and finished in the late afternoon. Duncan had a job moving maps, with his shift starting at 5 p.m. and ending at 2 a.m. During the week, the boys only saw each other, sleeping! However, since the boys both had jobs and Peter eventually went to Kingston, the living arrangement in the cosy little apartment worked out just fine.

During Peter's first year at Queen's, the family got together every two weeks. Either Peter would come home to Ottawa or Valerie and Ben would drive down to Kingston. Valerie recalled that, when Peter came home, Ben and Duncan would compliment the meals and comment on how she always made an effort to prepare Peter's favourite meals whenever he came home.

In 1975, Ben was promoted to Director of the Program for Export Market Development. In this new position, Ben had a large staff and many political issues. Valerie and Ben would discuss their respective problems over dinner and in the evenings, they supported each other in developing solutions. Furthermore, Ben's promotion required him to have a specified knowledge of French. This meant he had to take French lessons at the Government's French School. Ben was not at all excited about this as he was not good with languages and struggled with the whole concept.

Chapter 18 A New Chapter

Valerie tried her best to support Ben in his new role and finally, after almost a year of countless French lessons, Ben met the standard and could start his new job. Meanwhile, Valerie continued her job at the library with great enthusiasm and passion.

With boys grown up and at university, Valerie and Ben started to travel on vacations. Their first trip was to Victoria, B.C., in 1976. Then, in September of 1976, the entire family travelled to Saint John, New Brunswick, to attend the wedding of Nick and Pat's daughter, Pam. Valerie, Ben, and Peter flew to Saint John, while Duncan drove his car, visiting Valerie's parents and Diana's family enroute.

1976 – Duncan with his new car "Yellow Peril", co-purchased with Valerie – Ottawa, Ontario, Canada

While her personal life was eventful, Valerie's professional life was also busy. Her job required her to travel for work and in 1976, she attended conferences in Columbus, Ohio, and Halifax, Nova Scotia.

In addition to dutifully fulfilling her responsibilities, Valerie also believed it was important to contribute to the library profession. This resulted in her co-authoring *"User satisfaction in accessing multiple bibliographic databases online"* in 1976 for the Canadian Association of Information Science (CAIS) Conference held in London, Ontario, with her colleague, D. Foster, and her boss, M. B. Stone.

In addition to that, Valerie was also an active member of the Council for Federal Libraries where she was a member of the Committee on Classification from 1976 to 1978 and Chair of the Working Group on Charging for Library Services from 1976 to 1982. Valerie was also a member of the Canadian Library Association and Chair of the Canadian Association of Special Libraries and Information Services, Ottawa Chapter, from 1977 to 1978.

With the boys now busy with university, Ben started looking for other things to do to stay busy. In 1977, Valerie and Ben bought two bicycles and they would ride on the beautiful trails in Ottawa, which were close to Park Square and along the Ottawa River. That same year, Valerie took the Library Administration Development Program at the University of Maryland. Later that year, the couple visited Fort Myers Beach, Florida, for two weeks. Nick and Pat also joined them for this trip.

In November of 1977, Park Square was finally completed, and the family moved in. Having an extra bedroom now, after having lived in a small two-bedroom apartment for two years, was greatly appreciated by all.

Chapter 18 A New Chapter

1978 – Park Square Living Room – 151 Bay Street, Ottawa, Ontario, Canada

The condo turned out to be exactly what they wanted, so the wait did not seem too bad now that it was finally over. The kitchen was located on the immediate right side as you entered the large suite foyer. The kitchen was small but had enough space for a small table and two chairs, which was fine since it was mostly only Valerie and Ben at home. There was a short hallway beside the kitchen, which led to a large area for the dining room and the living room.

The living room had windows looking north and west, and a door leading to a small balcony. Unfortunately, the view to the north was blocked by a hotel and an office building. The views to the west and northwest, however, allowed you to see the Ottawa River, Gatineau Hills, and the sunsets.

On the left side of the foyer was a large closet and the hallway that led to three bedrooms. Down the hallway, the first bedroom was Duncan's room until he left, when it became a den. The next bedroom, also on the right, was initially Peter's room and later was turned into a guest room. On the left was a full bathroom. Finally, at the end of the hall was the master bedroom, with an ensuite bathroom and a large walk-in closet.

Like the living room, the master bedroom also had windows looking north and west. Valerie and Ben also had a storage room and laundry room on their floor, located just past their entrance. They had a large parking space near the elevator on level 3 in the basement. The building also had a swimming pool, and, after Ben retired, he worked with some of the other residents to create a hobby room in the basement.

Being downtown was very convenient for the couple as Ben could walk to work, while Valerie was much closer to her job at Tunney's Pasture. However, when Valerie changed jobs, her new office was situated in the south end of the city, near Micmac Street, so she had to drive to work. Valerie would go against the traffic, though, so driving to work was not too bad after all.

In 1978, Duncan graduated from Carleton with a Bachelor of Science and, shortly after, secured a temporary job debugging software programs working for the Department of Energy, Mines and Resources. He later got a permanent job with a small computer company in Ottawa called Versaterm Systems, and Duncan continued to live at home. Now that he had graduated and had started working at a permanent job, Valerie and Ben figured he should start paying rent, which he dutifully did until, in August of 1979, he found an apartment close to work and moved out.

In 1978, Valerie's parents celebrated their 50th wedding anniversary. The whole family got together in Simsbury to celebrate the occasion.

Chapter 18 A New Chapter

1978 – Valerie, Kitty, David, Fred, and Diana – Simsbury, Connecticut, USA

Valerie's leadership skills continued to grow with her new job as a manager, inspiring her to consider taking on more responsibilities, and head her own library. In 1978, Valerie won a competition for the job as the Chief Librarian for the National Museums of Canada.

So, Valerie became the first Director of Library Services for the National Museums of Canada. Valerie was responsible for the libraries in the Museum of Science and Technology, the Museum of Civilisation, the Museum of Man, the Museum of Nature (which later became the Museum of Natural History), the future Aviation Museum and the Canadian Conservation Institute. In total, the National Museum staff were in 17 locations in Ottawa. The National Art Gallery was also part of The National Museums but due to its sheer size, the library was a separate entity.

Despite its chequered history, The National Museums Library had just created a central administration under the National Museums of Canada. The library, which served the four National Museums, was housed in a warehouse on

Walkley Road. Similar to Ben when he started his last senior position, Valerie needed to have a working knowledge of French. Fortunately, the French she had learned in school and reinforced by some of her courses at the University of Ottawa enabled her to pass the Canadian Government French test quickly.

Creating the library was the initial challenge Valerie faced at her new job. She was tasked with determining the best structure, creating new job descriptions, and hiring staff. The staff in the existing five libraries also had to be assigned their roles. In some cases, they stayed in the museum library, as a branch library to provide services to the museum staff. In other cases, the staff had to move to the central location on Walkley Road in specialised roles.

There were also new positions to head up the centralised functions of cataloguing and acquisition. Making changes to the current staff was particularly challenging due to their union status, so Valerie had to use all her problem-solving and personal skills to avoid any big problems or conflicts. In the competition for the head of acquisitions, Valerie selected a woman, Alicia, who had just moved from Winnipeg to take on a position working in another Government of Canada library in Ottawa. Feeling guilty for hiring Alicia after her current boss paid for her to move to Ottawa, Valerie phoned him to apologise.

In addition to staffing, Valerie faced resistance from some of the Museum Directors who opposed centralization of the libraries. However, Valerie remained firm in her mission and negotiated the budget that would be allocated to her department as well as the staff that would be transferred. In some cases, staff worked part-time in the library and part-time outside of the library. Moreover, the Assistant Deputy Minister, who was Valerie's boss, was young and ambitious. Valerie had to spend a lot of time educating him on the value of the library so he could support the library with senior management.

Chapter 18 A New Chapter

Valerie was determined to make the most of her new role and knew what she wanted as the result, so she reorganised her department and hired more customer-focused staff. To do this, she knew she had to be with her team at the Walkley Road office. Her boss wanted her to have her office near his office in downtown Ottawa. Valerie was insistent that she wanted to be with her team.

The Museums had Branch Librarians responsible for various locations, and a centralised Technical Services department for the cataloguing and purchasing. One of the reasons Valerie was hired was to implement a Library Committee where users from each of the Branches were represented. Although the National Gallery was not part of the centralisation, Valerie worked very closely with the librarian, whom she got along with very well. This allowed all the libraries to work together.

When it came to work attire, Valerie always dressed very professionally—something which Valerie believed was essential to be respected in the workplace. Every day, she wore a brooch on her jacket. Over the years, she inherited or received over 60 brooches, mostly given to her by Ben, from his worldwide travels!

Valerie soon obtained a good reputation as a leader. The library had a total staff of 23 in professional, technical and support roles. Her initial objective was to recruit staff with the necessary skills and attitude—those willing to work hard and embrace new challenges. While Valerie was aware of her strengths, she also recognized her weaknesses and made sure to hire competent people in the areas in which she lacked. For instance, she had no interest in cataloguing, so she hired a person who was skilled and keen about cataloguing.

Given her numerous responsibilities – including securing support from coworkers and Museum Directors, educating her boss, and managing a budget of approximately $1.75 million – Valerie needed a competent team. Valerie had to constantly keep an eye on the library expenses to ensure she did not go over the budget and prepare the budgets for the coming years to ensure she had enough money for the staff to keep providing services to the Museums. This was a tricky matter as estimating the cost of subscriptions to technical publications was difficult. Publishers would rarely provide much notice of price increases, and those increases did not always align with inflation. Since the publications were very specific, Valerie was locked into the publisher.

Besides the annual budget, Valerie's responsibilities as the Director also included the two-year resource and operational plans which linked the results to resources and strategic goals. However, Valerie's direct reports lauded her management style; she avoided micromanagement, offering freedom to operate independently while remaining accessible for guidance as needed.

Valerie understood the importance of communication, especially with her direct reports and all her staff. She would have regular meetings with her directors to identify any issues they had, and she also shared with them what was happening with the Museums. She would also have staff meetings to update them on what was happening.

Even though Valerie had a secretary, one of the ways she communicated with her staff was by going to the office kitchen to get her own coffee. This way, she could "casually" bump into her staff and have a quick chat with them. Valerie also never ate her lunch at her desk. The office location on Walkley Road was isolated, and there were not any restaurants nearby, which meant everyone brought their own lunch and ate in the kitchen. Valerie would do the same. This gave her more opportunities to interact with the staff.

Back in the 1960s, when the family still lived on Micmac Street, Ben started making wine and beer. It was harder to do after they moved to Park Square, so the beer and winemaking came to an indefinite halt. However, once Duncan moved out, and there was an extra bathroom at his disposal, Ben had Duncan's bathtub was repurposed to hold beer-making equipment. During the winter, Ben would make beer which he could enjoy in the summer at the cottage. This was a lot cheaper and, according to Ben, tastier than store-bought beer. Once the beer was brewed, it had to be bottled and Valerie was usually called in to help.

One Monday, Valerie recalled, the staff were talking about what they had done over the weekend. One of the staff asked Valerie what she did. Although Valerie generally kept her personal life to herself, for some reason, she could not ignore this question. So, she replied that she "bottled beer." The staff was so surprised by her answer since that was not something they had expected her to be doing at all.

In 1978, Valerie and Ben went on another two-week trip to Fort Myers Beach, Florida. In September, a conference was scheduled in Paris, France, which Valerie had to attend. Ben accompanied her to "carry her bags" and the couple added a two-week vacation to the trip in celebration of their 25th wedding anniversary. They visited Rome, Florence in Italy, and Geneva and Zurich in Switzerland.

In 1979, Peter also graduated from university with a Bachelor of Science (Engineering) and got a job with Bell Canada in Toronto. Valerie and Ben were very proud of their boys; they both had graduated from university and had good full-time jobs.

In August of 1979, Valerie's friend from New Zealand, Ginny, and her husband Mike came to Canada and spent a week with Valerie and Ben. Although Valerie and Ginny had stayed in touch by mail, it was the first time she had seen her since New Zealand. That summer, Diana's daughters Kristi and Lynda also came to spend a week with Valerie and Ben, dividing their time between Park Square and the cottage.

Valerie and Ben were constantly on the hunt for new activities, and in 1979, they began square dancing again. This was one of the many activities they took up but then abandoned because of their demanding jobs and travel.

Trips to Florida continued throughout 1978 and 1979 and, in 1979, Valerie and Ben bought a townhouse in Satellite Beach, Florida. One of Ben's colleagues at work knew a builder in Florida who was building small developments. Ben liked the builder's work and, after a discussion with Valerie, they decided to buy a unit there. A year later they bought a second unit in Paradise Park, about 4 miles south of Satellite Beach. They already enjoyed travelling to Florida and, with the second unit, they thought that when they retired, they could spend the winters in Florida while renting out the other unit. Until then, they would rent both units year-round.

1980 – Paradise Park – Melbourne, Florida, USA

Chapter 19
Big Milestones

1980 to 1985

1983 – 30th Wedding Anniversary – Ottawa, Ontario, Canada

During her time at the library, Valerie brought in automation. Computers were gradually being introduced to workplaces and that included libraries. Computerization improved efficiency and helped to meet budgetary pressures. It also became necessary to fulfil the library services for the Museums, especially as other libraries were also adopting automation. Valerie then had to ensure that she had staff who were willing to learn new technology and that she had enough funding for her and the staff to attend conferences and learn what other libraries were doing to improve their operations and services.

Another area of interest for Valerie, where she also spent considerable time, was policy development. Valerie felt having policies in place would enable staff to know what their exact roles were and what was expected of them so they could perform their duties efficiently.

One aspect of her job that Valerie enjoyed was reviewing the diverse and interesting books the library acquired.

While observing how other libraries were operating, Valerie noticed that the Museum Library was supporting basic research, whereas the Health and Welfare Library supported applied research. Furthermore, the museums were all supporting research in different areas.

Valerie stayed active in professional associations and attended several conferences. As the Director of the library, Valerie realised she needed to support her staff. However, due to limited funds, only one person could attend. The conferences, so, Valerie decided to take turns with her direct reports to attend the conferences.

In 1980, Valerie attended conferences in Edmonton and Whitehorse, with Ben joining her for the trip. After they left Whitehorse, they flew to Vancouver to visit Nick and his family. Later the same year, Valerie also attended the Joint Annual Meeting, American Association of Museums/Canadian

Museums Association Conference in Boston where she co-presented "The Role of the Library in a Museum" with Rhoda S. Ratner. She also managed to visit David in Maine.

In 1980, after living in Simsbury, Connecticut, for over six years, Valerie's parents decided to move because of the harsh weather. Although they liked being close to Diana and being able to visit her family, the streets were very icy during the winter, and they were afraid of falling. On the other hand, it was so hot and humid during the summers that they were reluctant to go outside. So, they were unable to enjoy the city in any weather and, after not being able to adjust even after six years, they decided to move.

In December of 1980, they rented an apartment in Vero Beach, Florida, for four months. Valerie and Ben thought that the whole family should go down to Florida to spend Christmas with her parents. Valerie and Ben flew down to Melbourne, Florida. Duncan came in from the Bahamas, returning from vacation. Peter flew in from Edmonton after attending a friend's wedding in Calgary and visiting friends in Edmonton.

Valerie's parents really enjoyed their stay in Florida and in November of 1981, they moved to John Knox Village in Orange City, Florida, where they lived for the rest of their lives. John Knox Village is a life care facility that supports seniors at various stages of their lives.

Initially, Valerie's parents lived a very independent lifestyle at the facility, going to the main dining room for most meals and arranging trips to local shops and restaurants. However, as they got older, they required increased support from their family.

Between Christmas and New Year's in 1977, Peter had a skating party with some friends from Queen's University who also lived in Ottawa. After skating, they returned to Valerie and Ben's apartment for some hot chocolate just as Duncan was returning home from curling. Naturally, Duncan interacted with Peter's friends and ended up being invited to a New Year's Eve party organised by one of Peter's friends in Kanata, a suburb of Ottawa. Others at the New Year's Eve party were some of the Queen's group and their friends from Kanata, including Shirley Marshall. Duncan and Shirley hit it off immediately and danced and talked most of the evening. At the end of the night, Shirley agreed to go out with Duncan in the New Year. After an on-again, off-again courtship Duncan proposed to Shirley in January of 1981. The wedding was set for October 10, 1981, the same date as Valerie and Ben's wedding. Even the time was the same – 2 p.m.!

1981 – Peter, Duncan, Shirley (seated), Valerie, and Ben – Ottawa, Ontario, Canada

In December of 1981, Duncan and Shirley purchased an end-unit condominium in Kanata. They moved in on July 1, 1982, just in time to accommodate Diana and her family, who were in town for Peter's wedding on July 3rd.

Peter met Lyne Pharand in Toronto in July of 1981. That Christmas, Valerie and Ben were delighted to learn that Peter had proposed to Lyne who accepted. Lyne's parents lived in Ottawa and her father was a Chief Warrant Officer in the Royal Canadian Air Force. So, the wedding was held on the Uplands Air Force Base, near the Ottawa International Airport, on July 3, 1982. This served as another occasion for a family reunion. The day after the wedding, the whole family gathered at the cottage for a get-together.

1982 – Ben, Valerie, Peter, and Lyne – Ottawa, Ontario, Canada

With the boys now on their own, ready to start their own families, Valerie and Ben were freer to travel than ever before. Although their jobs were busy in the early 1980s, they did get four weeks' vacation and Ben was determined to make the most of it. The couple quickly fell into a pattern of spending a week or two in Florida in March to get away from the Ottawa winter and then saving at least a week to spend at the cottage – leaving them with one or two weeks for special trips. In 1981,

Valerie and Ben joined Nick and Pat for a two-week trip to Hawaii. The first week was spent at Waikiki and the second on Maui. In 1982, after visiting Valerie's parents, they drove down to the Florida Keys.

In 1982, Valerie attended a conference in Halifax. The next year, in 1983, Valerie spent five days in Washington, D.C., working at the Smithsonian. She also attended a conference in Saskatoon later in the year.

In the fall of 1983, Valerie and Ben celebrated their 30th wedding anniversary. They went on a three-week trip to Europe, starting in Venice. After six days in Venice, they took a ferry to Piraeus via the Corinth Canal and then on to Athens. In Athens, they took a four-day bus tour to visit some of the famous archaeological sites in Corinth, Mycenae, Olympia, and Delphi. They then flew to Crete, where they had time to simply relax, before heading back to Ottawa where Peter and Duncan, along with their wives, took Valerie and Ben out to dinner and to see Swan Lake.

In 1984, Valerie's job took her to Toronto and Calgary to attend meetings. That summer, Diana's sons, Doug and Mike spent a week with Valerie and Ben at the cottage.

On July 1, 1984, Peter and Lyne bought their first home. Valerie and Ben travelled to Toronto to help set up the place and spent a couple of days painting the living and dining rooms while Peter and Lyne went to work.

In June of 1984, Valerie and Ben found out that Duncan and Shirley were expecting their first child. On December 3, 1984, Devon was born at 4:30 a.m.—a healthy baby boy. Valerie and Ben rushed to the hospital right after work that day to see their first grandchild. Valerie could not believe how much Devon resembled Duncan at that age.

Chapter 19 Big Milestones

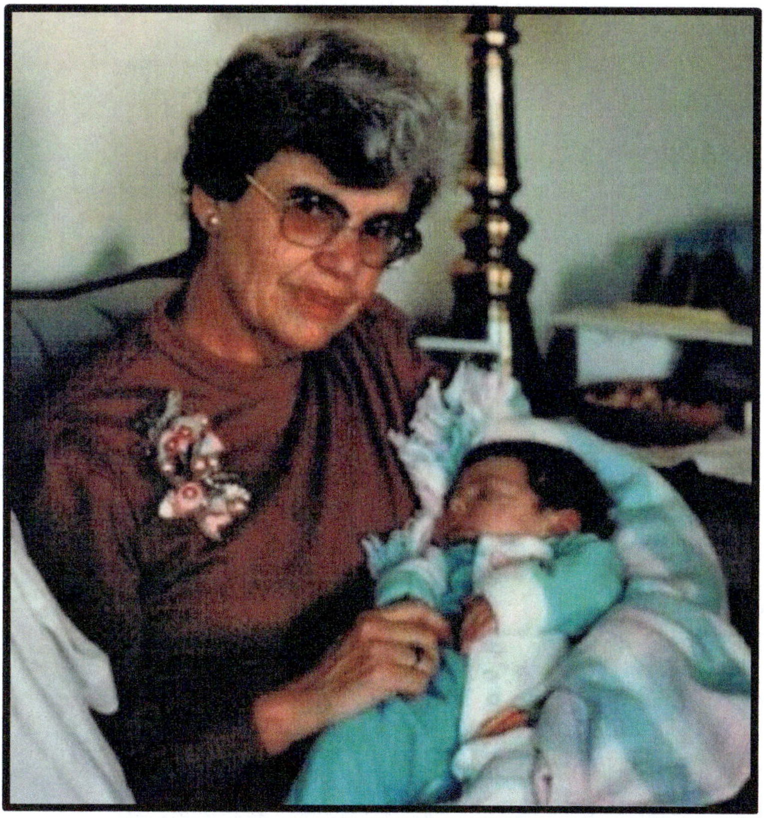

1984 – Valerie and Devon – Ottawa, Ontario, Canada

During the late 1970s and throughout the 1980s, there was a flurry of weddings of Valerie and Ben's nieces and nephews. The first was Nick's daughter Pam's wedding in 1976. Next in line was David's daughter, Jennifer, who was married in a beautiful location in Sugar Loaf Mountain, Maine, in 1985. Then, in 1986, both of Diana's daughters got married, Kristi in June and Lynda in August. They both got married in the same place in Springfield, Massachusetts. Then in October of 1988, Nick's son, Neale, was married in Los Angeles. Valerie and Ben enjoyed attending all the weddings and seeing the whole family together.

Life was busy and eventful as always, even with the boys now on their own, and Valerie and Ben looked forward to what the rest of the decade had to offer them.

1988 – Valerie and Ben – Ottawa, Ontario, Canada

Chapter 20
Life at the IDRC

1986 to 1990

1986 – Valerie – 151 Bay Street, Ottawa, Ontario, Canada

In January of 1986, Ben retired. The timing allowed him to accompany Valerie to a conference she was scheduled to attend in Victoria. They added a one-week vacation to the trip so they could visit Nick and Pat in Vancouver and enjoy Expo 86.

With regard to her work, Valerie did not seem to be slowing down in her role and was always striving to achieve new heights in her job. She was on the Board of the Canadian Museums Association. She also worked with the Northern Colloquy Group, a group of libraries with holdings in the Arctic. Then, from the beginning of June to the end of October 1986, she was assigned to lead the Administrative Reform for Staffing Study Team at the National Museums of Canada. This project involved Valerie working in downtown Ottawa, so she walked to work every morning, which she thoroughly enjoyed.

As the years passed, Valerie and Ben's relatively small family continued to grow. In April of 1986, almost two years after their first son Devon, Duncan and Shirley welcomed another baby boy, Andrew. Then, in the fall of 1986, Peter and Lyne shared the news that Lyne was pregnant with twins! These would be the first set of twins in the family, so everyone was very excited to welcome them. Unfortunately, the twins were born prematurely on December 5, 1986. Katherine Marie lived for only a few hours and Elizabeth Marie for two days.

Chapter 20 Life at the IDRC

1987 – Andrew, Valerie, and Devon – Ottawa, Ontario, Canada

In May of 1987, Valerie attended meetings of the International Council of Museums in Europe. Ben accompanied her once again and they vacationed in Paris. They also paid a visit to Valerie's friend Ginny, who owned a vacation home in the Loire Valley. Later in September of that year, Valerie went to Cambridge, England, for a week this time alone, for meetings with the International Council of Museums.

In 1987, for political reasons, it was decided that the National Museums Corporation would split, and each museum would become an autonomous unit - this meant that the centralised library, which Valerie had worked so hard to build from the ground up, would be broken up.

During her time at the library, Valerie had planned and managed the implementation of three applications to automate library systems, participated in the development of management information systems for the federal government libraries and participated in the development of policies such as the conservation and research policies for the National

Museums of Canada.

After spending over a decade building the library services for the National Museums of Canada, Valerie now had the lead in the dismantling of the library. This was certainly not going to be an easy task, not only because of the logistics involved but largely due to the significant effort and dedication. Then, there was the emotion of dismantling the library Valerie had invested so much in creating. Staff needed to be reallocated and, perhaps the hardest part of all, the collection had to be divided among the individual museum libraries.

One of the major challenges Valerie faced was a massive collection of more than one million photographs dating back to the early 1800s that had come from the Geological Survey. The collection had a lot of material which overlapped with the mandates of the Museum of Nature and the Museum of Civilization; however, as luck would have it, Valerie had two excellent librarians on board who were able to appropriately split the collection.

Another challenge she faced was the Museology collection. It was a good collection that all the museums were interested in, but after much discussion, it was finally taken over by the Canadian Conservation Institute.

Other than those specific challenges, Valerie's whole year was spent trying to find placements for the staff. They were all promised they would have a place at one of the libraries; the challenge was finding a suitable position for them that would not impact their current levels and a position in which they would be interested. This was quite the task as Valerie's direct reports would have fewer staff, smaller budgets, and fewer responsibilities. This gave way to the possibility of them being "red-circled". This meant their salary would not decrease when they were transferred to a lower-paying job. However, it also would not increase until the pay levels for the lower positions caught up to their current pay.

Chapter 20 Life at the IDRC

As for Valerie, she was offered a job to manage one of the branch libraries. This would have been quite a downgrade for her, considering she had been serving as the Director of Library Services for the National Museums of Canada. She thought this might be okay for a few years since she only wanted to work for three more years until she was 60. However, Valerie knew the Museum Director and knew right away this was not the place for her. So, she started looking for other opportunities within the federal government.

Valerie came across a few jobs that piqued her interest. She was called for panel interviews for two jobs, with only a week between them. It was quite an experience for Valerie as she had not done a panel interview in ten years. In fact, in the past ten years, she had been on the panel conducting the interview, not the one being interviewed!

Of the two jobs she applied for, one was for the Research Group for the Department of Defence and the other was for the Associate Director in the Information Sciences Division at the International Development Research Centre (IDRC).

Valerie was offered a three-year contract with the IDRC, which she readily accepted. As it turned out, one of the people who had interviewed her was her previous boss, Martha Stone, who she worked for at Health and Welfare. At IDRC there was a main library in Ottawa and six branch libraries around the world in Colombia, Egypt, Kenya, Senegal, India, and Singapore. Perhaps, one of the biggest advantages of this new job was that her office in the main library was an easy walk from Park Square, which meant Valerie walked to work.

1988 – Valerie in her office at IDRC – Ottawa, Ontario, Canada

Ivan Head was the President of the IDRC. He was a very active individual, full of energy, and he expected his staff to keep up and match his enthusiasm. The job at IDRC was very busy, and Valerie worked 50 hours a week, focusing on automating the procedures in all the libraries.

In 1983, the World Commission on Environment Development (WCED, also known as the Brundtland Commission) was set up by the United Nations under the leadership of Gro Brundtland. In 1987, the Commission produced its report, *Our Common Future* (also known as the Brundtland report), which focused on sustainable development. Once the report was published, the commission was dissolved, and its papers ended up in the IDRC library.

Chapter 20 Life at the IDRC

In her personal life, Valerie was delighted to hear that Lyne was pregnant again in the Fall of 1987 after having lost her twin babies the year before. On April 26, 1988, Lyne gave birth to Valerie's third grandson, Joseph Frederick. Both Valerie and Ben went to Toronto to see their new grandson.

For the July 1st weekend in 1988, Peter, Lyne, and Joe came to Ottawa to visit Valerie and Ben. This would be the first of what would be many trips to Ottawa for Joe in the years to come. Peter and Lyne left at about 3 a.m. in hopes of avoiding holiday traffic and the July heat during the drive. They also had their fingers crossed that Joe would sleep for most of the trip (which he did). When they finally reached Ottawa, they handed Joe over to Valerie and Ben and proceeded to take a nap.

That year, Valerie and Ben had a two-week vacation in Vancouver, visiting Nick and Pat after Valerie left National Museums and before she started her role at IDRC.

Part of Valerie's job at the IDRC was to visit the six branch libraries. In November of 1988, Valerie visited the libraries in Delhi, India, and Singapore. Once again, Valerie got to travel around the world, but this time, it was by plane and in business class. During her trip to Singapore, she visited the Singapore Botanical Gardens, which she had last seen in 1937 as a girl on the way from Japan to England. It was a pleasant trip that brought back many memories.

In January of 1989, after spending a few weeks in Florida, Valerie travelled to Bogota, Colombia, to visit the IDRC office. In March, she went on her second big trip visiting the IDRC office in Cairo, Egypt, where she attended a meeting at the foot of the pyramids, an astounding experience. Ben accompanied Valerie on this trip and kept himself busy going sightseeing every day while Valerie was working.

1989 – Valerie – Egypt

After Cairo, Valerie and Ben flew to Harare, Zimbabwe, to visit Ben's Henderson relatives, in particular cousin Michael Henderson who had attended their wedding as well as Duncan's. They had a wonderful trip. Michael and his wife, Pippa, drove Valerie and Ben to see Victoria Falls, Hwange Game Park and travelled the length of Lake Kariba by car ferry. When they returned to Harare, Michael invited Ben's three other cousins and their families to his farm for a buffet lunch. The trip ended with a visit to the office in Nairobi, Kenya. Ben went to a game park while Valerie was working.

Chapter 20 Life at the IDRC

1989 – Valerie and Michael Henderson – Zimbabwe

That year, Valerie's cousin Brian came to visit them from Scotland for a weekend while he was in North America on a business trip. The last time Valerie saw Brian was back in 1964 when he was 16, so it was a much overdue reunion.

In 1989, Valerie and Ben welcomed yet another new addition to the family—a personal computer. Although Valerie used a computer at work, it was a new and different experience having one at home. There were some frustrations finding her way around it, but Duncan and Peter were very generous in providing technical support. Over time, the home computer became integrated into Valerie's life as she began to use it for sending emails, typing letters, tracking finances, using Skype, and playing FreeCell in her leisure time.

1990 – Andrew, Joe, and Devon – Ottawa, Ontario, Canada (Valerie's favourite picture and was on her desk)

In 1990, Valerie was asked to take on a consulting assignment with IDRC to help the International Red Cross. The IDRC had sponsored a professor to work on a special assignment in Geneva and he was appalled by the state of the library, leading him to advocate for improvements.

Valerie went to Geneva for a couple of weeks to interview staff members and review the situation. She prepared a report that was well received. Then she was asked if she could write an additional report on the Archives. However, at this juncture, Valerie needed time to consider what she wanted to do next. She was not familiar with Archives operations, and she would still have to run the IDRC library. After three years working at IDRC, she was feeling burnt out, particularly following three months straight of working long days to finish the report. Upon some reflection, Valerie decided it was time to retire. Her parents needed more support, she had three grandchildren to enjoy, and she and Ben had plans for their retirement. And so, in December of 1990, Valerie retired from IDRC.

1990 – Retirement Day with Peter and Duncan – Ottawa, Ontario, Canada

Chapter 21
Retirement Life

1991 to 1999

1997 – View from the House – Ottawa, Ontario, Canada

After almost three decades of work, Valerie retired and was ready to sit back and relax. When she retired, one of the things she decided to do was to look up some family history. She started working on this about half a day a week. Initially, none of the information (census, births, deaths, and marriages) was available online, so Valerie spent a lot of time at the Ottawa Stake Family History Centre (at the Church of Latter-day Saints) in Ottawa, going through those records on microfiche. She would then record the information in the Personal Ancestry File application on her computer.

As she spent more time researching the family history, she learned about the newly formed British Isles Family History Society of Greater Ottawa (BIFHSGO) and started to volunteer for the organisation to help them with their book sales and welcome desk. At the time, the BIFHSGO meetings were initially held at the Legion on Kent St. near Park Square and, later, at The National Library of Canada which was just two blocks from Park Square.

A few years after Valerie and Ben bought the cottage in 1971, Ben noticed a 'For Sale' sign on a vacant lot four doors from the cottage. They decided to buy it and figure out what to do with it once they retired. That time had come.

Every year, Peter and Duncan, with their families, would visit the cottage once or twice. However, due to space constraints at the cottage, Valerie and Ben would have to stay at Park Square during these visits, but this meant they were not close to their grandchildren. Once Ben retired, he knew what to do with the empty lot: build a house on it! This way, they could stay near the cottage and visit with Peter and Duncan and their families when they were there. Additionally, the cottage was not built for colder weather. By building a house on the lot, they could ensure that it was a three-season home suitable for residence from May to October.

In late 1990, Valerie and Ben bought a three-bedroom house and moved it to the lot. The house needed some work, so a contractor was hired to build the foundation to set the house on, replace the roof, move some doors and windows, and enclose the porch. They removed one of the bedrooms to make a front entrance and added larger windows to overlook the river. They also had some kitchen cabinets made and purchased a new sink for the kitchen. They finished off the master bedroom and bathroom, with lots of help from Duncan.

1997 – House on the Ottawa River – Ottawa, Ontario, Canada

On April 7, 1991, Lyne gave birth to a beautiful baby girl, the first in the family. After many wonderful grandsons, Valerie and Ben, and the whole family for that matter, were excited beyond measure at the arrival of their first granddaughter, Michelle Kathleen.

Michelle was born at 2 a.m. EST, during the transition to daylight savings time. After sorting things out at the hospital to make sure that mother and baby were fine, Peter called his parents to tell them about the big news at 6 a.m. EDT.

Although the call had woken Valerie and Ben from their sleep, they just could not seem to go back to sleep after hearing the news. So, they got up, got dressed and drove down to

Toronto to meet their granddaughter and see if they could be of any help.

Lyne had to have a minor medical procedure after the birth. So, while Lyne was in surgery, Valerie was left in charge of Michelle, who was just a few hours old at that time. Shortly after Michelle's birth, Peter had to present at a conference in San Jose. So, while Peter was away, Valerie stayed in Toronto to help Lyne — mostly taking care of Joe — allowing Lyne to focus on Michelle.

Valerie and Ben used to visit Toronto once or twice a year to spend time with Peter, Lyne, and Joe. Following Michelle's arrival, they planned to visit Toronto a couple more times a year to spend time with their grandchildren. Peter and Lyne also travelled to Ottawa a few times to visit Valerie and Ben as well as Lyne's parents.

1991 – Valerie with Michelle – Ottawa, Ontario, Canada

Chapter 21 Retirement Life

Most of the trips to Toronto were uneventful, simply family spending quality time together. However, Valerie remembered one trip to Toronto that was anything but uneventful. Once, before Joe was born, Valerie and Ben drove to Toronto to visit Peter and Lyne on November 11 which was Remembrance Day. In 1991, it fell on a Friday, making it a long weekend. As Ben was driving on Highway 7 (a two-lane highway), a tire came off a tractor-trailer and started rolling down the middle of their lane. There was nothing Ben could do; the tire hit the car. Luckily, the couple was not injured but the same could not be said about the car. It was left in no condition to be driven and the two were stranded in the middle of nowhere. Valerie and Ben managed to get back to Ottawa as the car was towed to a repair shop.

Now that Valerie had also retired, she and Ben could finally see their retirement plans through. The framework had been decided years earlier: the winters would be spent in Florida near the ocean and away from the snow and cold of Ottawa while the summers would be spent at the cottage on the Ottawa River. Now, it was time to implement the plan—but it was not so easy.

By the late 1980s, it became apparent that Valerie's parents needed more support, leading Valerie to travel to Florida a couple of times a year to help them out as needed. Valerie and Ben had thought of living in one of the units in Satellite Beach during the winter, but because they were rentals for the full year and Valerie's parents lived in John Knox Village, which was a 90-minute drive away, they decided to rent a place closer to John Knox Village.

Valerie and Ben managed to find a suitable ground-floor apartment in the Edgewater Condominiums of Enterprise, Deltona, Florida, only about 20 minutes from John Knox Village. The complex had three swimming pools, was across the road from Lake Monroe, had nice walking paths and had plenty of stores nearby for daily necessities.

In 1991, the couple went down to the condo for a month to check it out and did not want to come back to Canada. As they settled into life in Enterprise, Florida, they met three other couples who were snowbirds. One couple was from Minnesota and, coincidentally, the other two were from Ottawa! They enjoyed a nice and happening social life thanks to their new friends. Compared to their previous trips to Florida, when they would find something to do on their own, they now had companions to go out for lunch with, go to the local theatre or other events.

Every Friday, the four couples took turns hosting drinks. Valerie and Ben also discovered that they could participate in community programs and classes offered by the local school. One winter, they signed up for a computer course. Ben also signed up for a woodworking course. He did not really need to join the course since he was already very skilled at making things. However, he just wanted access to the tools that came with the course.

In fact, during that time, he had several ongoing projects, such as making small rocking chairs for the grandchildren, a doll house and barn for Michelle and two grandmother clocks for Peter and Duncan. Work on all of these projects continued in Ottawa.

Valerie and Ben's presence in Florida served as a great attraction for Peter and Duncan, who made numerous trips to visit them. The apartment was small; it only had two bedrooms. However, they also had a pull-out couch, enabling them to accommodate Peter and Duncan's families for short visits, at separate times.

Apart from their time in Florida, Valerie and Ben continued to travel and visit family. In the summer of 1991, they drove to Maine to visit David and his family. It was the first time in 17 years that they had been to his house in Orono. In August of that year, they flew to Vancouver to visit Nick and Pat and went to Victoria to visit friends. In October, they drove to visit Diana, enjoying the fall colours in Vermont. It was safe to say that they had been very busy since Valerie retired!

In May of 1992, Valerie and Ben flew to England for a month, where they stayed at the house of Valerie's friend Ginny and her husband Mike. They travelled to visit Eversley, the boarding school Valerie attended in 1946. Valerie also visited her cousins Brenda, Bill, and Barbara, whom she barely knew. The trip ended with them travelling to Scotland to visit Brian and his family.

The following year, 1993, Brian and his family came to Canada for their summer vacation and spent time at the cottage before going to the Rocky Mountains. In the fall, Janie, the daughter of one of Ben's first cousins, came to visit from Zimbabwe.

1993 – Kitty, Michelle, and Valerie – Orange City, Florida, USA

1993 – Valerie's favourite picture of Joe and Michelle – Toronto, Ontario, Canada

For Christmas 1993, Ben had a special surprise Christmas present, a star! Ben arranged for star Camelopardalis RA 3h 26m 36s 61°11' to be redesignated to Valerie Sanger Monkhouse (starregistry.com/).

Certificate from International Star Registry

As Valerie and Ben got older, they also faced some health problems. Valerie had good health for most of her life, and the last time anything major had occurred in her life in terms of health was when she had her appendix removed in 1945. In 1994, however, while in Florida, she was not feeling well. When she returned to Ottawa, she underwent some tests which revealed that she had gallstones. She had laparoscopic surgery to remove her gallbladder. Valerie also had shingles in her 60s.

In 1994, Valerie and Ben decided to build a two-car garage onto the house, which was finished in 1995. Now, all the pieces of the puzzle were in place for them to enjoy their retirement together. They would spend three months in Deltona, Florida, stay in Park Square until mid-May, and then go out to the house on the Ottawa River until Thanksgiving in October. Afterwards, they would return to Park Square until the end of December. They continued this routine until 2008.

1995 – 65th birthday celebration with Devon, Andrew, Joe, Michelle, and Peter at the Cottage – Ottawa, Ontario, Canada

There was a covered area behind the garage that overlooked the river. This was a great space where they would sit and admire the river, eat lunch and dinner, and hold family gatherings. However, the beach was not great, so for swimming, it was back to the cottage.

Valerie's Journeys

One of the many things Valerie enjoyed about the house was being able to indulge her gardening hobby again. Since leaving Micmac Street, they did not have a garden. Now, living at the house, she could start a small vegetable garden, growing tomatoes, squash, spinach, beets, carrots, potatoes, and cucumbers. The rabbits and deer soon got wind of it and helped themselves to Valerie's garden. This started a twenty-year battle between Valerie and the animals.

In 1995, Valerie's cousin Brenda and her husband Nick visited during their trip to Canada. In 1996, Kitty fell and broke her hip. She had to rest for quite some time after that and since she was the main support for Valerie's aging father, this meant that both parents needed someone to look after them. It was obvious to Valerie and her siblings that their parents could not live independently, so they were moved to an assisted living unit within the John Knox complex.

In August of 1996, Valerie and Ben drove to Nova Scotia to visit Cape Breton Island, where they drove the Cabot Trail and visited Louisburg. They then drove to Grand Manan, in New Brunswick, where they met up with David and Mary Jo.

Valerie and Ben took another trip to Vancouver to visit Nick and Pat in May of 1997. On this trip, they went to Beaver Cove, where Ben had had a summer job working in a logging camp back in 1951. Ben was shocked to see the site being turned into condos.

Among the things that brought Valerie and Ben immense joy, aside from spending time with their children and grandchildren, was watching their sons advance in their careers.

Peter initially started working for Bell Canada in their engineering department. Bell would transfer Peter to different departments, unrelated to engineering, every few years. Eventually, Peter got frustrated with the bureaucracy of a large organisation and, in 1986, decided to join a USA based start-up software company, Telic. Unfortunately, Bell eventually partnered with Telic to create Bell-Telic and Peter was back working at Bell, this time in its IT division.

Peter joined the Project Management Institute (PMI) in 1996 and started volunteering for the local chapter. Valerie was pleased to see Peter had found a professional organisation as she knew the value of networking through her volunteer work with the Library and Museums Associations.

In 1997, Peter joined Saville Systems, a Canadian company. Saville was bought by ADC, an American company that sold the Saville division to Intec, a UK company. While at ADC/Intec, Peter started travelling and had trips to Australia, Brazil, South Africa, Ireland, and the USA.

After Duncan and Shirley's children were born, Duncan got tired of the long hours that his work at Versaterm System entailed and left, in 1987, to join the federal government as an employee with the Royal Canadian Mounted Police, initially as a computer programmer, then changing to computer forensics. In 2001, he transferred to the Competition Bureau. In 2001, when the local chapter of the High Technology Crime Investigation Association was formed, Duncan joined and was soon involved at the executive level both locally and internationally.

1998 began with Valerie and Ben attending the wedding of David's youngest daughter, Stephanie, on April 11th in Savannah, Georgia.

Kitty's health was slowly deteriorating, and she sadly passed away on May 8, 1998. It was a big loss for the family. Valerie was already in Florida at the time so she could be with her mother. Peter also happened to be in Orlando for business at the time and headed to John Knox once he heard the news.

In August of 1998, Valerie's family gathered at Diana's house to celebrate their mother's life. In total, twenty-six family members attended the event. In preparation for the gathering, Valerie prepared a booklet about the life her mother had lived. (Appendix D)

In 1999, they drove to Pembroke for the wedding of Ben's cousin's grandson, Matthew, Ann's son.

While Valerie was healthy for the majority of her life, Ben had a series of health issues. In 1999, his high blood pressure worsened, and he had to undergo triple bypass surgery that fall. Valerie was concerned about his health and wanted to ensure he was taking care of himself.

Life after retirement brought many changes: travelling, enjoying more family time, but also experiencing a big loss. However, Valerie accepted it was just part of life and looked forward to the future.

1995 – Valerie, David and Diana, Valerie's 65th birthday – Ottawa, Ontario, Canada

Chapter 22
The Greatest Joy

2000 to 2010

2000 – Valerie's 70th Birthday with Peter, Ben, and Duncan at the House – Ottawa, Ontario, Canada

Valerie's Journeys

After Valerie's mother passed away, her father, unable to live on his own, was moved into the nursing home wing of John Knox Village where he passed away in March of 2000. Nick and Pat happened to be visiting Valerie and Ben when her father died, providing extra support to her. It was both of Valerie's parents' wishes not to have a funeral but to be cremated instead and have their ashes scattered over the Atlantic Ocean. They arranged for this prior to their deaths and, to fulfil their wishes, which is what Valerie, and her siblings did.

Having lost both of her parents, Valerie was understandably saddened, but soon got back to doing the things she loved, she had realised the best way to honour her parents' memory was to live life to the fullest.

Even after Valerie's parents' deaths, Valerie and Ben enjoyed their life in the Edgewood Condominiums in Enterprise, Florida, with their friends and the community, and continued to rent there and only to change units once, in 2000 when they moved to the adjacent Lakeside condominiums. They were fortunate to have good landlords who only rented their units to them. This arrangement allowed them to leave some items there during the summer instead of transporting everything back to Ottawa.

Valerie and Ben would usually drive between Ottawa or Toronto and Florida as soon as the weather cleared after Christmas, always with the sole aim of arriving in Florida on January 1st. They would usually drive eight hours a day, switching the driving role every two hours. If they left from Ottawa, they would cross into the US at the Thousand Islands Bridge and head south to intersect with I-95 near Washington, D.C. If they left from Toronto, they would cross the border in Detroit and take I-75. In 2000, Valerie and Ben left early for Florida as they had invited the boys and their families to spend Christmas with them.

Valerie enjoyed the trip down, leaving winter behind and getting into warmer weather. Over the years, Valerie and

Ben found some motels they liked and would return to them every year. They also realised the necessity of a larger car, not only for a more comfortable ride but also to accommodate the numerous items they had to take both ways.

Valerie and Ben usually left Florida to return to Ottawa at the end of March. The northward journey took a bit longer as they stopped to visit places of historical interest or to visit Diana. However, they could not take too long to go north as they had doctor appointments booked and income tax forms to file by the end of April. As Michelle got older, they would return to Ottawa via Toronto to see her on her birthday, April 7th.

July 8, 2000, marked Valerie's 70th birthday. To celebrate, David, Mary Jo, Diana, and Ken came to the cottage. Unbeknownst to Valerie, Peter had arranged for Brian and his family to join them as well. Valerie was so surprised when she came over to the cottage for lunch and found Brian there!

In September of 2000, Valerie and Ben flew to Newfoundland for an eight-day trip. Then, after Thanksgiving, they headed to London, Ontario, to visit Ann, the daughter of Ben's cousin Colin, and her daughter, Julie. They also paid a visit to Tracey, Judy's daughter, another of Ben's cousins. Subsequently, they drove north to the Bruce Peninsula and took the ferry crossing to Manitoulin Island.

In 2000, Peter started teaching part time at The Chang School of Continuing Education at Ryerson University (now Toronto Metropolitan University). Valerie was thrilled to hear this news as she always thought Peter would make a great teacher. However, although exciting, this new opportunity made Peter even busier; he had a full-time job, a family, travelled for work, and volunteered at PMI.

In June of 2001, Valerie and Ben travelled around western Canada on a three-week vacation. They flew to Vancouver, where they were joined by Nick and Pat. The trip included visiting Salt Spring Island, Pender Island, Okanagan

Valley, then they travelled to Alberta to visit Head-Smashed-in Buffalo Jump, the Badlands, and the Royal Tyrrell Museum in Drumheller. After all that, they ended up in Edmonton, where Pam was living.

In September of 2001, Valerie and Ben visited David and Mary Jo in Orono, and then visited Diana and Ken in East Longmeadow.

In 2001, a frustrated Duncan left the RCMP to join the Competition Bureau, a government agency. There he worked as a computer forensic investigator until his retirement in 2017.

In the 1960s, Fred hired Cynthia Wilson, who worked at McGill, to do some research for him on the weather in northern Canada. Cynthia was only a few years older than Valerie, and, over the years, they became good friends. In 2002, Cynthia moved back to Ottawa after taking care of her parents. Valerie started picking up Cynthia when Valerie went grocery shopping. Valerie enjoyed Cynthia's company and their conversations about many things, especially tennis.

The year 2002 passed quietly with nothing very memorable happening. After a quiet year in 2002, Valerie and Ben went to Fredericton to celebrate the 50th anniversary of Ben's graduation from UNB in May of 2003. While in Fredericton, they went to Chatham to visit some of Ben's old haunts and then visited David and Mary Jo, followed by Diana and Ken.

To celebrate their 50th wedding anniversary in 2003, Valerie and Ben travelled to Europe in the fall. They visited family in England, France, and Scotland. They also saw some of the places where Ben grew up. Upon their return, they invited the family to Montebello, Quebec for Thanksgiving weekend and to celebrate their wedding anniversary.

Chapter 22 The Greatest Joy

2003 – 50th Wedding Anniversary (Andrew, Ben, Valerie, Devon, Michelle, and Joe) – Montebello, Quebec, Canada

In June of 2004, Valerie and Ben drove to Minnesota to visit their friends from Florida who lived there. The next year, they took a trip to New Brunswick, this time to St. Andrew's, where Pam now lived, and where Nick was visiting. In the fall, Ben's cousin Philippa and her husband came to visit Valerie and Ben in Ottawa. Ben had last seen Philippa 57 years earlier. Then, Valerie's cousin Barbara and her husband, Allan, came for a visit. So, 2005 was full of many long overdue reunions.

In September of 2006, Valerie and Ben visited Nick and Pat in Kamloops and drove to Tofino on Vancouver Island. On the way back to Nick's, they also visited Joe, who was at the University of British Columbia.

In 2007, Dr. Murray Watson interviewed Valerie, as part of his study on the lives of English immigrants who came to Canada after the war. Some of Valerie's story was included in the resultant book, *Invisible Immigrants: The English in Canada since 1945*, authored by Marilyn Barber and Dr. Watson, published in 2015.

In 2007, Peter's job at Intec came to an end after almost ten years. He then got a job as Program Director at the Chang School at Ryerson University. Valerie was glad that Peter had interesting jobs, but she was concerned about the constant moving around and that none of the companies offered a good pension. Now that she was retired, she realised the benefits of a pension that was indexed and wanted the same for her sons.

In 2008, Valerie and Ben embarked on another trip to the West Coast to visit Nick and Pat in Kamloops, British Columbia and their friends in Victoria.

Starting in 2007, Valerie and Ben began to find the drive to Florida to be too taxing. Over the years, they had observed people aging very well in Park Square, so they decided it was now time to spend their winters in Park Square, too. Therefore, in January of 2008, they went to Florida for three weeks to say goodbye. Once back in Ottawa for the winters, they got involved in activities, in particular, an exercise class for the elderly so they would have an excuse to get out of the building.

In 2009, Valerie travelled to Leeds with Peter to attend the wedding of Brian's son Mark. Shirley and Duncan, who were already travelling in Britain, joined them for the wedding. While in Leeds, Valerie's cousins, Barbara and Brenda, with their husbands, came to visit her.

Chapter 22 The Greatest Joy

2009 – Mark and Tola's wedding – Leeds, England

In July of 2010, Valerie and Ben travelled to Edmonton, Alberta to attend the wedding of Pam's son Nick. For Valerie's 80th birthday that year, Peter arranged for tickets to see the men's tennis quarterfinals at the Canadian Open in Toronto featuring Roger Federer in the first match and Novak Djokovic in the second match.

Duncan, while working as a computer forensic investigator, was involved with the High Technology Crime Investigation Association, both with the Ottawa Chapter and on the International Executive Committee. He went on to become the association's first non-US president in 2010. Valerie was always eager to hear about the work that Duncan was doing and assisted him in navigating the bureaucracy of the Canadian Federal Government.

Valerie and Ben absolutely adored their grandchildren and wanted very much to be an active part of their lives. As much as their health and other activities would allow, they would rearrange their schedule to be present at as many events as possible. They would travel down to Toronto for Michelle and Joe's birthdays and graduations. When in Toronto, they would stay with Peter and Lyne, which gave them a chance to see a day in the life of Joe and Michelle. Valerie felt she really got to know Joe and Michelle on these visits. With Devon and Andrew in Ottawa, it was easier for them to attend their events.

When each grandchild turned six, Valerie and Ben would treat them to a day out to visit the sights around Ottawa. As they got older, this turned into a sleepover. The sleepover usually started with a trip to the grocery store, where the grandchild was instructed to pick their favourite food. Then there was a trip to a place to sightsee. Valerie really enjoyed this time with her grandchildren and being able to spoil them.

It is often said that grandchildren are life's greatest joy, and Valerie could not have agreed more. Her grandchildren kept her occupied and made her realise just how blessed she was.

Chapter 22 The Greatest Joy

Christmas 2010 – Front row: Lyne, Valerie, Shirley, Alexandra, Back Row: Peter, Michelle, Joe, Ben, Duncan, Devon, and Andrew – Toronto, Ontario, Canada

Chapter 23
Growing Old

2011 to 2014

2013 – 60th Wedding Anniversary – Toronto, Ontario, Canada

Valerie's Journeys

The second half of 2010 was rather uneventful. After watching the Canadian Open in August, there was not much to write home about in Valerie and Ben's life. Life went on as usual, with the couple continuing their regular activities and spending time with their grandchildren.

The year 2011, however, started off on quite a devastating note. On the morning of February 17, 2011, Michelle, who was Peter and Lyne's daughter, and Valerie and Ben's only granddaughter, was in a fatal car accident north of Toronto.

Being the only girl in the family, Michelle was dearly loved by all, and it was very hard to process and accept her sudden and untimely passing for everyone. The next day, Duncan and Shirley drove Valerie and Ben to Toronto, where they stayed for a week to support Peter, Lyne, and Joe in any way they could. Valerie never said very much about Michelle, but she missed her dearly.

In October of 2011, Ben's cousin Philippa and her husband came to visit them, and they all went to Montebello for the weekend. The last time they saw them was back in 2004, so it was a great reunion.

In 2011, Devon married his long-time girlfriend, Alexandra LeBlanc. The two had met when they were in grade 9. They both attended Carleton University and after they graduated, Alex continued her training as an opera singer at the Glenn Gould School of Music in Toronto. Valerie had enjoyed going to Alex's Ottawa performances. On October 9, 2011, Devon and Alex were married in Ottawa on a beautiful, warm day. Nick, Pat, Pam, and Neale were also able to attend the celebration, and it was a wonderful day.

Devon and Alex now live in Toronto with Devon working as a real estate agent and involved in local politics. Alex pursued her music career and started working for the Toronto Symphony Orchestra in 2018.

Chapter 23 Growing Old

Joe graduated from Ryerson University (now Toronto Metropolitan University) in the Fall of 2011 and started working in Toronto, initially in part-time jobs then after a few years settled into a professional career in the paint industry, and in 2012, he met his partner Florencia Esteverena, a schoolteacher, and her son, Joaquin.

As mentioned before, Peter had been volunteering at the Project Management Institute's (PMI) local chapter since 1996. He was elected to the PMI Global Board of Directors in 2008 and by 2012, he was the Chair of the Board. One of the perks of being on the PMI Board was that Peter had the opportunity to travel a lot. Valerie was particularly interested when he managed to arrange a trip to New Plymouth, New Zealand. By a stroke of luck, he was able to visit the house on 16 Somerset Street, where she had lived so long ago, and brought back pictures for her. On another trip, Peter went to Shanghai and found the location of some of the places Valerie had lived. However, most of the buildings were gone by then.

After graduating from Carleton University, Andrew enrolled in the law program at Osgoode Hall in Toronto, the top law school in Canada, in the fall of 2009. He was part of the Osgoode Mooting Team and participated in a mooting (simulated court, legal debating) competition in Vienna in March of 2011, where he met Alexandra Neacsu. She was from Romania and doing her Master's in Paris. They fell in love and were married in Toronto on March 10, 2012, and Valerie and Ben went to Toronto to attend the wedding and stay with Peter. Valerie's cousin, Brian, and his wife, Margaret, also joined them. In July of 2012, Andrew and Alexandra had another wedding in Romania, so that Alexandra's friends and family members could join the celebration. Valerie, however, left the attendance of that wedding event for Peter, Duncan, and their families.

While 2012 was filled with exciting events, it also revealed some hard-to-swallow revelations—that Valerie and Ben were getting older, and their best days were behind them.

In 2012, it became increasingly clear to them both that it was time for a change. They were finding it increasingly difficult to cope with everyday life in Park Square. For a few years, Duncan had been dropping by every week to help them with odd jobs around the house. Valerie also grew concerned about Ben driving due to his health, while her confidence in driving lessened. They realised it was time to transition to the next stage of their lives.

Ben's health was slowly declining. He now had to use supplemental oxygen, then needed a walker, to move around, which further limited his mobility. Valerie also found it difficult to go shopping, especially in winter. Besides their physical limitations, it was becoming harder to visit with friends. Some had already passed away, and many no longer drove. Ben was increasingly frustrated with being in Park Square all the time. In his words, he felt like a "caged lion."

Valerie and Ben had seen their parents and many of their friends grow old and both of them had definite ideas of what they wanted their lives to be like in their old age. Both their parents had lived far away from their family in their last years. This made it very difficult for Valerie and Ben to support them, so they were determined to be in close proximity to their family.

However, Valerie was adamant about not living with her sons. Em had lived with them for five years, during which Valerie had to take care of her along with her own family. Consequently, she did not want to burden her daughters-in-law with the same responsibilities.

Valerie and Ben also did not want to move into a nursing home. Valerie's father had spent his last two years in the nursing home wing of John Knox Village in a room with another man, and very little privacy. When Em, Ben's mother, came to Ottawa after Flump died, she spent a year in a nursing home while the addition was being built on the Micmac Street house. Valerie did not like the idea of spending her final days in a nursing home.

The last thing Valerie and Ben realised while thinking of all these things was how simple it was to settle Valerie's parents' estate because they did not own any property. They had seen the challenges their friends faced when their parents passed away, and they had to sell their property. In addition, Valerie and Ben were very concerned about the possibility that one of them would have to go into a nursing home—not just the cost but also the challenge of seeing each other. They had spent almost six decades together and could not imagine staying apart for very long.

Over the previous few years, Valerie and Ben had been developing a plan to address all their thoughts and wishes. In fact, their plans had been set in motion almost two decades before. In the 1990s, they had done two things to make life easier. First, they sold the cottage to their sons for a dollar and love. Peter and Duncan enjoyed visiting the cottage with their families. This move allowed Valerie and Ben to continue enjoying the cottage too without having to worry about its maintenance and other things. Second, they got Peter and Duncan involved in the management of the properties in Florida. By the end of 2012, they had decided it was now time to implement the plan fully.

For Christmas of 2012, Peter and Lyne came up to Ottawa. Since Peter had just finished his term as Chair of the PMI Board of Directors, he had more available time. Valerie and Ben took this opportunity to discuss their plans with Peter and Duncan. It was time to sell the apartment in Park Square and move into a retirement home in Toronto.

At the beginning of 2013, Valerie and Ben started getting their finances in order. First of all, they had to decide what to do with the house on the river. Neither of their sons wanted it, so they put it up for sale.

Luckily, it sold quickly. Valerie and Ben gave the proceeds of the sale to Peter and Duncan, which allowed

Duncan to buy out Peter's share of the cottage, to receive money and enabled Peter to own the properties in Florida.

In 2013, Andrew completed articling and was called to the bar. However, he decided that instead of working for a law firm, he would start his own, hence Monkhouse Law was created. This was a great source of pride for Valerie.

On March 19, 2013, Alexandra gave birth to Valerie and Ben's first great-grandchild, a baby girl, Maria Cristina Valerie. In addition, Alexandra was also accepted into Osgoode Law School and later joined Andrew at Monkhouse Law.

For their 60th wedding anniversary in 2013, Valerie and Ben decided to celebrate in Toronto. They booked three nights in the Old Mill and invited the whole family there for an anniversary dinner. A few days later, on October 14, Peter and Lyne invited everyone to their house for Thanksgiving dinner. It was a great weekend and a memorable visit.

Valerie and Ben travelled to Toronto a few times in 2013. They used to drive to Toronto, but driving had now become a difficult task for both of them, so they opted to travel by air. They started flying on Porter Airlines, which flew small turboprop planes to the Toronto Island Airport, which is a small airport in downtown Toronto. Peter could drive to meet them at the airport. It involved a ferry ride to and from the airport to "mainland" Toronto, and it was nice to see the Toronto skyline while flying in.

While in Toronto, they visited two retirement homes, both about a 10-minute walk from Peter and Lyne's house. They settled on Delmanor Northtown. It was fairly new, with the building having been constructed only five years earlier. The home consisted of an eight-story building with a rooftop terrace. They also had a nurse on duty seven days a week, 24 hours a day, which Valerie felt was important. In addition, they had a doctor who came around weekly and also a hairdresser. One of the things Kitty did when she went to John Knox Village was to have her hair done every week at the hair salon. Valerie wanted to do the same thing and, with the hairdresser in the building, she could do just that.

Regrettably, the building was full at the time of their decision, so they added their names to the waiting list to await a unit becoming available. They had their eyes set on a two-bedroom unit with two bathrooms at the end of the hall. It also had a small kitchen with a fridge and a microwave, but no stove. There was a living room that had enough room for a television and chairs. For their meals, they would go down to a nice dining room on the main floor.

In March of 2014, Valerie and Ben were notified that a unit on the fourth floor was available at Delmanor in April. Peter came to Ottawa and with Duncan, assisted them in deciding what furniture they would take with them to Toronto and what they would leave behind.

The furniture going to Duncan was moved to his Ottawa house, while the furniture meant for Peter was moved to Toronto. A few days before they moved into Delmanor, Valerie and Ben flew to Toronto and spent some time with Peter and Lyne. During that time, the movers arrived at their home in Ottawa, and Duncan instructed them on what to take and where it was going. At the other end, when the movers arrived, Peter worked to have the furniture placed correctly. Valerie was pleased with the way things worked out, but it was strange not to be as involved in the process as she once would have been.

On April 15, 2014, Valerie and Ben officially took up residence in Delmanor. Afterwards, Park Square was put up for sale. The market was tough, but the property eventually sold in the fall of 2014. In fact, it was the only unit in Park Square to sell that year. Valerie and Ben had now achieved two of their goals: no property and living in a retirement home.

2013 – Valerie and Maria – Toronto, Ontario, Canada

Chapter 24
Final Days

2015 to 2022

2019 – Valerie – BIFHSGO Meeting – Ottawa, Ontario, Canada

Valerie's Journeys

Slowly but surely, Valerie and Ben settled into their new life at Delmanor. They had settled into a routine that they quite enjoyed, starting their day with breakfast in their suite while reading the newspaper and solving crossword puzzles. After years of getting up early and rushing off to work, Valerie and Ben refused to get dressed before breakfast and be rushed any longer. They were retired now and wanted to enjoy a carefree life after decades of working and building a life together—they deserved it.

So, they opted to arrange their own breakfast in their own time rather than go downstairs to pick up what Delmanor offered, they would then head down for lunch later and return when it was time for Ben's nap. In the afternoon, they had tea and then went down again for dinner.

The couple would usually talk or Skype with family in the evenings. Ben had a regular weekly Skype session with Nick, and Valerie would have weekly conversations with her sister Diana and the occasional call with her brother David.

Delmanor was a block away from the Metro grocery store. Once or twice a week, Valerie would walk to Metro to buy food for breakfast and other treats that Delmanor did not have. Valerie and Ben always enjoyed doing jigsaw puzzles and they would be always working on one at any given time. They had often had one set up at the cottage, and it was no different here. Luckily, Delmanor had a considerable supply of jigsaw puzzles that they could borrow. Valerie would also have a book of Sudoku and crossword puzzles that she would work on while the television was on or as a break from reading The Economist or a book.

There was always some kind of program going on at Delmanor and it also had a shuttle bus that made a variety of trips which Valerie and Ben could sign up for. Some of the trips were to the local shopping malls, but others were to some of the sites in Toronto. One of the more memorable trips Valerie and Ben enjoyed was to the Aga Khan Museum. In addition to that, Valerie also attended some concerts in downtown Toronto with some of the other women.

The three grandsons, all living in Toronto, would visit Valerie and Ben and occasionally take them out for a meal. In addition, Peter and Lyne would take them to their house for meals and family events such as birthdays, Thanksgiving, Easter, and Christmas.

One of the projects Valerie got really involved in at Delmanor was to straighten up the library. Delmanor had a small library where people would donate books. It was a mess and Valerie decided it needed to be organised. She approached the Director of Delmanor, and he agreed to her proposal. Valerie asked for volunteers and formed a small group to work on organising the books and keeping them that way.

In 2014, Nick and Pat came to visit twice. The year 2015 was a year of many family visits. That year, Diana and her husband Ken came to visit along with Nick's son and daughter, Pam and Neale, Valerie's nephew Doug and his family, and Ben's cousin Ann. The next year, in 2016, Valerie's brother David and his wife Mary Jo also came to visit. For Nick and Pat, Diana and Ken, and David and Mary Jo, Valerie was able to arrange accommodation for them at Delmanor.

On September 17, 2016, Ben had a serious stroke while having lunch at Delmanor. Duncan rushed to Toronto from Vancouver where he was working. Ben fought hard, but the damage was too severe, and in the early morning hours of September 29, Peter got the call from the hospital saying it was time. By the time the family got to the hospital, Ben had passed away.

Valerie and Ben were prepared for all eventualities. They completed powers of attorney and living wills and made sure Peter and Duncan had a copy and knew their wishes. They had purchased a plot in Beechwood Cemetery in Ottawa where they could both be buried and paid for the burial. Finally, they had clearly indicated there was to be no service.

Valerie's Journeys

After Ben's death, arrangements were made to transport his body to Ottawa to be buried at Beechwood. Peter and Lyne drove Valerie up to Ottawa. While there, Valerie saw some of her old friends.

Valerie had known Ben for 66 years and had been married to him for 63; she missed him dearly. However, she was so pleased to see how smoothly everything went according to plan because of the efficient teamwork of her sons, Peter and Duncan.

After Ben's death, Valerie continued to live in Delmanor in the same suite. She got used to her new routine. She continued to have breakfast in her suite, while reading the newspaper, and doing the crossword and Sudoku puzzles. The other residents at Delmanor were very supportive and Peter and Lyne dropped in once or twice a week to check on her. In addition, Valerie took over Ben's Skype calls with Nick, and continued to keep in touch with David and Diana.

The fall of 2016 included of visits by Brian and his wife Margaret, Valerie's niece Pam, nephew Neale and several more visits from Duncan and her grandsons. And of course, there was always a jigsaw puzzle on the go.

In 2017, Valerie realised that she was strong and could still travel. So, in April, she travelled to Vancouver to visit Nick, Pat, Pam, Neale, and some of her friends. In July, Peter and Lyne drove her to Ottawa to visit her friends there. Valerie also visited her grandsons' homes and enjoyed seeing where they lived. On November 21, Andrew and Alexandra welcomed their second child and Valerie's second great-grandchild, this time a boy they named John Paul Alexander.

In April of 2018, Duncan took Valerie to St. Augustine, Florida, to visit David and Mary Jo. After a long and successful career at the University of Maine, David decided to retire to Florida near his youngest daughter Stephanie and her family. The visit to David was followed by a trip with Peter to East Longmeadow, Massachusetts, to visit Diana and Ken. While there, Valerie also attended the wedding of Diana's grandson, Adam. Valerie enjoyed visiting her siblings, seeing where they lived and visiting their families.

In June of 2019, Peter and Lyne drove Valerie to Ottawa to visit friends and celebrate the 25th anniversary of the British Isles Family History Society of Greater Ottawa (BIFHSGO), where she volunteered and was member, member number 14, one of the earliest members. Valerie was pleased to see how BIFHSGO had grown and was very proud to see her son, Duncan, in action as President of the organisation.

In October of 2019, she travelled to Vancouver with Duncan to visit Nick, Pam, and Neale.

In early 2019, Valerie began to think that the two-bed apartment was too big for her. With Ben gone, she had changed his room to house the television and computer and she was not using the living room anymore. So, she asked about moving into a smaller unit to save some money and to be closer to the elevator. In December, a one-bedroom apartment with a small den became available on the third floor. She decided to take it and move in at year's end. The unit was just perfect, although the bathroom was a little further from the bed than she would have liked.

There were also a couple of women on the third floor who provided good company to Valerie. One of the women, Ann, was known as her twin as they were both born on July 8, 1930.

The year 2020 was a year of expectations of seeing family, as it was going to be Valerie's 90th birthday that year. Unfortunately, this all changed in March when the COVID-19 pandemic set in. Delmanor was very aware of the risk to the residents' health and the building went into lockdown. This meant that Valerie was confined to her unit. She could not even go to the dining room; meals were delivered to her suite.

It felt like her life had come to a sudden halt—which it

had, not only for her but the whole world. She could not go to Metro. Instead, Peter or Lyne would drop food off at the front door for delivery to her suite and, worst of all, the hairdresser could not come into the building! Her whole routine was disturbed.

Nonetheless, with her family's support, Valerie managed to keep herself busy. She talked to Nick on Monday and Thursday evenings, Joe and Florencia on Tuesday, Diana on Wednesday, her friend Cynthia from Ottawa every second Friday, Devon on Saturday, Duncan, and Lyne on Sunday. She also talked to David, Brian, and Andrew. Peter would call her frequently during the week and when he came over to drop off the food, he would make sure to let her know in advance so they could wave through the glass.

After going through the worst of COVID-19, the restrictions were relaxed a little but not enough to have a big family gathering. So, for Valerie's 90th birthday, she went to Peter and Lyne's house for a celebration and joined the rest of the family on a Zoom call.

During this time, Delmanor added Peter, Lyne, and Duncan to their essential caregiver list allowing them to visit Valerie in her suite. Valerie was very grateful that she could finally have visitors in her suite.

In the summer of 2021, many of the restrictions were removed and Valerie was free to travel again. When Duncan retired in 2017, he started planning to replace the cottage with a permanent house for himself and Shirley. Work started in 2019 and was finished to the point where they could move in by January of 2021. Valerie had heard all about it and had seen pictures but wanted to see the house in person. Thus, her first trip was to Ottawa, to see Duncan's new house.

In July, Peter and Lyne drove Valerie up to Ottawa where she stayed with Duncan for two days. The time spent there was wonderful. The house had a porch where Valerie could sit and look up the Ottawa River. It was so nice and peaceful that she did not want to leave.

Valerie was also able to visit her grandsons and their families in their homes in Toronto, which she thoroughly enjoyed.

2021 – Valerie visiting Maria and John – Toronto, Ontario, Canada

Valerie's health had been gradually deteriorating during COVID-19 pandemic. In August, during a Skype call with Nick, and he felt she was not well, Nick called Peter, Peter called Delmanor, and the nurse went to check on her. The nurse decided she should go to the hospital. After a week in the hospital, Valerie had recovered, and she was sent home. She continued to get better but was still not strong enough to walk to Metro.

There was another scare and another visit to the hospital in February of 2022 and, once again, after a week Valerie was sent home. This time, it took a while for her to get her strength back. By Wednesday, March 23, Valerie was finally feeling better. Peter had come over for a nice visit in the morning to work on Chapter 9 of this book and she planned to go to the dining room for dinner for the first time in six weeks.

2021 – Family Christmas with Lyne, Valerie, Duncan, John, Alexandra, Peter, Maria, Florencia, and Joe (missing Shirley, Devon, Andrew, Alexandra, and Joaquin)– Toronto, Ontario, Canada

Valerie talked to David in the afternoon and went to dinner. When she got back from dinner, she spoke with Diana, mentioning that she did not feel well. She called the nurse who suggested she should go to the hospital. Lyne went to the hospital to accompany her, staying with her for the night and into Thursday. There were still restrictions on the number of visitors she could have and the duration of their stays.

Peter planned to go over mid-Friday afternoon. The doctor called at noon to say Valerie had taken a turn for the worse. Peter headed right over to the hospital. However, it was clear at that point that Valerie was not going to make it.

Peter got Duncan on the phone with the Palliative Care doctor and the decision was made to invoke her living will. Duncan made arrangements to come to Toronto and the grandsons were called. At approximately 6:30 pm on Friday, March 25, 2022, Valerie breathed her last breath with Joe and

Florencia by her side.

On Saturday, April 16, 2022, Valerie was laid to rest in Beechwood Cemetery with her husband. All her family was in attendance, and there was a small celebration of her life after the burial.

Valerie achieved her end-of-life goals. She lived independently, avoided nursing home care, and didn't move in with either of her daughters-in-law. She left behind a clear estate that provided financial security, cherished memories, and inspiring guidance for her family on their journeys.

2021 – Valerie visiting Peter – Toronto, Ontario, Canada

Appendix A
Valerie's Ships

SS Rajputana[10]

A Peninsular and Oriental Steam Navigation Company (P&O) ship built by Harland & Wolff in Belfast in 1926. The ship weighed 16,568 tons, measured 547 x 71 feet, and carried 600 passengers. Named after the Rajputana region of western India, she sailed on a regular route between England and British India. During WWII, she patrolled as an armed merchant cruiser in the Denmark Strait before she was sunk by the German submarine U-108.

Valerie sailed on this ship with Kitty, departing from Southampton, England on December 22, 1934, to Shanghai, China.

---

10 https://en.wikipedia.org/wiki/SS_Rajputana#/media/File:SS_Rajputana,_color.jpg

SS Comorin[11]

A P&O liner of 15,132 tons, 524' by 70' and built by Barclay Curle & Co. in Glasgow in 1925. She carried 320 passengers. (On April 6, 1941, she sank after suffering a fire in the North Atlantic while serving as an armed merchant cruiser).

Valerie sailed in the ship with Kitty and David from Japan in October 1937, joined by Fred in Hong Kong disembarking in Marseilles, France.

11 https://www.google.com/search?q=SS+Comorin&rlz=1C1CHBF_enCA925CA925&oq=SS+Comorin&aqs=chrome..69i57j0i390l4.12642j0j7&sourceid=chrome&ie=UTF-8

Appendix A Valerie's Ships

SS Rawalpindi[12]

A P&O liner built in 1926 at the end of September. The ship was 16,619 tons, 547' by 71', and was constructed by Harland & Wolff in Greenock. She carried 600 passengers. (On November 23, 1939, while serving as an armed merchant cruiser, SS Rawalpindi was sunk in an engagement with the German battleship Scharnhorst, which was patrolling in the Iceland-Faroes gap).

Valerie sailed on this ship with Kitty, David and Diana, departing from Southampton, England on September 24, 1938, for Shanghai, China.

---

[12] https://en.wikipedia.org/wiki/HMS_Rawalpindi

SS Tjisadane[13]

A Royal Interocean Lines (RIL) ship that served Japan, Hong Kong, Philippines, Malaya, Singapore, Indonesia, Australia, New Zealand, East, West & South Africa and South America. The Tjisadane was built as a cargo-passenger vessel by N.V. Nederlandse Scheepsbouw Maatschappij, Amsterdam for the N.V. Java China Japan Lijn, Amsterdam in 1930. The Tjisadane was then used in the service between Java, China and Japan. Towards the end of 1941 the Tjisadane under command of Captain WFH Burger sailed unarmed to China to evacuate European women and children from Shanghai, Amoy and Hong Kong (departing December 4th) for Surabaya. The Tjisadane was scrapped in 1962.

Valerie sailed on this ship with Kitty, David and Diana departing from Shanghai, China on November 30, 1941, to Surabaya, Indonesia in December 1941.

---

[13] https://www.derbysulzers.com/shiptjisadane.html

SS Gorgon[14]

A Holt & Blue Funnel Line ship built in 1933 by Caledon Shipbuilding & Engineering, a single screw ship of 3,600 tonnes.

During the second half of World War II, she served as a naval-requisitioned support vessel running between Australian east coast ports and the islands north of Australia, principally New Guinea. In April 1943 the *SS Gorgon* was bombed and damaged in Milne Bay. Sold for scrap in 1964.

Valerie sailed on the ship with Kitty, David and Diana from Tjilatjap, Indonesia to Fremantle, Australia on December 20, 1941.

[14] https://birtwistlewiki.com.au/wiki/MS_Gorgon

SS Rimutaka[15]

Built in 1923, the Rimutaka was a 16,500-ton, 573' by 71', P&O ship acquired by the New Zealand Shipping Co. It could carry 840 passengers.

Valerie sailed on this ship with Kitty, David and Diana from Wellington, New Zealand departing on February 26, 1941, travelling through the Panama Canal to New York, United States arriving April 12, 1945, in Liverpool, England.

---

[15] https://en.wikipedia.org/wiki/SS_Mongolia_(1922)

SS Cavina[16]

A 6,907 tonnes twin-screw banana-carrying refrigerated steamship built by Alexander Stephen & Sons of Govan, Glasgow in 1924 for Elders & Fyffes. She only carried a few passengers. Scrapped in 1958.

Valerie sailed on this ship with Fred, Kitty, David and Diana departing December 19, 1946, from Southampton, England arriving on January 1, 1947, in Halifax, Canada.

[16] https://www.clydeships.co.uk/view.php?ref=17027

Appendix B
Valerie Monkhouse's Resume

Valerie Monkhouse

1008 - 151 Bay Street
Ottawa, Ontario
K1R 7T2
Telephone: (613) 233-2285

CAREER SUMMARY:

1988 - 1990	Associate Director, Information Sciences Division, International Development Research Centre.
1978 - 1988	Director, Library Services, National Museums of Canada.
1973 - 1977	Head, Public Services Section, Departmental Library Services, Department of National Health and Welfare.
1972 - 1973	Head, Readers' Services Section, Health Protection Branch, Department of National Health and Welfare.
1970 - 1972	Librarian, Environmental Health Library, Department of National Health and Welfare.

As a member of the Information Sciences Division management team, my responsibilities included the management of the IDRC library and archives and functional responsibility for the Regional Office Libraries in six locations around the world.

Policy development

- Developed operational policies for the Library. Participated in developing policies for the Information Sciences Division.

FUNCTIONAL SKILLS USED IN MOST RECENT POSITION

Planning

- Planned and managed the implementation of the writing of the post-project abstracts for inclusion into a data base which is available world-wide.
- Planned and managed the implementation of three applications to an automated system.
- Planned and managed the service to microfilm the additions to the archives collection.
- Managed the Information Packages Service for the Information Sciences Division.
- Managed an evaluation on library services to projects funded by IDRC and an evaluation on the Development Data Bases Service.
- Participated in the development of a Management Information System for the federal government libraries.
- Planned and coordinated the publication of two brochures describing library services and ensured the publication of an acquisitions list.

Advising

- Advised the North-South Institute on the reorganization of their library and the hiring of a new librarian.
- Advised the Design Institute on the setting up of an Information Centre.

Personnel management

- Was responsible for the management of 23 employees in the professional, technical and support categories in the specialized areas of information sciences including library science, archives and abstracting.
- Was responsible for the preparation of the Library's Training Plan.
- Participated in the management of the Information Sciences Division.

Financial management

- Negotiated for and managed a budget of approximately 1.75 million dollars.
- Was responsible for the preparation of the Two-year Resource and Operational Plan and work plan linking the results to the resources by deciding on priorities and

allocation of resources based on plans submitted by Library managers.

- Had full financial signing authority for the purchase of library material.

ADDITIONAL FUNCTIONAL SKILLS USED IN PREVIOUS POSITION

Policy development

- Participated in the development of corporate policies such as the Conservation and Research Policies by reviewing drafts prior to approval by Senior Management of the National Museums of Canada.
- Developed operational policies for the Directorate in consultation with the Library Advisory Committee.

Project management

Managed two projects at the Corporate level:

- The development of the text for the National Museums of Canada into the first edition of the Access register.
- Leader, Administrative Reform for Staffing Study Team. All optional solutions recommended by the Team were approved by the Management Committee of the National Museums of Canada.
- At the interdepartmental level, managed a project on exploring charging for library services which resulted in two publications under the auspices of the Council of Federal Libraries.

Planning

- A mandate was prepared based on a Library users' survey in consultation with the Library Advisory Committee.
- Two new branch libraries were created and, one in particular, required careful planning as it amalgamated six collections.
- Managed feasibility and systems studies produced by consultants in order to implement an automated integrated library system.
- Developed a management information system both at the Directorate level and at the federal government level for libraries.

ACADEMIC AND PROFESSIONAL TRAINING

- Senior Management Orientation Course, Public Service Commission, 1987.
- Library Administrators Development Program, University of Maryland, 1977.
- Bachelor of Library Science, University of Ottawa, 1967.
- Bachelor of Arts, University of New Brunswick, 1951.

RELATED ACTIVITIES

International

- International Council of Museums, 1985-88.
    - Member, CIDOC Documentation Centres Working Group, 1985-88.

National

- Canadian Library Association, 1967-1990.
    - Member, Program Committee, Third World Interest Group, Canadian Library Association, 1990.
- Chairman, Canadian Association of Special Libraries and Information Services, Ottawa Chapter, 1977-78.
- Canadian Museums Association, 1980-1988.
    - Member, CMA Council, 1982-1985.
    - Chairman, Research and Editorial Committee, 1982-1984.
    - Chairman, Awards Committee, 1985.

Interdepartmental

- Council of Federal Libraries.
    - Member, Committee on Classification, 1976-1978.
    - Chairman, Working Group on Charging for Library Services, 1976-1982.
    - Member, Steering Committee, 1979-1983, 1986-1988.
    - Chairman, Priorities and Planning Committee, 1987.
    - Member, CFL/MIS Working Group, 1985-1990.

Intradepartmental

- International Development Research Centre
    - Member, Records Management Committee, 1989-1990.
    - Member, Subcommittee on Electronic Filing, 1989-1990.
- National Museums of Canada.

  - Member, Collections and Research Committee, 1983-1988
  - Member, Sub-committee on Key Job Descriptions, 1986-1987
  - Chairman, Implementation Committee, Administrative Reform for Staffing, 1986-1987
  - Project Manager, NMC input into the first edition of the Access Register.

Publications

- "Medicine and books", Living, Winter, 1975, p. 8-9.
  - "User satisfaction in accessing multiple bibliographic data bases on-line", Proceedings, 4th. Annual CAIS Conference, 1976. (Co-authored with D. Foster and M. B. Stone)
- "National resource collections: the federal libraries' perspective", Proceedings of the workshop on collection development and rationalization, 1982.

February, 1991

Appendix C
Red Cross Letter

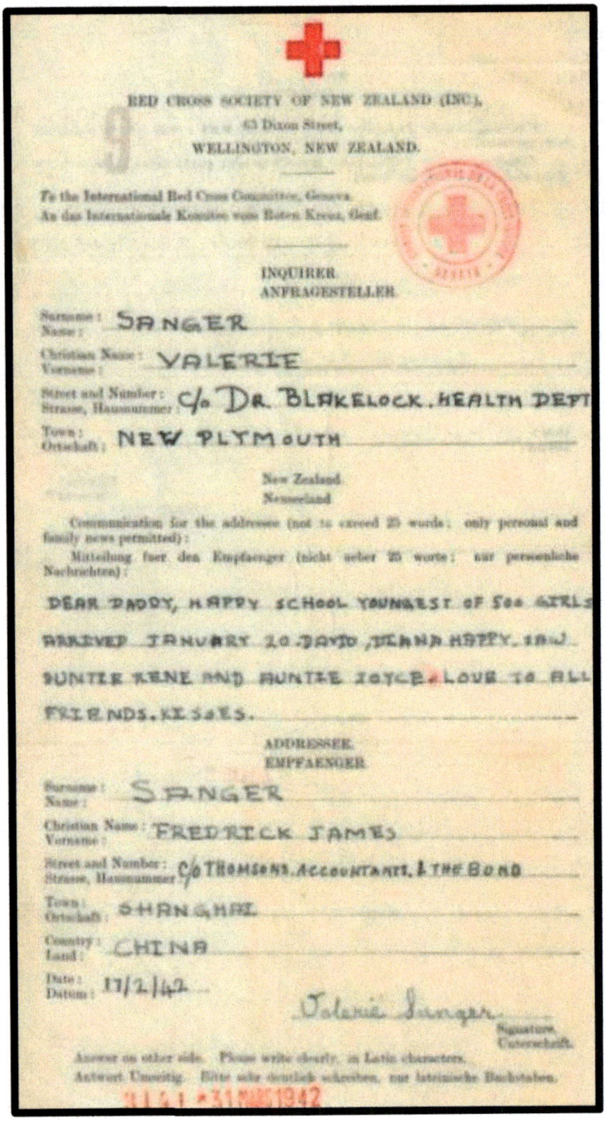

RED CROSS SOCIETY OF NEW ZEALAND (INC.),
63 Dixon Street,
WELLINGTON, NEW ZEALAND.

To the International Red Cross Committee, Geneva.
An das Internationale Komitee vom Roten Kreuz, Genf.

INQUIRER
ANFRAGESTELLER

Surname: / Name: SANGER

Christian Name: / Vorname: VALERIE

Street and Number: / Strasse, Hausnummer: C/o DR. BLAKELOCK. HEALTH DEPT

Town: / Ortschaft: NEW PLYMOUTH

New Zealand
Neuseeland

Communication for the addressee (not to exceed 25 words: only personal and family news permitted):

Mitteilung fuer den Empfaenger (nicht ueber 25 worte: nur persoenliche Nachrichten):

DEAR DADDY, HAPPY SCHOOL YOUNGEST OF 500 GIRLS ARRIVED JANUARY 20. DAVID, DIANA HAPPY. SAW AUNTIE RENE AND AUNTIE JOYCE. LOVE TO ALL FRIENDS. KISSES.

ADDRESSEE
EMPFAENGER

Surname: / Name: SANGER

Christian Name: / Vorname: FREDRICK JAMES

Street and Number: / Strasse, Hausnummer: C/o THOMSONS. ACCOUNTANTS. 2 THE BUND

Town: / Ortschaft: SHANGHAI

Country: / Land: CHINA

Date: / Datum: 17/2/42

Valerie Sanger
Signature.
Unterschrift.

Answer on other side. Please write clearly, in Latin characters.
Antwort Umseitig. Bitte sehr deutlich schreiben, nur lateinische Buchstaben.

31 MAR 1942

Appendix C Red Cross Letter

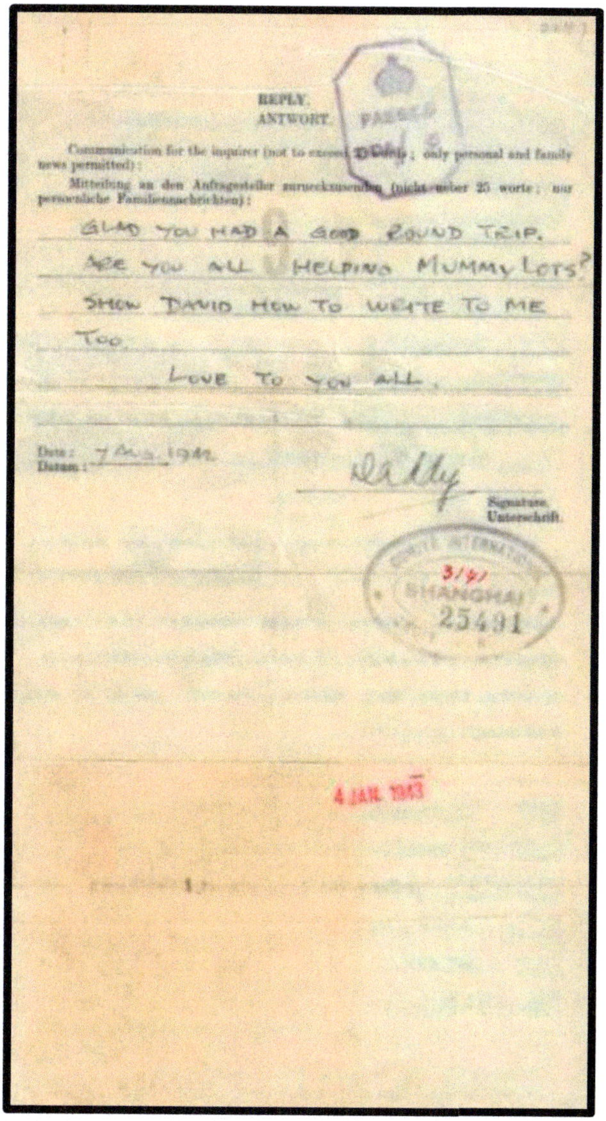

REPLY.
ANTWORT.

PASSED

Communication for the inquirer (not to exceed 25 words; only personal and family news permitted):

Mitteilung an den Anfragesteller zurueckzusenden (nicht ueber 25 worte; nur persoenliche Familiennachrichten):

GLAD YOU HAD A GOOD ROUND TRIP.
ARE YOU ALL HELPING MUMMY LOTS?
SHOW DAVID HOW TO WRITE TO ME
TOO.
LOVE TO YOU ALL.

Date: 7 AUG 1942
Datum:

Daddy

Signature
Unterschrift

COMITE INTERNATIONAL
3/41
SHANGHAI
25491

4 JAN 1943

Appendix D
Kathleen Mary Sanger
1906–1998

THE FIRST FORTY YEARS

Kathleen Mary Thorn was born on January 11, 1906, in Portsmouth, England, the eldest of three daughters of William John Thorn and his wife Lily Harriet Cuell. Her father was born in Kimberley, South Africa where his father prospected with Cecil Rhodes. Her mother came from an old Hampshire family who had lived for generations in the Winchester area.

Her mother was not a particularly well person and her father, who was in the Royal Navy, was away for all but 17 months of the 17 years that they were married. Her mother had an elder sister who had no children and she offered to bring up Kathleen, so she grew up with her aunt and uncle from the age of two and a half. At first, they lived in Croydon, near London, so Kathleen used to go by train to visit her family.

When Kathleen was twelve, she moved with her aunt and uncle to live next door to the Sanger family in Portsmouth. Her parents lived nearby too so she was able to visit them more frequently. Later, she moved to Waterlooville where she nursed her aunt until she died. Her uncle remarried and Kathleen returned to live with her father and stepmother. By this time, Kathleen and Fred Sanger (See Appendix E) were engaged to be married and were to be so for three years until Fred graduated from the University of London. During that time, Kathleen made her trousseau and embroidered her wedding dress. Kathleen played the piano and sang in church choirs and one of her happy memories was singing in a massed choir under the direction Sir Malcolm Sargent. Fred graduated at the top of his class in 1928 but was unable to find a job until the middle of August as there was a depression in England. They postponed their wedding for six weeks and Fred had been on the job a couple of weeks when he asked for next Saturday off—people worked six days a week in those days. When his boss asked him why, he replied that he wanted to get married to which his boss replied, "You may have Monday off too". They went to live in Brixton, a suburb of London, in one room on the fourth floor and sharing a bathroom. Shortly after, Fred was transferred to Stockport, near Manchester for three months so Kathleen was on a train to find somewhere to live—the first of many times that she moved during her married life.

In 1929, Fred got a job as an Education Officer in the Royal Air Force, so they moved to Tring just north of London. A year later Valerie was born at home. After a while, Fred decided he wanted something more exciting and Kathleen wanted to travel so he applied for positions outside England and, in 1934, he took the position of Head of the Department of Engineering and Building in the Lester Institute of Technical Education in Shanghai, China. Because there were disturbances in Nanking at the time, he went on ahead. When he arrived in Shanghai, he discovered all was quiet there so Kathleen and Valerie followed a few months later. At that time, one went by boat from Southampton through the Suez Canal stopping at various ports on the way. This took six weeks. Life on board ship was very different from the life that she had led. At that time, one dressed for dinner every evening in a long dress so she had to buy a whole new wardrobe for the trip. Once on board, she had to decide which sitting she would have her meals, when she would have her bath which was always drawn by the bath steward with sea water with a large bowl of fresh water in which to rinse oneself off. She had never been out of England before so she was exposed to many new cultures as the ship stopped in places like Marseilles, Port Said, Bombay, Colombo and Hong Kong.

In 1936, David was born in Shanghai and the following summer the family went to Karatsu, Japan with their amah for a holiday. While there, the Japanese-Chinese war broke out in the Shanghai area so the Lester Institute was closed and the faculty were told to go back to England and take their sabbaticals. We arrived in England around Christmas and Kathleen and Fred found a delightful gardener's cottage to rent just south of London. Fred worked on his master's thesis and Kathleen produced Diana at King's College Hospital in London.

Fred had to return to Shanghai and the rest of the family with Amah were to follow early in 1939. However, the Munich crisis loomed so Kathleen managed to get us aboard a ship leaving in September, 1938 as she decided that if there were going to be a war she wanted to be with her husband. When we arrived at Marseilles we heard that the crisis had been averted.

Life in Shanghai was pleasurable for the children. Kathleen had servants to do the housework, cooking and gardening in which she took a great interest. Instead of bridge parties, women had mah-jongg parties and she regularly went shopping which usually necessitated bargaining over the prices. She was very active in the King's Daughters Society.

In late November of 1941, conditions worsened, and it looked as if war would break out in the Pacific. Friends of theirs, the Blakelocks had settled in New Zealand and had cabled them saying that they could provide accommodation if they decided to leave Shanghai. With a week's notice, Kathleen organised the packing up of the most precious things in their home as well as useful things and we set sail on November 30th. On the way to the ship we saw several Japanese tanks parked on a road near our house. She had thirteen pieces of luggage and three children aged 11, 5 and 3 and a half. Fred had resigned and he was to follow ten days later when he had tied up all the loose ends at work and met the family in Java for a holiday before he went to India to join the British army when the rest of the family would go to New Zealand. Unfortunately, the Japanese took over Shanghai two days before he was to leave. We were a day and a half out from Hong Kong when Pearl Harbor was raided so we proceeded directly to Surabaya. On our arrival there, we spent a very hot day in the customs shed where the customs officers insisted on doing a body search of every adult.

Kathleen went to the British Consulate and they recommended that we should leave as soon as possible. As we were originally booked to go to New Zealand three weeks later, she received part of the refund for that part of the passage from Java to Auckland. This enabled her to book transportation as far as Sydney, Australia via Perth. She got us a passage on board a small ship of 4000 tons from Tjilitjap a couple of days later. This necessitated an unexpected 12 hour train journey 300 miles across Java, an island in what is known as Indonesia now, during which we had four bananas to eat. We stayed in a soldiers' barracks overnight as the only hotel was full and then boarded the "Gorgon" the next day. There was concern that there were Japanese submarines in the area so all the men aboard the ship took turns watching out for submarines and we had a boat drill of some sort every day. Everyone was on edge so there were many sightings which turned out to be whales or porpoises. David and Valerie shared a cabin and Kathleen told her to look after him. Well, the first day we had a boat drill, which we had not been warned about, she dashed out on deck leaving David behind! After six days, we arrived in Fremantle, the port of Perth in Australia. There, Kathleen made contact with a friend of hers whose husband had seen us off in Shanghai and we shared her two-bedroom apartment with her and her daughter for two weeks while we celebrated Christmas and Kathleen arranged for us to cross Australia by train. We had to change trains each time we crossed a state line as the gauges were different widths. The first two days we crossed the desert so it was around 120 degrees and there were only three air-conditioned cars for the whole train where one could sit. We all slept in the hot carriages. For four hundred miles, beside the railway line, was a huge pipe in which water was sent to Kalgoorlie. Then, from Port Augusta to Adelaide, we went through the worst sandstorm in fifty years so we were very grateful to find showers in the railway station at Adelaide. The scenery from Melbourne to Albury was spectacular but, at Albury, we had to change trains late in the evening and it so happened that we had to walk the length of ten cars to where our reserved berths were. Diana insisted on carrying the attaché case in which Kathleen had all her first aid equipment and medicines and the next day her legs were bruised from her effort. We arrived in Sydney and went to stay with another Shanghai friend of Kathleen's for a week during which time Kathleen received the rest of her refund and pestered the shipping lines to get a passage to New Zealand. We crossed the Tasman Sea aboard the "Rimutaka" and then took a train to New Plymouth to be met by the Blakelocks. She arrived there with the equivalent of $200 and no obvious form of income.

She, who had never written a business letter in her life before, contacted the New Zealand government who gave her four pounds a week on condition that she repay it when she was able. She also contacted the Henry Lester Foundation in London and they agreed to give her fifty pounds a month so she was able to repay the New Zealand government. Then, once or twice during the war, England froze all money leaving the country so then the family was back to four pounds a week! At first, we rented a furnished house for which she paid two pounds ten a week but then an unfurnished house became available for one pound fifteen. A woman she had met, Mrs. Symes who had lived in New Plymouth for some time, spoke to her friends and among them they helped Kathleen furnish the house. There she gardened and looked after the three of us. In May of 1942 she went to hospital for a couple of weeks with a suspected diseased gall bladder and it was just before she went that she heard that Fred was safe in Shanghai.

Contact with her husband was erratic during that time. One way was through the Red Cross. One wrote 25 words on a form, sent it to Geneva and they delivered it behind the war zone. Another way was Fred sent us letters through the underground where his ex-students, who were Chinese, would send the letters to the interior of China, usually Kunming, and they would send them by mail to us in New Zealand. Another way, once Fred was in Lunghwa camp, was that he could put messages in a box and the Japanese would broadcast them. There was a man in the South Island of New Zealand who sat up all night transcribing the messages and sending them to the families. So, essentially, she was on her own bringing up three children.

Early in 1945, the New Zealand government contacted Kathleen and suggested that she should return to England as that is where Fred would be repatriated and space on shipping would be hard to get after the war because of moving the troops home. Once she had satisfied herself that there were no prospects for Fred in New Zealand, she agreed and we left Wellington in February, 1945 on the "Rimutaka" to the sound of 'Now is the hour' for England via the Panama Canal. It took us three weeks to get to Panama without the sight of land. The sea was calm after the first few days and the temperature lovely but, even so, we were thrilled to see land again. After going through the canal, we stopped overnight in Kingston and in Havana before joining a convoy of three ships with four escorts to go to New York. Much to our disappointment we were not allowed ashore and the next day we joined a large convoy of some thirty ships with eight escorts. We were not able to keep up to the speed of the convoy so, once more, we were on our own as we neared Ireland. We arrived in Liverpool the day Roosevelt died in April, 1945. Because housing was very hard to get in England, Kathleen put us all in boarding school and she stayed with friends until Fred arrived in England in December of 1945.

After a year in England, Fred accepted a position at the University of New Brunswick, and we all came over by boat arriving in Halifax on January 1, 1947.

Kathleen, who was shy and had led a sheltered life but was always interested in travelling, came into her own when she had to take three children on her own halfway around the world under wartime conditions. In Worcester, she became

Appendix D Kathleen Mary Sanger 1906-1998

President of the Faculty Women's Club and the Home Club and gave a presentation of her trip from Shanghai to New Zealand to the Home Club. In later years, she remained a very private person but was always friendly. She was actively interested in the activities, problems and achievements of all her far-flung family giving counsel only when asked. One of her favourite phrases was "you gotta do what you gotta do". Her philosophy was to do the best you can, learn from experience, always look forward and, when things seem to be going the wrong way, perhaps it was for the best in the long run.

Appendix E
Frederick James Sanger
1905–2000

Frederick James Sanger, known in his family as Fred, Daddy, Grandpa, Tan-Tan and Uncle Fred, was born on September 8, 1905, in Wyke Cottage, The Avenue, Bishops Waltham, Hampshire, England. He was the second child in the family having an elder sister, Eva Louise and a younger one, Doris Edith. Their parents were James Augustus Sanger and his wife Edith May Wright. He spent a happy childhood until he was 11 in early 1917 when the family moved to Portsmouth as his father had joined the Medical Corps and was quartermaster for the Queen Alexandra Hospital, a hospital used especially for the war wounded. During his childhood, he spent 6 months in bed once for a tuberculosis hip and was hospitalised in 1919 for an abscess in his back following the Spanish influenza epidemic. While he was confined to bed on his back, he decided that he was just as smart as the other kids and all he had to do was study. This he did and improved his marks tremendously when he went back to school and became top of the class the next year and from then on.

At the age of 11, he won a scholarship to attend Price's Public School in Fareham to which he had a long walk to the train station, waited for the train, the train ride and a short walk to the school and then returned home which he did every day. At school, he practised playing chess as well as participating in sports. He was a soloist in the choir of the church until he was 16. At the age of 17 he enrolled as a shipwright apprentice in the Royal Dockyard Technical College in Portsmouth for which he was paid 12 shillings 6 pence a week, 10 shillings of which he gave to his parents for his board. It was a four-year apprenticeship which included three years in construction and one year in the drawing office. It was made up of classes and working on building warships. He spent some time building the aircraft carrier HMS Eagle[17] and going to classes in the evening. If he had a good supervisor, he would let him go into the bowels of the ship to study. At the end of each year, half the class failed. He graduated second in the class because he was sick when writing the final examinations. If he had been first, he would have automatically gone into the Royal Navy. Instead, he won two scholarships—Kitchener's Memorial and the Royal – which allowed him to go to the Imperial College of Science & Technology at the University of London where he achieved a B.Sc. (Engineering), with 1st. class honours in Engineering Sciences. He then took a Diploma of Membership of the Imperial College of Sciences and Technology in hydro-electric engineering. He fell in love with Kathleen Mary Thorn, known as Kitty, Mummy, Idasan, Grandma, Tai-Tai, and Auntie Kitty in the family, who had lived next door in Portsmouth with her aunt and uncle and in 1925 they became engaged to be married.

He graduated the top of his class in 1928 but was unable to get a job for six weeks as it was the heart of the depression in England, and they postponed their wedding until he had a job. He went to work as a structural engineer for Christiani and Nielsen, a Danish firm of reinforced concrete engineers and contractors, which contributed to the building of the Sydney Harbour bridge. Two weeks after he started, he requested Saturday morning off. When his supervisor asked why he replied that he was going to get married. In that case, his supervisor said he could have Monday off too! They were married in Fareham on September 1, 1928.

While at Christiani and Nielson he was given unusual problems for solution including a roadway to be built along an

[17] https://www.youtube.com/watch?v=vXb6MVhpEKM

existing vertical sea-wall of stone blocks: a skew bridge (road over railway) with construction plans to maintain rail traffic without interruption: a new kind of wharf-wall, devised by Christiani and Nielsen, the first in England but since then a widely used design of a large rectangular coal bunker with a water tank over its roof: the first reinforced concrete aeroplane hangar built in England and unusual foundations for gasworks structures.

Within a short period of time, he was transferred to Manchester, so Kitty went north to find lodgings which started the many times that they moved during his life. In 1929, he was successful in obtaining a position as an education officer for the Royal Air Force where he taught aeronautical engineering in a school of technical training. He was stationed at Halton, so they moved to Tring, Hertfordshire where their eldest child, Valerie, was born. He was a founding member of the British Gliding Association and worked on the Technical Committee checking proposed designs of gliders and sailplanes, almost entirely of wood construction. At this time, he also played chess for the county of Hertfordshire.

He did not find the work challenging enough and he and Kitty were anxious to travel. He applied for several positions out of England and was accepted as Head of the Department of Engineering and Building at the new Henry Lester Institute of Technical Education in Shanghai in 1934. This Institute was affiliated with the University of London and gave its engineering degrees. In the last year, students would write examinations sent out by boat from London which took five weeks. They would then be returned by boat to London to be marked after which the results would be sent once more by boat to Shanghai. The Institute was just being set up so he was involved in the early planning which involved all the curriculum and the setting up of the laboratories. The students were primarily Chinese and later a high school was created to feed into the Institute. During this time, he would get up at 6 am. to take lessons in the Chinese language. Over the years, he talked a lot about his students and how hard they studied to do well. He told of how one of his students was so nervous that he had to speak to him, which was generally not allowed, to settle him down. Also, how when the Chinese started coming to the U.S., his students would look him up and visit. One of them painted a scroll entitled "The Pine and the Stone" which was a "gift in honour of the birthday of Mr. Sanger given by the Lester Institute Student Society. Painted in California by Wei Lee Tang. He is as righteous as the pine and is as steadfast as the stone." He maintained contact with some of his students until his death some sixty years later.

In 1936 his second child, David was born, and in July of 1937, the family went to Karatsu, Japan for a month's holiday which turned out to be 4 months because of the fighting which had broken out between the Chinese and Japanese in Shanghai. It was decided that all the faculty of the Institute should return to England for their 6 months' leave which normally would have occurred every five years. While he was there, he completed his master's thesis and was awarded his M.Sc. from the University of London in the Albert Hall when Valerie remembers being present. He returned to Shanghai in May of 1938 after his third child, Diana, was born. The family followed in September and, as war in Europe seemed imminent, Kitty decided that it would be better and safer for the family to be all together rather than leave in December which was the original plan.

From 1934 to 1941, in addition to his work at the Institute, he managed to find time to consult various organisations as well do research into soil mechanics. From 1938–1941 he allotted half an hour to each of his children every day by reading to David and Diana and often playing Chinese checkers with Valerie.

The family left for New Zealand on November 30, 1941, and he was to follow on December 10". at the end of the semester, to meet them in the hills of Java for a three-week holiday and then to go to India to join the army. The Japanese took over Shanghai on December 8th, so he was trapped there. Early in 1942, the Japanese took over the schools and Institute. Before he went to camp, he lived in the same house, where he had lived with his family before the Japanese took over Shanghai, with two other men, Dr. Bernard Read and Dr. Herbert Earle, both of the Lester Medical Institute. Electricity was very expensive, so they cooked on a small coal stove with a brass tank on the side for hot water. There was a small oven on top of the stove. They used 20 pounds of coal balls a day. Earlier there had been a small vegetable garden. They enlarged it by doing the gardening themselves as gardeners were too expensive. Prices had skyrocketed and were about twenty times what they were when the Japanese first took over.

In 1942–1943 he was very active as a volunteer in the British Residents' Association when he was asked to organise an office to register the 7500 people and to coordinate with other offices giving clothing and bedding to those in need. The Civilian Assembly Office of 4 sections and 50 workers was organised for the movement of all British nationals into internment camps known as "Civil Assembly Centres". A suggested list of belongings that people should take into the camps was made. Before he went into camp, he wrote individual letters to all his children and his wife which were taken by his students underground to Kunming and then they airmailed them to New Zealand. Once in camp, there were two methods of communication. One was writing 25-word letters, courtesy of the International Red Cross, which took six months to arrive as they had to go to Geneva first. There was a place to write a return message of 25 words which also took six months to arrive if it ever did. The other was that he put messages in a box which the Japanese said that they would broadcast. The first one was broadcast in December of 1943. There was a man in the South Island of New Zealand who would stay up at night and write down the messages and then mail them to the families.

In camp, he was elected Labour Officer making sure that essential camp work was done by the people interested in a particular occupation and assigning duties to all able-bodied people. He also directed cultural activities, organised air raid defence groups, lectured and acted as Chairman of the School Examining Board. Red Cross parcels were sent in as well as, in his case, a food parcel arrived once a month from Chinese students and friends. Ken Flemons was in the same room as Fred with ten other men. He remembered that Fred gave lectures on various topics and tutored in mathematics, physics and mechanics to those who were interested in taking up engineering. Ken had great respect for him as he helped a lot of young people to further their studies. He recalled vividly Fred helping a group of them to make telescopes using old spectacle lenses and cardboard tubes. They spent hours looking out of their window towards the Japanese airfield nearby watching the activity. At the end of the war, Fred gave Ken a letter of introduction to his old professor, Professor Peppard at the University of London, who remembered him.

In August, 1945, Fred was freed by the Americans. In September, permission was granted for him and Mr. Jeppersen to live in the two flats available in the Henry Lester Institute. On November 5, he sailed on the SS Arawa, a Shaw Saville refrigeration ship of 14,500 tons which had been converted into a troop ship. It was a single funnel ship which burnt oil. There were 800 passengers on board when it was supposed to have only 500. He was one of 75 men in what was initially a cold storage department. They slept on canvas. bunks which could be folded up so that they could eat at tables in the same location. There were no portholes but there was blower ventilation. There were nine men at a table, so they were divided into groups of three for jobs. That meant that every three days he had to help by fetching food from the kitchen, washing up, sweeping and mopping the deck. Fred represented the 75 men on the Ship's Passengers' committee which met daily to ask for various things as the crew were not ready for women and children. They experienced bad weather soon after leaving Shanghai and, by the time they reached Singapore where the weather was good, the Arara had speeded up to 14 knots. Some passengers left there to go to Australia, and more were taken aboard so now they had 900 passengers. Fred used his evenings to play bridge or chess and to read. They had a very rough crossing on the Mediterranean when he was seasick and, lying in his bunk, he calculated how far up and down he went. He arrived in England in the middle of December to be greeted by his wife and a few days later by his children as they arrived from school. Kitty had made arrangements to rent a house for the month of January when their children were on holiday so that we could all be together again. It was during this time that Fred took Valerie to the Albert Hall to hear Myra Hess play a Tchaikovsky piano concerto. Valerie suffered from chilblains and couldn't stop moving when they started to itch as they warmed up much to his annoyance.

He spent the next year working on his doctorate thesis based on his research in Shanghai but was unsuccessful in receiving his doctorate degree as it was based on old research and someone else had done similar research. He taught science for one term at the boarding school where his daughters were before obtaining a position as Professor of Engineering Drawing at the University of New Brunswick in Fredericton in January of 1947. In the summer of 1947, he took a bus to Urbana, Illinois to study with Dr. Ralph Peck, a noted expert on geotechnical engineering, to bring himself up to date in his subject. The following summer he taught at Mount Allison University in Sackville, and, in the fall of 1948, he obtained a position as Professor of Civil Engineering at the Worcester Polytechnic Institute in Worcester, Massachusetts where he remained for nine years teaching Geology, Hydraulics, Soil Mechanics and Foundations, Concrete Technology and Testing of Materials. He also taught land surveying going out into the field for three weeks twice a year. He became an American citizen in June of 1954.

It was while he was in Worcester that he started to consult once again, which he did for the next twenty-five years. During the nine years when he was in Worcester, he did 28 different consultations on problems for which there were no precedents. The first one was when the City of Worcester had contracted a major repaving job on 57 roads which had begun to break up. They approached Worcester Polytechnic Institute and the professor, who was the expert on roads, did not want the job as he felt it was too political and asked Fred if he would be willing to do it. He accepted, hired four students, and spent the summer taking samples. As the result of his report, a lawsuit ensued when he was called upon to be an expert witness and the City won the case. While consulting he solved a tricky soil problem for a nearby Trappist monastery as well as undertaking many other consulting problems. In 1955–1957, he was hired as a soils consultant to Clarkson Engineering, Co. Inc. who had the $40 million contract to build the Massachusetts toll road from Weston to Westboro. This involved advice on the location and type of test borings to be taken, evaluation of terrain conditions and the best way to take the new road over swamp areas. He was also consulted on bridge foundations, problems on excavation and control of groundwater. As a result of his consulting, he was called to be an expert witness three times.

In 1957, he joined the U.S. Army Corps of Engineers as a Special Assistant in writing manuals for military construction and serving as a general consultant to the Services and Public, mainly when frozen ground was the basic difficulty. He had previously worked for them during some summers. He wrote three manuals: Computation methods for freeze and thaw of soils; Terrain evaluation in the Arctic and Subarctic; and Foundations in areas of deep frost penetration which became standard for Army and Air Force construction in cold regions.

He was involved in numerous research projects. The first one was an involvement in the Army Corps northern construction projects. David remembers that "in 1957, he spent the summer in northern Greenland at camp Tuto, a tent city a few miles outside Thule, where he worked on several projects: the ramp road project—putting gravel road up onto the ice cap so vehicles could cross the highly dissected face of the ice: drilling in the ice cap in preparation for Camp Century (100 miles into the ice cap and a major research station for years); and generally trying to find out more about ice movement and permafrost action at the fringe of the ice cap. Much of this was experimental. He also worked on foundation problems for the DEW Line radar stations from Alaska to Greenland. These were tricky because the weight on permafrost will eventually melt the permafrost unless a suitable pad—usually gravel—is put below to insulate the permafrost."

In Canada, he was involved in the design of the extension for Frobisher (Iqaluit) airport on bad permafrost, a study of Kelsey Dikes in Manitoba and assisted power companies on transmission-tower foundations in thawing permafrost. In 1958 he went on a cross-Canada speaking tour and consulted for the National Research Council in Ottawa.

From 1959–1970 he planned and directed a monograph series of 51 volumes entitled "Cold Regions Science and Engineering Monographs" of which 30 were published under his editorship with 20 more in progress. It was during this time that he realised that the Russians were ahead of the United States in building on permafrost, so he learnt to read technical Russian.

One of his consultants was Dr. Cynthia Wilson who wrote "In the 1960's, I was so fortunate to work with Fred Sanger at CRREL on the monograph covering the Climatology of the Cold Regions. There were few women in Meteorology and Climatology at that time, and I was very aware of the wonderful opportunity that Fred had given me (and the responsibility) in granting me the contract. Working with him was both a welcome challenge and a very happy experience. I learnt so much from his very practical approach which freed up my strictly academic upbringing:

"Cynthia, you need to get your feet wet" which I did as soon as I could. He was always very considerate in administering my contract and facilitating my needs in every way. In discussion he was incisive, but patient and generous. Above all he was a good listener, and in the final discussions on the reviewed manuscript, a very fair judge." In a letter written November 26, 1969 to him, Dr. Wilson stated "I want to thank you very sincerely for your generous help and direction both on technical matters concerning the engineering aspects of the subject, and on style in report writing. Our healthy battles with the final manuscripts were very instructive to me and added greatly to the quality of the end product, I know!

There was also your considerate administration which made my path so smooth, both here and on visits to Hanover, and made it a very real pleasure to work with CRREL". He was appointed Adjunct Professor of Engineering at the Thayer School at Dartmouth College in 1963 where he advised doctoral and master candidates in engineering and gave occasional courses on Soil Mechanics, Foundation Engineering and Transportation Engineering.

From 1960–1970, he was a private consultant for Conch-Methane Services, London who were liquefying gas to—160 degrees Celsius and storing it at different ports around the world. Work began with an experimental tank excavated at Lake Charles, Louisiana when the ground was artificially frozen, and the tank excavated so the frozen ground would support the earth and provide a liquid-tight wall. These tanks were to be up to 200 feet across and 185 feet deep in all kinds of soils and rocks and costing up to $5 million. Work included the writing of many reports and a Manual of Design (Company restricted) of original techniques developed for the work for which he was paid $15,000 and which resulted in one patent for the connection of a concrete wall to frozen ground. He was encouraged to patent his soil freezing technique by Conch-Methane Services who talked him into letting them have the patent for $1.00 in exchange for a guarantee of so much work for a few years and calling him in when they were planning new storage locations. He agreed to this because what he really liked was the challenge of the problems. Later four copies of the manual were sold by the company for $125,000 each. He was further restricted not to do similar work for other companies for five years. Unfortunately, he was only called in after they had run into trouble instead of before so he could have got them to perhaps locate the tank where there was more suitable ground to freeze. He also consulted for two other companies to design construction procedures and engineering specifications for artificial freezing for shaft and tunnel construction and problems in tunnelling under difficult soil conditions and advising when tunnels that were being made with conventional freezing technique began to admit water in San Francisco and New York. He travelled to Japan, Algeria, London, Elizabeth, New Jersey, and Montreal to provide advice based on the particular soil conditions. It was on his trip to London that he took a couple of days off to visit his sister in Portsmouth. His nephew, Brian, remembers his visit when he explained to him that "the pipeline was built on flexible stilts set into the permafrost, which stopped the pipe buckling due to ground heave and also about the storage of liquid gas in tanks which were dug directly into the ground and unlined." Brian took every opportunity when he was travelling for his work to spend a day or two with him in later years.

In 1970 he retired from the U.S. Corps of Engineers and went to work for the U. S. Geological Survey in Palo Alto, California as Senior Government Engineer on the Alaska Pipeline and where he remained for eighteen months. David wrote that " part of his assignment also involved the planning of ideal locations for future cities in the United States based on environmental considerations, etc. He was also involved in a metrification program, but both these latter projects died with the change in administration in Washington."

David wrote "that from 1971–1973 he was appointed Chairman of the Technical Advisory Board on Trans-Alaska Pipeline Project, Department of the Interior. He had worked on the Alaska Pipeline as a consultant and the Department wanted his expertise to chair the Board which was to consider the Alaska Pipeline Environmental Impact Statement. David wrote that "At an earlier date, when consulted by the oil companies, he had voiced the opinion that the pipeline should not be buried in the permafrost, as the oil companies wanted, because the heated oil (heated to thin it and make it flow) would melt the permafrost and create a huge canyon that would impede caribou migrations, break the pipeline, etc. He was thanked for his opinion and dismissed. When he became Chair of the Technical Advisory Board, he could insist on an above-the-ground pipeline. Further, he insisted that it be put on a sliding bed so that, in case of an earthquake the pipeline, could slide laterally about 100 feet each way. In the event, there was a bad (7.9 magnitude) 'quake a few years ago (November 7, 2007) and the design worked as planned as there were no ruptures. He used to call me late at night getting his thoughts on the pipelines' potential impact on Native Peoples, because at that time social considerations were not strongly integrated into EIS (Environment Impact) Statements." He was under tremendous pressure as " every day that the pipeline was not delivering oil to Valdez meant millions of dollars lost." He received a Certificate of Commendation from the Department of the Interior for his work. He then suffered two heart attacks and retired once again. He moved to Simsbury, Connecticut in 1973 and from then to 1978 he became a consultant part-time if the subject interested him. He also did some technical auditing. He was Editor of the USSR contribution Permafrost, Second International Conference, July 28, 1973 which was published by the National Academy of Sciences in 1978.

In 1981, he moved to Orange City to a retirement home, John Knox Village, where he actively participated in the Food Committee. He was particularly interested in diabetic diets as he had had diabetes from the age of forty-five. He was also responsible for looking after the wing where he lived in and preparing for hurricanes and tornadoes until his health no longer enabled him to do so.

Over the years, he participated with his children and grandchildren by talking to them about the many subjects which interested him (as he was an avid reader), as well as his experiences. He enjoyed playing games with them such as mahjong, Oh Hell and paper games such as battleships. He enjoyed showing them how to make paper aeroplanes. He taught them how to play bridge, chess, crib, double pack solitaire and how to perform a couple of card tricks. He introduced them to jig saws. Later, it was difficult to keep him provided with crossword puzzles when he particularly liked double-crostics.

At the age of 41, he had to start from scratch to develop his career again after having been cut off from the many developments in his field during the war as well as having to compete with returning veterans in the tight job market. It was also a time when his children were entering an expensive stage. He took on consulting again which enabled him to ensure that his three children received a university education. He also supported his grandchildren in following their particular interests in encouraging them and in assisting financially. His belief in a good education has endured in that his grandchildren and great grandchildren of university age have all participated in post-secondary education.

Prepared by his daughter Valerie, with the great assistance of son David, daughter Diana, grandsons Peter and Duncan, son-in-law Ben (Andrew), nephew Brian, Dr. Cynthia V. Wilson, and Ken Flemons.

The Lester School and Henry Lester Institute of Technical Education – Shanghai, China

Appendix E Frederick James Sanger 1905-2000

Frederick James Sanger Notes

BIRTH: Born at Wyke Cottage, Bishop's Waltham. Source: Frederick James Sanger. Source: EVR 1905 4th. quarter, Droxford, 2a, 143.

MARRIAGE: Kathleen Mary Thorn. September 1, 1928 in Holy Trinity Church, Fareham, Hampshire. Source: daughter, Valerie Sanger and EVR 1928 3rd. quarter, Fareham, 2b, 1563.

OCCUPATION:

- 1930 Education Officer. Royal Air Force.
- 1934–1941 Head of Department Engineering and Building, Lester Institute of Technical Education.
- 1947 Professor of Drawing, Engineering Geology, University of New Brunswick.
- 1948 Professor of Civil Engineering, Worcester Polytechnic Institute.
- 1957 Corps of Engineers.
- 1970 Consulting Civil Engineer, U.S. Geological Survey.
- 1971 Chairman, Technical Advisory Board on Trans-Alaska Pipeline Project, Department of the Interior.
- 25 years as a private consultant in Civil Engineering.

DEATH: Source: death certificate. Died at 5.20 p.m. in Memorial Hospital, Deland, West Volusia, FL.

CHRONOLOGY:

- 1905 Wyke Cottage, Bishops Waltham, England.
- 1916 34 Gladys Avenue, Portsmouth, Hants.
- 1925 London.
- 1928–1929 Brixton, Manchester, London.
- 1930 The Cottage, Highfield Road, Tring, Herts.
- 1932 Sherborne, Aylesbury Road, Wendover, Herts.
- 1934 July 21 sailed on the SS Mantua for Shanghai.
- 1934 Kiaochow Road, Shanghai.
- 1937 Karatsu, Japan
- 1937 109 Hookrise New Malden, Surrey
- 1938 Tolworth, Surrey.
- 1938 May 14 sailed on the SS Schamhorst for Shanghai.

Valerie's Journeys

- 1938 Great Western Road.
- 1941 99D, Jessfield Road.
- 1943 Entered Lunghwa Camp, Shanghai.
- 1945 Henry Lester Institute.
- 1945 November 5 left Shanghai on the SS Arawa.
- 1945 December 14 arrived London.
- 1946 Ealing, Middlesex.
- 1946 Lymington, Hants.
- 1947 January 1 arrived on the SS Cavina in Halifax, N. S.
- 1947 WAC Officers Hut, Alexander College, Fredericton, N. B.
- 1948 August arrived in Worcester, Massachusetts. U.S.A.
    - 47 Clark Street.
    - 10 Hackfeld Road.
    - 15 Homer Street
    - 18 Berkmans Street.
- 1958 26 Berwick Road, Belmont, Massachusetts.
- 1960 Moved to Evanston, Illinois
- 1961 August Hanover, New Hampshire
    - Lyme Road.
    - 6 Wren Lane.
- 1970 Moved to Menlo Park, California
- 1971 4000 Massachusetts Avenue, Washington, D.C.
- 1974 76 Library Lane, Simsbury, Connecticut.
- 1981 November. 218B, John Knox Village, Orange City, Florida.

Find my Past records.
Sanger, Frederick 28 M 1934 Southampton, destination China, Shanghai. July 21, 1934 on the S. S. Mantua.
Sanger, Frederick J 33 M 1938 Southampton, destination China, Shanghai. May 14, 1938 on the S.S. Scharnhorst.

Appendix E Frederick James Sanger 1905-2000

APPENDIX E-1

FROZEN ORDER OF HAIRY EARED ARCTIC ENGINEERS

By those present let it be known to all that F. J. Sanger is hereby appointed a member of the "Frozen Order of Hairy Eared Arctic Engineers" and is awarded this certificate as proof that upon entering the Arctic Circle the has braved the seat in icy latrines;
eaten blubber when it wasn't lean;
shared his bath with a pair of seals;
dined on frozen "C" ration meals;
he has shaved in water covered with ice;
lost his pay on a roll of the dice;
he has been without mail for a month or two;
and then when it came the postage was due;
he has withstood the winds
and blinding white of the endless days and womenless nights so the Frozen Engineers welcome a Brother Hairy Ears.

Source: A plaque, which was awarded to him when he left Greenland, lived in his bathroom.

APPENDIX E-2

Article written by Valerie Monkhouse for the *Anglo-Celtic Roots* in 2008

LUNGHWA, A CIVIL ASSEMBLY CENTRE

My father, Frederick James Sanger, was born in Hampshire in 1905. In the thirties he went to teach in Shanghai at the Henry Lester Technical Institute which was affiliated with the University of London. On November 30th., 1941, I left Shanghai with my mother, brother and sister and my father was to follow, leaving on December 10th. We were to meet in Java after which my father planned to go to India to join the British army and we were to travel to New Zealand. As is well known, the attack on Pearl Harbor occurred on December 7th, 1941. What is not as well known is that the next day, December 8th, the Japanese took control over the International Settlement and French Concession in Shanghai so that my father was trapped in Shanghai for the duration of the war.

Within days, all the Allied nationals over the age of 13 had to register with the Japanese gendarmerie and were prohibited from moving, selling or transferring property. Later, they were required to wear arm bands with different colours for different nationalities. It also became a time of long queues to withdraw money from the banks as there was a limit as to how much could be withdrawn. Long queues for food were also common. Inflation was rampant so people started to share living accommodations in order to save money and planted vegetables in their gardens and as well as finding ways to keep animals for food.

During the period from the takeover of the International Settlement and when the residents were relocated to the camps, the British Residents' Association of China (BRA) started to play an important role for the British residents. By the end of 1942, the Japanese ordered that all British and American civilians were to be placed in camps called Civil Assembly Centres. They contacted the BRA and gave them the option of either organising the placement of the British nationals into the camps or the Japanese would place them. The BRA accepted the challenge as they decided that that would be the best way to take care of the British and those with British passports by being able to keep families together as much as possible. Some men, deemed dangerous by the Japanese, had already been arrested and tortured. The conditions were that all nationals were to be moved to the camps by June of 1943 with the bulk to go by March of 1943. Correspondence from the Japanese was received suggesting what should be taken to camp and this list was augmented by suggestions from the BRA. Each internee was permitted to send a bed and three boxes in advance plus what they could carry. The difficulty, of course, was that they had no idea how long they would be interned. On their assigned date to be interned, they went to the Columbia Country Club to wait for buses to take them to a Civil Assembly Centre.

Little has been written about the lives of civil internees held by the Japanese during World War II compared to that about the prisoners of war. Treatment was different as the Civil Assembly Centres, also known as camps, were under the aegis of the Japanese Consulate rather than under the jurisdiction of the Japanese army. There were several of these in China with most of them being in the Shanghai area My father was interned in Lunghwa from June of 1943 to August of 1945, so I have had a particular interest in this camp.

Lunghwa camp was located eight miles southwest of Shanghai and covered 35 acres. The group of buildings had originally been a boarding school for Chinese which sustained damage in the 193 7 air raids as it was within a mile of an airfield. Then the Japanese had used the area as an army base and had built three long huts for barracks. There were seven large concrete buildings which had originally been used as classrooms or dormitories. There were also about twenty-four outbuildings used for various purposes and an assembly hall with a stage. They were all in poor condition. The Japanese supplied the buildings such as they were as well as 100 tons of low-quality soft coal and 100 units of electricity per month. One of the uses of the electricity was to run the motor for the well which supplied polluted water to the buildings for toilets and cleaning. The Japanese instructions were that the internees were to operate their camp with the minimum of interference from them. The ruins in the camp provided material for repairs.

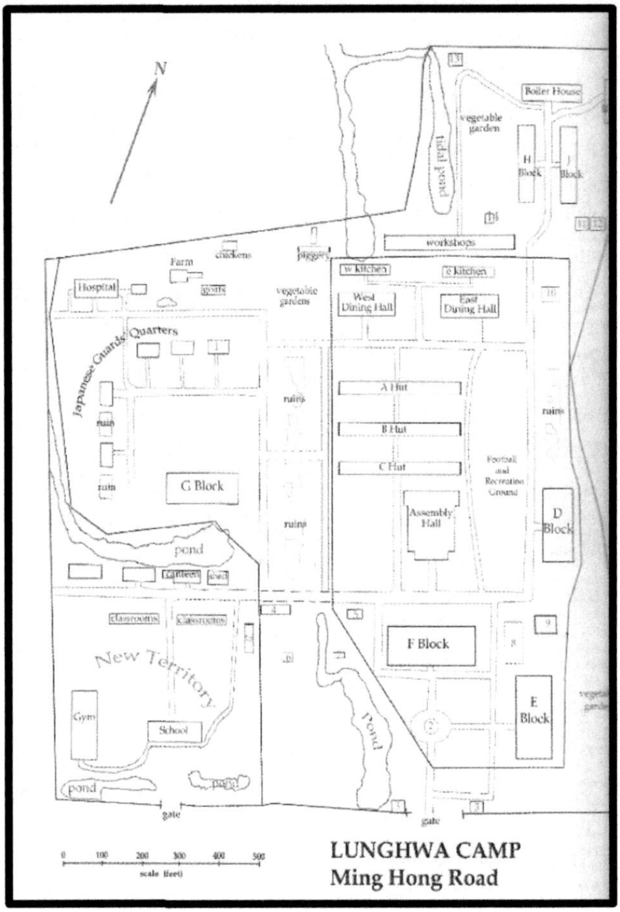

LUNGHWA CAMP
Ming Hong Road

Each person was allotted 48 square feet and families were kept together in one area There were 700 men, 800 women and 300 children in the camp. There was no heat or air conditioning in the accommodations. Internees suffered greatly in the Shanghai summer of heat and humidity and also in the winter when the temperature can go below freezing especially during the winter of 1944–1945 when there were 79 days of freezing or below freezing temperatures. On August 11, 1943 there was a typhoon which damaged the West dining hall when the roof was blown off. Several of the other huts lost their roofs as well, and many internees were forced to seek refuge in the Assembly Hall. Peggy Abkhazi gives a graphic description of the typhoon and the efforts of everyone to evacuate the huts and take care of the leaks which appeared in the other buildings.[2] The Japanese Commandant was concerned and "did his best to console them by serving out a tot of saki to each one"[3]. In addition, the typhoon destroyed so much which the internees had done to make the camp a little more attractive by planting flower beds and providing some shade.

To begin with, the Japanese allotment was 1,600 calories per day per person which included mainly rice and bread. Out of this, extra food was given to those who were assigned heavy work by the internees. Internees were also allowed one twenty-pound parcel from friends outside every month. As there was a lot of land, three large gardening teams planted vegetables. The internees were also able to keep two cows, a herd of goats, hens and up to sixty pigs. In time, there was enough milk to give all children under six years old half a pint of milk daily. "Private gardens provided vegetables to their owners. There was also a shoe repair shop, a sewing room, a hospital laundry, a library, a bookbindery, and numerous other workshops."[4]

Water was a major problem. The BRA managed to negotiate with the Japanese that 2000 gallons of drinking water would be delivered daily. This amounted to one gallon a person per day—half a gallon was served boiling, and the other half was reserved for kitchen use. The polluted water from the well was used for washing and was distributed from two depots known as Bubbling Well and Waterloo. In addition, the internees also collected water from a pond which they hauled to Dew Drop Inn where they received a bucket of hot water for washing clothes in exchange for a bucket of cold water. Internees also collect rainwater. "Lunghwa's showers were opened with fanfare and viewed as a technological achievement. Entering in groups of forty-eight, the users were driven by sharp whistle blasts announcing each stage. A whistle moved them to the shower, where they had one minute to get wet. Water was then turned off to apply soap. Water back on for one minute to rinse."[5] Internees conducted a deep well study[6] when less water was pumped up in June 1944 using the same power consumption and, in December it started to contain much sand and silt. There is no evidence to explain how this was resolved.

In the beginning, the Japanese requested that two internee representatives be appointed to be in charge of the camp. This arrangement was not liked by the internees so only lasted six months when a constitution was presented to the camp by qualified internees, voted upon and adopted. It allowed a democratic form of self-government to monitor and organise the camp activities. For each block or hut a house monitor, floor monitors and room captains were elected every six months. The house monitors reported to a House Committee the chair of which reported to Council. A Council of fifteen was elected every six months at the same time. Elections were held by secret ballot for everyone over 18 who was working or who had medical exemption. Every ballot paper had to show 15 votes, including two women candidates. Candidates had to be 25 or over. There was an Executive Committee of three chosen by the Council from themselves. Council met weekly or more often as required. The Executive Committee handled everyday affairs, each Executive being responsible for several Departments in which he/she could contribute the most. Department Heads were confirmed or appointed by the Executive Council for such activities as Public Services including Public Health, Education, Cultural activities, Billeting including Labour were appointed or confirmed in office by each new Council. There was a committee for each Department with a Chairman and a Councillor and consisted of about six people with special knowledge and interest.

Everyone in the camp except those who had a medical exemption had to contribute four hours of work a day with the Executive Council spending about eight hours a day. The Labour Committee was chaired by my father and comprised a labour officer, two women labour officers, one male assistant and one clerk. In order to make the duties fit the qualifications of the person as much as possible, the Committee had to have a good knowledge of personnel and sources of supply and of job requirements as well as be prepared to make transfers as necessary. Detailed records were kept on each person.[7]

Because the internees represented the different occupations in a society as large as Shanghai, the Council utilized this expertise in camp. There was a 'hospital' staffed by doctors, nurses and a dentist with clerical support. Malaria and dysentery were the most common medical problems. Those cases which they could not handle were sent to a hospital in Shanghai. The clergy led by the Dean of the Cathedral decided that they would look after unblocking the drains which needed constant attention.

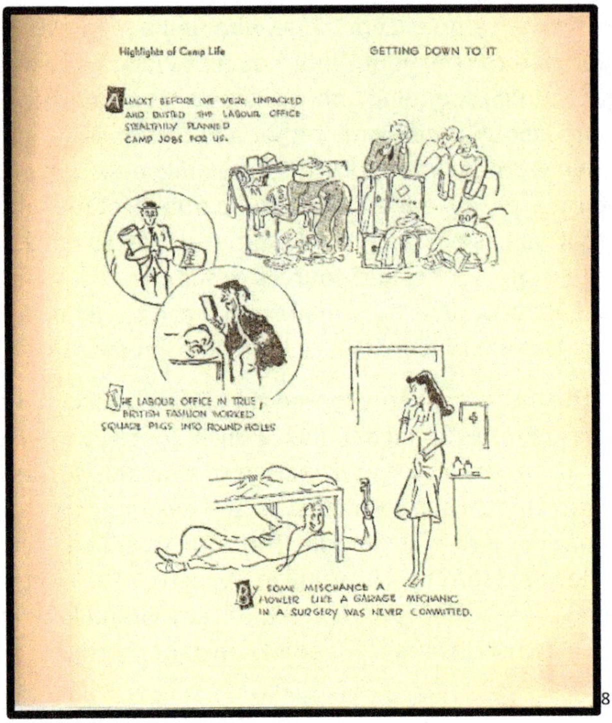

[8]

The Lunghwa Academy provided a curriculum for the children in the camp. As an example, the head mistress of the school I attended in Shanghai took in a lot of textbooks and those of age passed the school certificate examinations on their return to England and some of them matriculated. A special programme was arranged for the "Sophomores" who were those aged eighteen to twenty-six. There were cultural activities as well consisting of public lectures, dances, games, dramatic presentations, adult courses, discussion groups, concerts, choral singing, and art exhibitions. All through the internment, the internees obtained the news of the outside world through a hidden radio, 'Jimmie', which the Japanese never found. Information was also obtained from the Shanghai newspaper and from people who were delivering goods to the camp. The internees could write twenty-five-word Red Cross letters to the outside which often took up to six months to be delivered as they had to pass through Geneva, Switzerland. Later, the internees were able to write a note to their family to be broadcast by the Japanese. For instance, there was a man in New Zealand who sat up nights taking these messages down and sending them to the family in question.

There were four escapes involving twelve men altogether, the last one in late 1944. Each time there was an escape the internees suffered a cut in rations, additional roll calls, confinement to their rooms and having the electricity cut off earlier than usual not to mention the confiscation of such items as books, records and tools. Much interrogation went on with former neighbours of the escapees and with the Chinese villagers living in the countryside near the camp. After the last escape, the Japanese ordered that all single men aged sixteen to sixty be billeted in E block around which they placed extra barbed wire. My father was in charge of the move of over nine hundred people which was accomplished in a two-month period[9]—a remarkable accomplishment under the especially poor conditions of the last winter.

On August 15, 1945, the control of the camps became the responsibility of the Swiss Consulate but many of the internees had no homes to go to so remained in camp until arrangements were made for their return to their homelands. In the case of my father, he stayed on until November and then left for England where he was reunited with his family in time for Christmas. In 1946, we emigrated to Canada arriving at Pier 21 in Halifax on January 15, 1947, where we received a memorable welcome from an immigration officer. He invited us to his home for dinner and later put us on the train for Saint John as our destination was Fredericton where my father had obtained a teaching position at the University of New Brunswick.

Lunghwa camp has returned to its original use and is now the Shanghai Middle School.

Lunghwa Camp Now Shanghai Middle School, the compound still retains the Assembly Hall, D Block, and F Block. The ground where huts A, B, and C, as well as the football pitch, were located, is now covered by tall trees. The water tower was pulled down some time ago. The two kitchen buildings are still standing. Again, few of the people on the grounds knew of its past history.

[10]

I would like to thank my son Duncan for his great assistance in the research for this article.

ENDNOTES

1. Leck, Greg. Captives of Empire, the Japanese internment of allied civilians in China 1941–1945. Shandy Press, c2006, p. 460.
2. Abkhazi, Peggy. *A curious cage, life in a Japanese internment camp, 1943–1945.*Victoria, BC, Sono Nis, c1981, p. 97-99.
3. Ibid., p. 100.
4. Leck, op. cit. p. 462.
5. Ibid., p. 140.
6. Sanger, F. J. Deep well breakdown: report on meeting of a special panel convened to discuss the deep well of the Centre. December 14., 1944.
7. Ibid., Labour Office: Terms of reference and organisation, September 18., 1943.
8. Cumine, Eric. Lunghwa cackles, cartoons of camp life. (1945). "Getting down to it", n.p.
9. Sanger, op. cit. Rebilleting, Oct.–Dec., 1944. December 6., 1944.
10. Bamboo wireless. Association of British Civilian Internees, Far East Region. Issue n. 38, March 2007, p. 9

Source: Monkhouse, Valerie, "Lunghwa, a Civil Assembly Centre", Anglo-Celtic Roots, Ottawa, v. 14, number 4, Winter 2008, pp. 92-95.

Appendix E Frederick James Sanger 1905-2000

Appendix E-3

CURRICULUM VITAE

NAME: Frederick J. Sanger
DATE PREPARED: March 1972
DATE OF BIRTH: September 8, 1905. Bishop's Waltham, Hampshire, England.
Naturalized U.S. Citizen, 1954.
EDUCATION:
Public elementary school. Private secondary school.

- Royal Dockyard Technical Coll. (Shipbuilding, etc.) 4 yr part-time.
- Royal Scholar. Kitchener Memorial Scholar. Imperial College of Science & Technology at University of London.
- Assoc. C & G Inst. (C. E. Technology).
- B. Sc. (Engr'g) London—1st class Hons: Engineering Sciences.
- M. Sc. (Eng) Lond. (Field research on Foundations in Shanghai).
- D.I. C. (Dip. of Membership of the Imp. Coll. Sci. and Tech.) Hydroelectric eng.
- Refresher course in Soil Mechanics Univ. of Illinois, summer of 1947.
- Continuous private study for more than 40 years.

EXPERIENCE:

- 5 years Shipbuilding (Appr. & Shipwright). (Including one year in drawing office)
- 1 year Struct. Des. (Reinforced Concrete).
- 5 years Education Officer, Royal Air Force {Teaching Aero-Sciences).
- 7 years Hd. of Dept. Eng. & Bldg. Lester Inst. of Tech. Education. Shanghai. Civil, Mech., Elec., Eng.; Bldg. Con., and Arch. (Dean in U. S. colleges). Cons. & Res. in Found. and Mech. Eng. for City and Public Utilities.
- Interned by Japanese in China during war. Executive, Teacher, Administrator and elected Councillor in Camp.

- 2 years Prof. & Hd. Dept. Drwg. & Lect. in Eng. Geology, Univ. N. B., Canada.
- 9 years Prof. of Civ. Eng. Worcester Poly. Inst. (Engineering Geology, Soil Mechanics, Foundations, Soil Engineering, major. Hydraulic Eng., Route surveying, R. C. design, Concrete tech., Testing of Materials, minor).
- 5 years part-time Consultant and Expert to Arctic Construction and Frost Effects Laboratory N.E. Division, Corps of Engineers, U. S. Army.
- 13 years Corps of Engineers and Army Materiel Command. Cons. to Eastern Ocean District on Ballistic Missile Early Warning Systems, Thule and Clear, Alaska, and Omaha District on Top Secret Project (artificial soil freezing) 1965. Managing Editor: Cold Regions Science & Engineering Monographs (51 in all). June 1970: 30 published; 20 in preparation.
- 20 years private consultant in Civ. Eng. incl. Worc. Street Investigation 1950, Soils Cons. Mass. Turnpike 1954, Storage of Liquefied Fuel Gases at cryogenic temperatures in artificially frozen ground since 1961: (Projects in Canada, Japan, Iran, Libya, Algeria Germany, England and ten of the United States). Site geological study. Feasibility study. Thermal, Rheological and Structural Design, and Construction Inspection. 1967: Consultant to Parsons, Brinckerhoff, Quade, Douglas, Tudor and Bechtel Corporations on Bay Area Rapid Transit System, San Francisco; Design and specifications for artificial freezing for shaft and tunnel construction. 1969: Cons. Perini Corp. on tunnel (East River, N.Y.C.).
- Appointed Adjunct Prof. of Engineering, Thayer School, Dartmouth College 1963. Advising D. Eng. and M. Eng. candidates. Occasional courses in Soil Mechanics, Foundation Engineering and Transportation Engineering.
- 2 years with U. S. Geological Survey (Cons. Civ. Engr.

Appendix E Frederick James Sanger 1905-2000

- 1971 Appointed Chairman, Technical Advisory Board on trans-Alaska pipeline project, Department of the Interior (super grade position).

SECURITY CLEARANCE—U. S. GOVT: Top Secret

PUBLICATIONS, LECTURES, ETC:

- Article on Aircraft for Harrap's Encyclopaedia, 1930.
- Internal Combustion Engines—Eng Soc China (ESC) 1935.
- Soil Exploration and Sampling (ESC) 1936.
- Trans-Ocean Air Communications (ESC)
- 1936. Laboratory Testing of Soils (ESC) 1937.
- Stabilization of Soils (ESC) 1937.
- Foundations Research in Shanghai (Limited circ.) 1937.
- Models in Engineering {Joint} ESC and Institution of Civil Engineers (UK) 1938.
- Design of Engineering Laboratories for the Lester Institute, Shanghai (Inst. Civ. Eng. as part of membership requirements) 1938.
- Prestressed Steel Structures (Joint) Inst. Civ. Eng. (UK) 1939.
- Natural and Artificial Flight, Royal Asiatic Soc. China, 1940.
- Many discussions in Eng. Soc. China Journal, 1934–1941.
- Piled Foundations in Shanghai (Limited circ.) 1946.
- Large number of newspaper articles and public addresses, mainly on China and Shanghai, 1946–1950.
- Moderator of conference on permafrost with Russian engineers at MIT 1958.
- Discussions in HRB Bulletin 225, 1959, on thermal interaction between atmosphere and ground.
- 'Construction of a gravel road on the Greenland Ice Cap", MIT,1959.
- Special report on Rampart Dam, Alaska, for a joint committee, 1962.
- Computations on Frost in the Ground. New Hampshire Waterworks Association, 1963.

- Resources and Logistics of the Canadian Arctic (Arctic Institute of North America Conf. Montreal), 1963.
- Plastic Deformation of Frozen Soils in Unconfined Compression, Int. Conf. Permafrost, 1963. (Extended CRREL Research Report, 1968).
- Time to creep-failure at constant stress from known time and stress values at two failures. Int. Conf. Permafrost, 1963.
- Degree-days and heat conduction in soils, Int. Conf. Permafrost, 1963. (Parts reproduced by Asphalt Institute and by Dow Chemical Corporation).
- Panellist on two sections. Int. Conf. Permafrost, 1963.
- Cryogenics—article in science encyclopaedia, 1964. Technical editing 19 Russian, and 1 Japanese, papers for Int. Conf. Permafrost, 1964, 1965.
- Planning of 1st Air Force School. 11 Introduction to Cold Regions." 1964.
- Lectures at Pavement Maintenance Schools, Wright-Patterson Air Base. Several years.
- Technical review of rough translations from the Russian, 1965:
- 11 Rheological properties and bearing capacity of frozen soils" by S. S. Vialov. 219 pp.
- "The strength and creep of frozen soils and calculations for ice-soil retaining structures" by S. S. Vialov et al. 301 pp.
- Computations on Frost in the Ground. New England Waterworks Association, 1966.
- Cryogenic Inground Storage of Liquefied Natural Gas. ASCE Lecture, 1966.
- Technical review of rough translation from the Russian, 1967: 'Construction under Winter Conditions! by V. N. Sizov. 300 pp.
- ASCE Seattle Meeting. 'Ground freezing in construction." 1967. Publ. ASCE. January 1968. Disc. 1969.

- 'Technology of Liquefied Natural Gas.' Lecture at University of New Hampshire, October 1967.
- Lecture tour of Canada at request of National Research Council. 19 Lectures (5 different ones) at 10 cities, coast to coast, on Principles and Practice of Frost Action in the Ground, 1968. (Selected from all Free-World engineers).
- "Technology of Liquefied Natural Gas." Lecture at University of New Hampshire, October 1968.
- Monograph on 'Foundations in Cold Regions". 1968.
- Technical review of rough translation from the Russian, 1969: 'Power plant in icebreakers! by Yudorin B. S.

MEMBERSHIPS:

- F. ASCE, F. ICE {UK}. Chartered Civil Engineer (UK). F. AAS.
- Registered Professional Engineer, Mass., 5831.
- Sigma Xi Society (Pres. of Worcester, Mass., Chap. I yr).
- Pi Delta Epsilon (Hon. Mem.) (College journalism).
- Nat'l Council & International Soc. for Soil Mech. and Fndn. Engr'g. Sometime committee member on piled foundations for USA.

COMMITTEES:

- Chairman, Training Committee. USA TSC (U. S. Army Cold Regions Research and Engineering Laboratory).
- USA TSC Representative:
  1. On Army Materiel Command, Engineering Design Handbook Advisory Group.
  2. Adhoc Committee on Handbook on Environment, for U. S. Army.
- Coordinator
  - USA TSC contributions to Arctic Test Center
  - Guide to Environment of Fort Greely, 1968
- Formerly (at Shanghai, 1934–1941)
  - Federation of British Industries Committee, China. Member of Council; China Comm. of Inst. Mech. Eng. (UK).

    - Chairman, Foundations Research Comm. Eng. Soc. China.
    - Member of Council—Eng. Soc. China.
    - Member War Inventions Comm.

TRAVEL:

- Has lived in England, China, Canada and USA, and has visited many countries including Japan and Algeria. Engineering in those countries, Libya, Iran, Greenland, etc. Travel in Alaska by air, rail, road and off-road.
- DISTINCTIONS:
- Who's Who in America (since 1956).
- American Men of Science.
- Who's Who in Engineering.
- Blue Book (London) 1970.

LANGUAGES:

- Reading technical literature in Russian and in French.

CLUBS:

- Shanghai Club etc. in Shanghai (1934–1941)
- Cosmos Club, Washington, D. C.

FAMILY:

- Married 1928. 3 children; 9 grandchildren

Appendix F
Sanger Family Tree

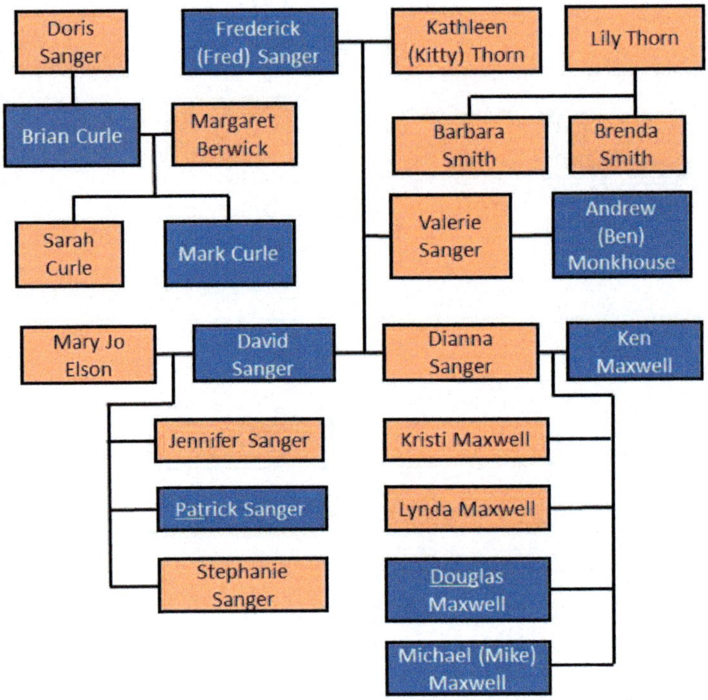

Appendix G
Monkhouse Family Tree

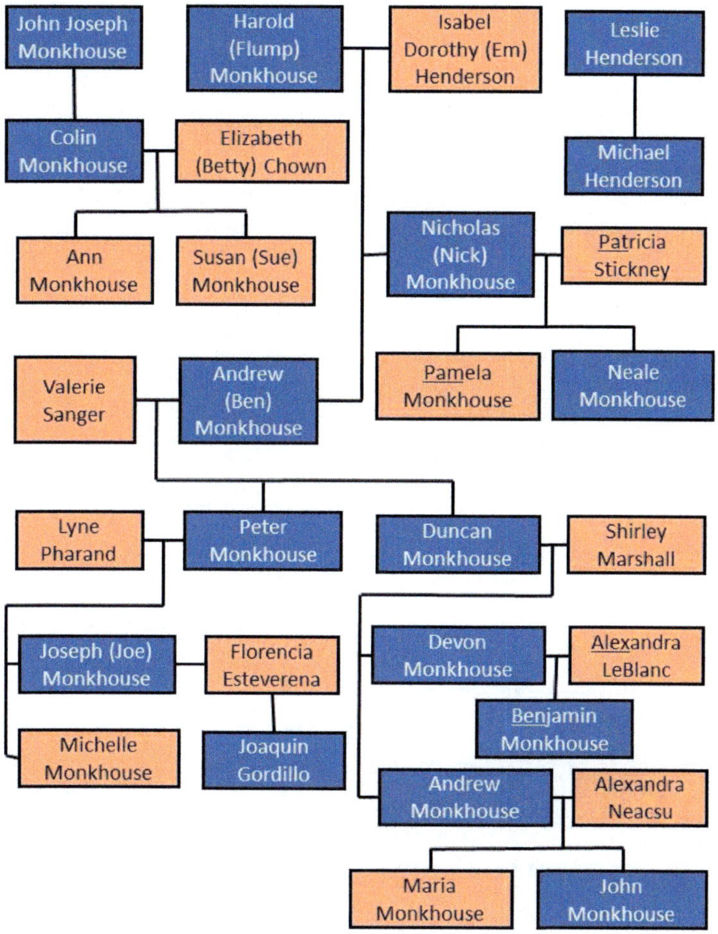

Printed in Great Britain
by Amazon

44808682R00178